STAGE PRE

Focusing on examples of live performance in drama, dance, opera and light entertainment, Jane Goodall explores the mystique of stage presence, a topic as compelling as the performers who demonstrate it.

The quality of 'presence' in a performer has strong resonances of the uncanny. It is associated with primal, animal qualities in human individuals, but also has connotations of divinity and the supernatural; it is defined in relation to figures of evil as well as heroism.

Stage Presence traces these associations through modern theatrical history. This challenging study also highlights the blend of science and spirituality that accompanies the appreciation of human power. The scientific imagery of electricity and magnetism is central to the way presence is described, but ghosts and deities are never far from the scene.

Case studies include: Josephine Baker, Sarah Bernhardt, Thomas Betterton, David Bowie, Maria Callas, Bob Dylan, David Garrick, Barry Humphries, Henry Irving, Vaslav Nijinsky and Paul Robeson.

Jane Goodall is a Professor with the Writing and Society Research Group at the University of Western Sydney. She is the author of *Performance and Evolution in the Age of Darwin* (Routledge 2002) and has published widely on experimental performance. She has also published several crime thrillers.

STAGE PRESENCE

Jane Goodall

Routledge
Taylor & Francis Group

LONDON AND NEW YORK

First published 2008
by Routledge
2 Park Square, Milton Park, Abingdon, Oxon OX14 4RN

Simultaneously published in the USA and Canada
by Routledge
270 Madison Ave, New York, NY 10016

*Routledge is an imprint of the Taylor & Francis Group,
an informa business*

Typeset in Goudy by
Saxon Graphics Ltd, Derby
Printed and bound in Great Britain by
TJ International Ltd, Padstow, Cornwall

British Library Cataloguing in Publication Data
A catalogue record for this book is available from the British Library

Library of Congress Cataloging in Publication Data
Goodall, Jane R.
Stage presence / Jane Goodall.
p. cm.
Includes bibliographical references and index.
1. Acting—Psychological aspects. 2. Acting. I. Title.
PN2058.G66 2008
792.02'8019—dc22
2007038429

ISBN10: 0–415–39594–1 (hbk)
ISBN10: 0–415–39596–8 (pbk)
ISBN10: 0–203–92858–X (ebk)

ISBN13: 978–0–415–39594–6 (hbk)
ISBN13: 978–0–415–39596–0 (pbk)
ISBN13: 978–0–203–92858–5 (ebk)

CONTENTS

ACKNOWLEDGEMENTS

I started work on this book in the idyllic surroundings of the Australian National University, with the assistance of a visiting fellowship at the Humanities Research Centre. For the opportunity to take up this fellowship, and for a generous period of study leave and a subsidised research trip to England, I am indebted to the University of Western Sydney, where I have benefited from the support of Wayne McKenna, Dean of Arts, and some wonderful colleagues. Ivor Indyk, as Whitlam Professor in the Writing and Society Research Group, created an environment in which writing of all kinds was the subject of vital and discerning interest; Kathleen Olive, who combines advanced editorial skills with her scholarly expertise, prepared the bibliography; Tessa Needham was a resourceful and canny research assistant; Chris Fleming, incurable polymath, has shared insights on the writing process. A book with such a wide-ranging brief creates a wonderful pretext for dialogue with brilliant minds from many spheres, and my promiscuity in this regard is such that I should not attempt to name them all here, but some of them were generous enough to read and comment on work in the draft stages. Helena Grehan, whose judgement I specially value, made suggestions that were spot on; Sylvia Lawson, a writer of unique lightness and verve, offered responses to Chapter 2; Talia Rodgers at Routledge was a marvellous person to talk to about the overall conceptual shape and style of the book. I also benefited from a set of thorough, insightful reports (anonymous, of course) obtained by the publisher at the proposal stage. At submission stage, Minh Ha Duong provided an illuminating reading of the work and judicious advice on many points. Julie Holledge of Flinders University agreed to an email interview, through which she provided me with invaluable comments on presence and the actor training process. While the internet is now a wonderful resource for scholars, libraries and the books in them remain our principal life support system. I have made particular use of the collections in The Bodleian Library, including the John Johnson Archive, in Oxford; Fisher Library at Sydney University; the State Library of New South Wales and the National Library of Australia.

I have never written a book without sharing the imaginative journey with my father, Paul Haeffner, and also with Margaret Haeffner and my two brothers Mark and Nick. From every conversation I have with them, I come away feeling that the world is somehow larger and more interesting. My son Jon has developed a startling propensity for running in at a topic laterally, often at lightning speed, opening it up in a way I never would have thought of. Peter, my husband, seems to have, over what is now a very considerable period of time, come to specialise in all the forms of mental talent in which I am most deficient. Perhaps I had better not confess what they are, but I must confess to having profited from sharing house with them, and from the constant patience and generosity with which they are made available.

INTRODUCTION

> 'To have presence' in theatrical parlance, is to know how
> to capture the attention of the public and make an impres-
> sion; it is also to be endowed with a *je ne sais quoi* which
> triggers an immediate feeling of identification in the spec-
> tator, communicating a sense of living elsewhere and in an
> eternal present.[1]
>
> Patrice Pavis, *Dictionnaire du Théâtre*
> (Paris: Messidor, 1987)

At the ancient Greek theatre of Epidauros, 20,000 people have
assembled to see an opera whose prima donna has a drawing
power that is unprecedented. Amongst the crowd is a ten-year-old
girl. It rains, the show is cancelled and a whole week passes before
the occasion can take place. By this time anticipation is at fever
pitch, but the singer's performance rises to meet it. The child is
'transported by the power of her voice and the dramatic truth of
her interpretation', but also by 'something deeper, by the intensity
of the fire I could feel raging inside her, consuming her at the same
time as it illuminated everything around her'.[2]

A stage-struck teenager working as a box office assistant at the
Old Vic Theatre in London goes into the auditorium one Monday
night when there is no performance and the theatre is 'dark'. He
approaches the stage and, unable to resist, sets foot on it. 'It
seemed to me a sacred space, Stonehenge', he recalls later. 'It was
throbbing with energies and a curious power – an altar without a
tabernacle'. So the young actor faces the vast black space of the
auditorium and speaks a few lines of *Hamlet*:

> It was a shock to hear my own voice so loud and resonant;
> but just as shocking was the physical, or even the psychi-
> cal, power released, a small earthquake.[3]

In a small town in the American mid-west, a special arrival is
anticipated at the local showground. A popular vaudeville wrestler
known as Gorgeous George is due in town with his troupe for a

1

performance that night. No-one is paying much attention to the boy practising his guitar on the crudely constructed platform stage near the entrance, but the boy himself has sharp antennae. He notices the level of activity around him has stepped up. He sees the doors burst open and the star make his entry, and later, when the boy is an adult, well advanced in a career of his own, he puts it all on record:

> He roared in like the storm... he came right through the lobby of the building and he seemed like forty men. It was Gorgeous George, in all his magnificent glory with all the lightning and vitality you'd expect... He brushed by the makeshift stage and glanced towards the sound of the music. He didn't break stride, but he looked at me, eyes flashing with moonshine.[4]

The first of these stories introduces a biography of Maria Callas by Arianna Stassinopoulos; the second is told by Simon Callow and the third by Bob Dylan in his autobiography. As three accounts of stage presence, they are widely different: they feature an operatic diva in one of the most ancient performance arenas in the world, a novice actor in a metropolitan theatre, and a vaudeville star in a small town showground.

Yet there are strong echoes in the language used by the three narrators, with its images of earthquake, storm, lightning, raging fire. These are elemental powers, greater than any natural strength belonging to humans, called up in the place and the act of performance. Something beyond the natural is being evoked. Callas, with her incandescent but consuming fire, is a being from a Greek myth, caught between the worlds of gods and mortals. Simon Callow feels he is in a 'sacred place', with the psychical potency of Stonehenge. The vaudeville wrestler with his moonshine eyes blazes onto the scene like some ancient Druid. Stage presence with its hieratic and archaic resonances is a phenomenon that exists through the eyes of the beholder, but, as Callow discovers, it is also experienced as very real by those who embody it. The narratives give us both sides of the equation, with Dylan switching from one to the other as he catches the eye of the Druidic figure and its telepathic message – 'You're making it come alive' – as if in that prophetic instant the boy with his guitar can also be a presence by virtue of the fact that he is performing on a stage, however make-shift.

The idea that someone may 'have presence' as an objectively real quality raises questions about what this quality consists of, whether it may be trained or cultivated, and to what extent it may be enhanced by the perceptions and expectations of those who witness it. Stage presence is a large topic, one that is addressed frequently in the writings of actors and directors as well as those of critics and theorists. Theoretical fascination with it has grown through the twentieth century as actor training programmes have diversified and cross-cultural awareness has expanded the range of approaches to performance. At the same time, a curious orientalist tendency has crept into the discussion of stage presence, as if it were necessary to go to Bali, or India, Malaysia or Japan in order to connect with the larger energies of theatre. One of the reasons for this is that the quest for an understanding of presence is often associated with the quest for unbroken indigenous traditions, which seem set apart from the comprehensively modernised cultures of urban modernity in the west.

The great poetic essays of Artaud's *The Theatre and its Double* (1936) were inspired by the Balinese dancers on a visit to Paris, not by any of the city's native artists. Artaud also looked back to the Eleusinian mysteries as the source of an 'alchemical' theatre that he hoped to revive, through dramas in which the fusion of matter and spirit would effect transformative experiences.[5] The theatre he invokes is characterised by modes of expressiveness that are 'poetic and active', veering away from psychological naturalism in order 'to recover the religious and mystic preference of which our theatre has completely lost the sense'. Having made this assertion, he immediately turns on an imagined home audience. 'If it is enough to pronounce the words *religious* or *mystic* to be taken for a churchwarden or an illiterate priest outside a Buddhist temple, at best good for turning prayer wheels, this merely signifies and condemns our incapacity to derive the full import from our words, and our profound ignorance of the spirit of synthesis and analogy'.[6]

Artaud was not the first European to look to the Orient for a model of the truly present actor. Edward Gordon Craig, writing a generation earlier, wanted to revitalise the stages of Europe with a reintroduction of the über-marionette, a life-sized puppet with its origins in Indian tradition. In its original form, this uncanny puppet stands as 'the direct symbol of the Divinity in Man', and is linked with the first record of the actor in the east.[7] Gordon Craig's call for the return of the über-marionette is echoed in Artaud's invective against a fallen culture no longer infused with hieratic power. Craig tells a story of how the puppet built in the likeness of a God and housed in a temple on the banks of the Ganges comes to be displaced through the determinations of vain humanity. Two 'foolish women' are dazzled by his appearance and conceive the desire to become like him through imitation. Mimesis then progressively distances the performer from the figure of the sacred puppet that channels divine energy. The puppet is a version of the hierophant, linking humans with the gods and serving as a channel for creative power, the kind of power that by-passes the work of imitation to bring things into being.

This craving for the revival of an ancient inspiriting force in theatre might be seen as a reaction against modernism, not just for its technologies, but for the quality of consciousness it fosters, and the ways in which it promotes constant change in a relentless future-bound drive that by implication devalues the past. How can a society trained in scepticism and pragmatism remain committed to metaphysics? How can a culture aware of its own progress through successive aesthetic movements, informed by new science and driven by the imperatives of commerce and industry, expect to be able to channel hieratic powers, or to be in touch with archaic energies?

The tendency to atavism and orientalism in European writing on presence may arise from a sense of incompatibility between modernity and metaphysics. Amongst those who seek vital forms of renewal for cultures that have been comprehensively transformed by science and industry, indigenous traditions can seem to speak more directly about deity and manifestation, and to have more powerful training regimes for cultivating the energies of the human body.

In modern Europe, according to Craig, this distancing process has been accentuated by new technologies. 'The actor looks upon life as a photo-machine looks upon life; and he attempts to make a picture to rival a photograph'.[8] If presence is quite literally about the here and now, technologies of representation may be seen as its enemies. Here we have the beginnings of a line of theoretical analysis that was to take on major importance through the twentieth century. At the start of his great essay 'The Work of Art in the Age of Mechanical Reproduction', Walter Benjamin quotes Paul Valéry:

> For the last twenty years neither matter nor space nor time has been what it was from time immemorial. We must expect great innovations to transform the entire technique

of the arts, thereby affecting artistic invention itself and perhaps even bringing about an amazing change in our very notion of art.[9]

In the future, Valéry predicted, the 'presence' of the work of art would be obedient to our call, across distances of space and time. What he identified here was a warp in the meaning of 'presence' as the word became divorced from any assumption of someone or something being present. This had large implications: it suggested a wider loss of connection to origins, a rupture in the lines of communication and vital impulse connecting the whole culture to its deepest sources of inspiration. Valéry was writing in 1928, and Benjamin in 1936, but it is as if across the stretch of less than a decade between them prophesy has been converted into current reportage and retrospective analysis. 'Even the most perfect reproduction of the work of art is lacking in one element', Benjamin challenges, 'its presence in time and space'. Lack and loss becomes the theme of the essay. Creativity and genius, eternal value and mystery, become 'outmoded concepts'. When the work of art is disseminated through techniques of mechanical reproduction, 'the quality of its presence is always depreciated'. Thus the medium of film produces an effect that 'shrivels the aura' of the actor.[10]

The Marxist philosophical dichotomy between transcendentalism and materialism is at issue here, but so is a more empirical view of how mystery and presence belong to a pre-industrialised natural world. In metaphysical terms, Martin Heidegger posited a change in the order of things that reversed the human/machine hierarchy so that 'in truth, it is the coming to presence of man that is now being ordered forth to lend a hand to the coming to presence of technology'.[11] Heidegger is an important influence on the work of Jacques Derrida, who associates the fascination of presence with an investment in lost origins and an illusion of the fullness of being. There is always something missing, and the quest for presence is itself an expression of lack. The very thought of presence implies a concept of absence, so that the two have a mutually dependent and oscillating focus in the mind.[12] Derrida writes for a culture with a cumulative history of self-knowledge, a culture that has long ago lost its innocence and can see its own most prized investments as delusory habits of thought. He has influenced a widespread movement in contemporary philosophy that has found it is easier to convert discussion of presence into a focus on absence. As Philip Auslander observes, there are also political concerns:

The suspicion of presence and of simple presentation of performer to audience that suffuses postmodern experimental theatre derives, then, from the anxiety created by historical demonstrations of collusion between presence as charisma or salesmanship and repressive power structures.[13]

Theatre, though, is a medium riddled with paradox, and with perennial tendencies to make conversions between opposites. Joseph Roach writes of these in a witty essay entitled 'It'. 'Theatrical performance', he suggests, 'is the simultaneous experience of mutually exclusive possibilities – truth and illusion, presence and absence, face and mask'.[14] The essay was published in 2004, and subsequently developed as a book, in which he moves with quicksilver adroitness between the figures of the current media-driven glamour industry and those of earlier periods in history. Roach demonstrates that it is indeed still possible to engage with notions of charisma, magnetism, attraction and presence or – perhaps more to the point – that they will not go away. The theatre perennially reverts to questions of origin and inspiration, and actors engage with them on very different terms from philosophers. The imaginative game of hypothesis is at the heart of theatrical experiment; it is a game that accommodates an unending process of reversal and contradiction, refusing to gauge 'truth' in factual or literal ways.

My approach in this book began with a sense of provocation in response to both the orientalist move and the shift to a focus on absence. Western theatre has a complex tradition of discourse on presence. Attempts to describe it persist, from the Restoration onwards, and the language surrounding it diversifies. Illusions play their part in this, but illusion is a vital element of theatre, one that is always renewing itself with catalytic fervour, even across those rupture-marking boundaries labelled 'modernism' and 'postmodernism'. The western tradition may carry a heavy burden of self-awareness; those who belong to it may be beset by a sense of distancing, displacement and dissociation; the scientific mind may set constraining parameters on fantasy and speculation: even so, theatre and performance continue to accommodate mystique. Endeavours to grapple with the contradictions between a scientific world-view and an ever-resurgent supernaturalism produce their own kinds of drama. And by 'supernaturalism' here I do not mean simply the ghost hunting kind, but rather the will to engage with energies and ideas beyond those that are comprehensible within the terms of naturalism.

The real challenge may be not to demystify presence, but to discover just how this mysterious attribute has been articulated and what kinds of imagery surround it. Far from being inexplicable and untellable as many commentators have claimed, the notion of presence has inspired some of the most memorable passages in the literature on performance. We can trace the evolution of a poetics of presence that works collaboratively with the artists it describes, surrounding their appearances with heightened recollection and anticipation. It is often when language is pushed to venture beyond familiar limits that it too takes on force and life: the paradox of encountering inspired eloquence accompanied by the insistence that, as Colley Cibber put it when writing of the Restoration actor Thomas Betterton, the effect 'is not to be told to you', is one of several anomalies attached to the notion of stage presence in western modernity.[15]

Since this book is about the poetics of presence – the rhetorics and imagistic language in which presence is evoked in different cultural and historical contexts, and across diverse forms of theatre and performance – I have taken some poetic licence, and followed the narratives of many different writers, allowing them to lead the process of commentary. From the point of view of my academic discipline, I have taken some liberties. A great deal of sophisticated work has been done on the demarcations between acting and performance, modernism and postmodernism, and on the changing terms in which 'presence' can be approached across the twentieth century. I am thinking here especially of Philip Auslander's *From Acting to Performance*, which charts the debates in a lucid and judicious way,[16] and of Joseph Roach's *It*, of which I have been able to take only brief account as it was published just as I reached the publisher's deadline for this work.[17]

I am attempting to offer something quite different but, I hope, complementary, by insisting on a resilient continuity in the western tradition of theatre. Although this study is concerned with concepts of stage presence in modernity, important bearings can be gained from the pre-modern etymology of the word *presence* and its symbolic associations. It is derived from the Latin *prae-sentia* so that it hangs very close to the word *presentiment*. We talk of 'sensing' a presence – that of a ghost, perhaps, or some other supernatural entity. A human being with presence may be said to have an aura – an energy field that extends around them in space and in time also, so that you might sense them coming, or feel that they've been here, after they've gone. A German visitor to England who attended a performance of David Garrick's *Hamlet* in the 1772–73 season at Drury Lane wrote of 'the almost terror-struck silence of the audience, which preceded his appearance'.[18]

In the *Oxford English Dictionary*, one of the earliest usages of the term 'presence' is in association with the Eucharist, which symbolises the Presence of Christ when Christ is no longer there. Mystical writings about the Presence of Christ or God give the word itself a highly charged value, that is transferred progressively to humans of pre-eminent status in their spheres. (Emperor, Sovereign, Cardinal, the Judge presiding over a Court). With the Tudor dynasty, a presence chamber was introduced as the ceremonial heart of the sovereign's court. Giordano Bruno on a visit to London celebrated Queen Elizabeth as the quasi-divine 'diva Elizabetta', who 'with the splendour of her eyes for the space of five lustres and more has tranquillised the great Ocean'.[19] But in the later Renaissance, presence is a quality that starts to leak out amongst the non-annointed, especially if they have regal or aristocratic personal attributes. By 1579 it can mean 'demeanor, carriage, or aspect of a person, especially when stately or impressive'. Sir Thomas More was described as 'a man of stately and handsome presence'.[20]

From here the word and its connotations start to split: there is divine or divinely ordained presence and there is worldly presence. Frances Yates gives evidence for this dichotomy as being essential to Renaissance humanism. On one hand there was the dignitary, the classically educated noble man identifiable by manners, speech and bearing; on the other was the hermetic model of the ideal man, whose dignity 'consists in his lofty relation to God and, when he is a Magus, in the power which he can draw from the universe'.[21]

These two models of human presence remain at the core of the western theatrical tradition. To the first belong all the regimes of training and technical prowess: elocution and vocal technique, deportment, the aesthetics of gesture and facial expression. The second is suggested in the more mysterious qualities of magnetism and mesmerism, a sense of inner power being radiated outwards. The sphere of the dignitary is the social world with all its power-play; that of the magus is a wider cosmos, governed by metaphysical forces. Key figures in theatrical tradition may belong more on one side of the equation than the other, but there is no simple binary in operation. The legendary players of the western tradition exhibit the doubleness of Renaissance man, wearing the Janus faces of the dignitary whose attributes are evident in trained physical and vocal qualities and the magus whose capacities are a mystery. The scientific and the uncanny, mystique and technique, may be frequently in tension but they are also hand in glove.

Patrice Pavis, who offers some astute commentary on stage presence in his *Dictionary of the Theatre* (1987), distances himself from idealistic and mystical interpretations, recommending a semiological approach in order to take the notion of a 'supreme attribute' and divest it of its 'halo of mysticism', so as to bring the enquiry back within the domains of sense and reason. This involves shifting the focus from the intrinsic qualities of the actor to the process of enacting a drama in the dual timeframe through which an audience experiences it: the fictional present within the narrative, and the social here and now of the performance. Identification between performer and spectator is at the heart of the matter, so that these frames of experience converge as a rediscovery of our own physical being through that of the actors: 'hence our consternation and our fascination in the face of this strange and familiar presence'.[22]

From the actor's point of view, the familiar is the domain of training and technique, which enables control over the communicative process that is the actor's art. From Thomas Betterton onwards, players and directors have devised training systems to assist in unlocking the secrets of what makes a powerful performance. Their techniques have often been closely correlated with new forms of scientific enquiry. Actor training has been influenced by knowledge of physiognomy, taxonomy, ethnology, evolution, electricity, psychology, sociology and semiotics, all of which have contributed to the demystification of what is compelling on stage.

Although by the twentieth century traditions of deportment and physical grace are no longer central to actor training, the qualities of the dignitary are adapted and reconceived in Stanislavski's approach. 'Our aim is not only to create the life of a human spirit', he teaches, 'but also to express it in a beautiful artistic form'. Before the trainee has grasped the founding principles of the technique, the simple act of sitting on stage makes him look 'stupid, funny, embarrassed, guilty, apologetic'. He learns that in order to give communicative fluency to his physical behaviour, whatever happens on stage must be for a purpose. The physical co-ordination involved in the graceful comportment of the dignitary is replaced by psychological co-ordination. As the instructor cautions: 'Until his goal is clear the direction of his activities will remain unformed. He will feel only individual movements in his role'.[23]

Once the 'through line' is established, the role becomes 'an integrated whole made up of individual acts and feelings, thoughts and sensations'. A kind of secular magic then takes place through 'the miraculous life-giving quality' of this connective principle, and the actor acquires stage presence or 'the state of "I am"'.[24] Michel Saint-Denis, one of Stanislavski's successors as a transformative influence on actor training, bore witness to the effects of his mentor's system on the performances of the Moscow Art Theatre:

> The deftness of the company's acting was absolutely incredible: without forcing anything, they were alive. They did not seem to touch the ground. Their movements seemed to flow through them as they communicated freely with one another. What struck me most was the lightness of their acting: these performers seemed constantly to improvise their movements and their text. Every movement had a prodigious creative invention about it, but nothing seemed ever to solidify; all was ephemeral...

The principles of the dignitary here reach a state that replicates the powers of the magus. 'Their performances were an enchantment'.[25]

Another successor of Stanislavski, Michael Chekhov (nephew of the playwright) was accused of taking enchantment too far under the hardline cultural policies introduced by the Communist government in the 1920s. He was accused of 'harmful mystical deviations' and warned against continuing to draw his influence from Rudolf Steiner. Chekhov's career in actor training was revitalised in 1940 after he settled in America, where he taught some of the great film and theatre stars of the post-war decades. For them, the 'mystical tendencies' were a radically enhancing influence. In Simon Callow's account, this was Stanislavskian work on behaviour, taken to an esoteric level:

> When the shaman does his dance, nobody says: could you do a little less, please. When the great comedians, the great clowns walk on stage, we know we are in the presence of something else, something well known to us but outside of our experience.[26]

Naturalism in its consummate form may produce something approximating transcendence, yet it seems that where stage presence is concerned there is no getting away from the strange and the uncanny. Joseph Chaikin prefaces his book *The Presence of the Actor* with a quotation from Paul Eluard: 'There is another world, and it is in this one'.[27] The moment by moment actuality of a live theatre performance perhaps appeals to some haunting sense that we are never quite present in our own lives and the stage performer who seems so fully and powerfully there in front of us, steering our reactions through unpredictable turns into spectacular terrain, can bring about a temporary reunion with lost aspects of our own being.

No rationalised approach can ever really explain why some performers are demonstrably more effective in creating this identification than others. There are certain figures in the history of theatre and performance around whom the rhetorics of presence collect – Betterton, Garrick, Kean, Siddons, Rachel, Irving, Bernhardt, Callas, Robeson, Nijinsky, Brando, Olivier – and in all these cases the description of a certain kind of figure and bearing is combined with the evocation of a radiating power that transcends the natural. These examples are from the 'high' or classical end of the theatrical spectrum. From there it has spread to the realms of popular performance, especially through the star system of the vaudeville tradition, but the concept of stage presence, with its connotations of the regal and the divine, originally developed around the figure of the classical actor. Since classical forms of theatre are themselves concerned with metaphysical questions about the nature and scope of human being, they may be said to have a thematic predisposition to endow those playing the major roles with an enhanced stature. This does not, however, mean that presence implies elitism, since one of its effects is to magnify the attraction of a work in performance, so that the audience base is widened. It lifts the individual to a higher plane, regardless of his or her origins. Stage history is full of examples of leading performers who were born in the most unhopeful circumstances.

The *OED* definition raises the question of how it is that actors, who may come from the humblest social classes, share an attribute that is the property of gods and kings, spirits and angels. Is Presence, capitalised as a proper noun that designates a form of supra-natural being, transferred through the work of personification or impersonation? Betterton, whose father was an under-cook to King Charles I, became a surrogate king for his era, praised for his 'commanding mien of majesty'.[28] In a fine essay on Betterton's funeral, Joseph Roach assembles comments from the actor's contemporaries to illustrate the ways in which they acknowledged his role as an impersonator of kings and emperors in a fifty-year reign over the 'Mimic State' of the London stage.[29] Betterton's interment in Westminster Abbey was at once the termination and culmination of this reign and Roach takes a statement from Richard Steele's eulogy as keynote for a new analysis. 'There is no invention so aptly calculated for the forming of a Free-Born people as that of a Theatre', wrote Steele. And Roach, focusing on issues of cultural memory and its means of accretion, extrapolates: performances provide the ways and means by which a 'Free-born people' can be *formed*.[30] The body of the actor serves as a medium or effigy for speaking with the dead, and especially with the regal dead, as George Farquhar claims:

> And that the same Person shou'd be Mr. Betterton, and Alexander the Great, at the same Time, is somewhat like an Impossibility in my Mind. Yet you must grant this Impossibility in spight of your Teeth, if you han't the Power to raise the old Heroe from the Grave to act his own part.[31]

In Betterton's 'royal' funeral, Roach suggests that we can see 'the early development of a particular kind of secular devotion' instrumental in the formation of a free-born people. I would suggest also that we see the beginnings of a democratisation of Presence, through the mediation of the actor who plays the sovereign, and is at once the king and the common man.

In Europe and America, the poetics of presence is linked with the cult of the individual and testifies to the changing meanings and tensions surrounding individuality in modernity. As the formally symbolic and religious connotations of Eucharistic Presence are diluted into a more generalised sense of 'indwelling power' and 'the state of "I am"', the language used to describe it begins to draw on the vocabularies and image banks of the dynamic sciences. Radiation, electricity, magnetism, mesmerism and chemistry provide the keywords around which the discourses on presence become organised from the mid eighteenth century. As these discourses mature and diversify, vocabularies borrowed from the sciences are often blended seamlessly with terminologies from magic and mysticism.

If mystery, genius and aura do not seem to belong in the world of mechanical reproduction, there may be other explanations for this besides Benjamin's. A growing stand-off between naturalist and supernaturalist views of the world is evident in the debates of Darwinism. Science has become almost synonymous with secularism, and always connotes scepticism. Yet this has not always been so clearly the case. Early experiments in magnetism were fraught with a sense of the uncanny as they began to make visible the presence of 'wondrous forces' and as 'novel, unheard-of properties came to light'.[32] Automatism was personified through the creation of mechanised beings that seemed to cross the boundary between natural and supernatural worlds. Images of magic and fairyland surrounded electrical invention from the early modern period through to the time of Edison and Tesla. In the late eighteenth century, it was impossible to separate the occult, pseudo-science of mesmerism from the legitimate science behind electricity and magnetism. The vocabulary and imagery associated with stage presence are drawn from all these areas of experiment. This is therefore an enquiry that breaks down the cultural dualisms of rationality and superstition, science and art.

The chapters to come will explore the phenomenon of stage presence from a range of angles, focusing on examples from the early modern period to the beginning of the twenty-first century and drawn from across the fields of drama, dance, opera, experimental performance and music theatre. Chapter 1 offers an exploration of the concept of presence as the 'supreme attribute', providing a survey of some of the performers whose special impact has triggered attempts to describe this supposedly indefinable quality. There is discussion of the term *charisma* and the concept of stardom, so as to clarify areas of overlap and distinction, especially with regard to the figure of the live performer on stage. Some attention is devoted to the question of presence in film acting as a way of highlighting what qualities are unique to the stage performer.

Chapter 2, 'Drawing power', focuses on the relationship between scientific experiment and interpretations of the actor's powers during the Restoration period and the early eighteenth century. Thomas Betterton, whose career spanned half a century, between 1660 and 1710, and who came to epitomise all that was best in Restoration theatre, is also a figure who defines the beginnings of modernity in acting, taking the profession to new levels of social and aesthetic stature. With David Garrick and Sarah

Siddons, we can see the development of the actor in the eighteenth century as a public celebrity, the subject of portraits, cartoons and satires, panegyrics and fan letters. The period of Betterton and Garrick is also that of the rebirth of science, with the foundation of the Royal Society in 1660 and the rapid development of an experimentally based culture of enquiry, in which magnetism and electricity were of primary importance. From its early stages, electrical experiment brought physics and metaphysics together. It was intimately related to the study of magnetism but the idea of physical bodies having 'drawing power' was profoundly unorthodox. Thus, though researches into magnetism and electricity produced new ideas about human presence and energy, the imagery took some time to come through from the realms of science to those of theatrical performance.

Performers who make a compelling impression are often referred to as 'mesmerising'. Chapter 3 considers the history of this, beginning with an account of the exploits and ideas of Anton Mesmer in the decade preceding the French Revolution. In mesmerism, a theory of universalised magnetic forces was applied in practical experiments, creating a pseudo-science that held sway over the cultural imagination long after its scientific credentials were exploded. The popular craze for mesmerism disseminated new ideas about human power and communication, which changed the terms in which actors related to their audiences. The French tragedienne Rachel is the first great mesmerist of the theatre, with Henry Irving and Sarah Bernhardt developing the hypnotic approach in popular and classical dramas. Each of these actors cultivated a unique form of personal power which combined elements of the demonic and the animal with an enhanced sense of human stature. In them the idea of stage presence acquires new mythical dimensions which are exhibited during the twentieth century by such figures as the Russian dancer Vaslav Nijinsky, the African-American singer Paul Robeson and the operatic star Maria Callas.

'Dash and flash' is a chapter concerned with the second major phase of electrical research, focused on industrial innovation. Nikola Tesla was a leading inventor at the turn of the twentieth century, but also a maverick personality who was fascinated by the human body as a generator and conductor. He enjoyed experiment as a form of public spectacle, with himself as the illuminated centre of it. By the end of the nineteenth century, the spectacular manifestations of electricity, especially at the Worlds Fairs, inspired a feeling that science and magic had finally met. Popular entertainers began to use costumes and settings that accentuated the brilliance of light and reflected it from their own bodies as they moved. Josephine Baker, whose career took off in Paris in the 1920s, gave the word 'dazzling' a whole new meaning and created a prototype of the electrifying star that became the dream of the Broadway musical. Glamour was reinvented with a dash of parody in the 1970s with the *Rocky Horror Show* and the advent of David Bowie in his Ziggy Stardust persona. The impact of the star performer was expanding in scale with mass media dissemination, but live interaction with audiences remained a generative source of star power, as Dame Edna Everage has understood so well. The razzle-dazzle tradition in entertainment has its dark side, with the mystique of smoke and mirrors. The chapter concludes with a discussion of Lloyd Webber's *Phantom of the Opera* as the revival of a romantic and mysterious emblem of stage presence.

Command over the time and space of performance marks out the actor with presence. Experimental performance often involves a confrontation with time, and leading theatre practitioners in the twentieth century were also concerned to create a confrontation with the present as a shifting and turbulent reality. 'Being present' is a chapter concerned with the factors in stage performance that contribute to a heightened sense of present time, whether experienced in its moment by moment passing, or as a *zeitgeist* demanding alert and immediate response. The two world wars of the twentieth century produced collective trauma on an unprecedented scale. It was as if the 'nervous system' of an entire culture was in crisis. Nijinsky's last dance, performed at a country house in 1919, was a definitive expression of this. Across the mid century, Brecht and Artaud envisaged polarised approaches to engagement with the conditions of a world in the throes of a nightmare transformation and both had a transformative influence on acting. Following the Second World War, Beckett's dramatic minimalism created a new kind of immediacy in the theatre through the imposition of stringent controls on spatiality and timing. Performances by Ryszard Cieslak, Simon Callow, Al Pacino and Billie Whitelaw are discussed as examples of how these major influences impact on the presence of the actor. Outside the domain of dramatic acting, there have also been presences who embody the spirit of the times in live performances with massive drawing power: Bob Dylan and Johnny Rotten are figures expressive of changing currents in the culture at large.

It will be evident from this summary that I have chosen as my examples actors and performers of iconic status. Stage presence does not necessarily imply star quality, or genius, and many lesser known performers demonstrate it in events that may attract modest numbers of spectators. A practised eye can pick it – or the potential for it – in the most raw of hopefuls at an acting school audition. Goethe, establishing a set of rules for actor training in the early nineteenth century, stated simply that 'an actor standing alone on the stage should remember that he is called to fill out the stage with his presence'.[33] By implication, someone who has presence is someone who can command the space of the stage so that the audience experiences it as 'full'. For Julie Holledge, who teaches student actors at Flinders University in South Australia, 'it is the ability to remove all residual and unnecessary tensions from the body that underlies "presence"'. This can be developed 'by training the actor to have control over his or her physical energy so that it can be shaped, held and released in accordance with the needs of the specific performance'.[34]

Another kind of study could be written based on what happens in the studio and the rehearsal room, or drawing on accounts of performers whose unique qualities do not cause them to register on the celebrity scale. And another study could be written featuring equally celebrated and remarkable actors and performers omitted from this one. I made the decision to focus on high profile individuals because they provide a widely shared point of reference for readers across different continents, and because the more celebrated figures in history are well documented so that we can reconstitute an imaginative picture of their impact. In consultation with the publisher, I have made the decision not to include illustrations. Presence is rarely captured effectively in a still image, and the focus of the account here is on visualisation through verbal description. As for my choices of who to include, they are to an extent arbitrary and based on personal enthusiasms, but my aim has been to create a map of representative examples to illustrate major trends in the rhetoric and imagery surrounding presence. If the reader is mentally spurred at every turn to offer alternatives, that is both inevitable and to be welcomed: it is how the picture is opened out to the fullness no single study can give it.

1

THE SUPREME ATTRIBUTE

According to current opinion in the profession, 'presence is
the supreme attribute for an actor'.
                    Patrice Pavis, *Dictionnaire du Théâtre*
                                (Paris: Messidor, 1987)

What is it that makes a performer compelling to watch? We might
explain the fascination in terms of the performance itself as a
display of exceptional talents, but history is full of examples of
stage celebrities who gained pre-eminence in spite of quite obvious
deficiencies in looks, technique or discipline. Even where
supremacy in skill is unquestionable, we may still find commentators struggling to describe how there was something more than this
in the performance, something experienced as uniquely powerful,
perhaps even transcendent or magical. It is the 'x' factor in the
actor's art. As Joseph Roach summarises: 'Poets have It. Saints
have It. Actors must have It'.[1]
    'Its' supposed indefinability is part of its fascination, and lends a
mystique that escalates the cultural values associated with
performance. Roach does not directly correlate 'It' with presence,
but surveys a range of attributes and associations of 'this hard-to-
define quality': it is radiance, genius, 'a singular chemistry', what
Stanislavski calls 'stage charm', charisma, magnetism, attraction,
an 'uncanny appeal'. Seeking to push beyond this kind of scatter-
gun evocation surrounding 'a census of worthies', Roach calls for a
theory that technically explains the special powers they possess.
For this, he goes to Zeami in the Noh tradition, before returning to
a range of commentaries from European traditions and offering an
interpretation based around paradox and opposition. 'Actors with
It', he suggests, 'have eyes that focus both outward and inward
because there is much of importance to be seen in each direction'.[2]
Such an approach is subtle and probing, and avoids trying to nail
down the factors in a way that denies the mystery and multi-
dimensionality of the nameless quality.
    Since my concern is with a quality that *does* have a name – and
one that carries complex cultural resonances – my work here has a

17

rather different orientation. Part of the task is to offer some steer-age between the word 'presence' and the set of terms associated with it. I will make the case that it is to be differentiated from charisma and has a strong relationship with genius, and that the metaphors of magnetism, attraction, electricity and radiance belong to it as ways of conceptualising its dynamics. Another part of the task is to stay close to the word and to make some particular explorations of its etymological range. Though my concern is not with the un-namable, however, there is a need to address and acknowledge the claims that it is somehow 'untellable'. The 'it' factor is undoubtedly part of the picture. Thomas Betterton, the first real star of the modern English stage, was praised above Vandyke and Shakespeare as a creator of human portraits:

> ... a Betterton steps beyond 'em both, and calls them from the grave, to breathe and be themselves again, in feature, speech and motion. When the skilful Actor shows you all these powers at once united, and gratifies at once your eye, your ear, your understanding. To conceive the pleasure rising from such harmony, you must have been present at it! 'Tis not to be told to you.[3]

Three centuries later, the claim of untellability is still being made in relation to the qualities of the supreme actor of the times, in this case Laurence Olivier:

> The experience of seeing him on stage was quite over-whelming in a way that's very hard to explain to anybody who hasn't seen him. To see him as Othello, Edgar in *The Dance of Death*, actually, later too, as James Tyrone in *Long Day's Journey*, was to experience a blast of sensuous energy, vocal and physical virtuosity...[4]

This is Simon Callow's testimonial and, characteristically, his gift for articulating whatever is most difficult to put into words gets the better of his apology about being unable to explain. No sooner has he made it than the beginnings of an explanation are under way. It has something to do with technical virtuosity, and something to do with energy. For Colley Cibber, writing on Betterton, it has some-thing to do with harmony and the orchestration of the senses.

Yet the claim that ''tis not to be told to you' is more than mere empty rhetoric. There is always a special cultural power in that which cannot be told, especially if the inability to tell is an indicator of some phenomenon beyond the limits of what is known and definable in human experience. The uncanny, the magical and the dangerous hover at the outer edges of these limits, and become part of the aura of the actor who is a strong presence. Peter Brook finds that outstanding actors 'have some mysterious psychic chemistry, half conscious and yet three quarters hidden, that they themselves may only define as 'instinct', 'hunch', 'my voices', that enables them to develop their vision and their art'.[5] Patrice Pavis is critical of this *je ne sais quoi* approach amongst theatre practitioners, but it has spirited advocates, like Jane Lapotaire:

> You cannot teach acting, you cannot. People either have it or they don't, it's as simple as that. You can teach them how to speak better, to breathe properly, to analyse a text, but the actual spark that transmutes words on a page into a living, believable human being... is a process of mystery and myth that no-one can analyse. That's what makes it so magical.[6]

Presence is a coalescence of energy, mystery and discipline. The way these dimensions relate to each other is different with every exceptional performer, but there are shared traditions and inspirations for them to draw on.

Energies

When Goethe states that an actor must always 'remember that he is called to fill out the stage with his presence', he begs a question: what is the actor to be filled with?[7] 'Energy' is the obvious answer, but this is a word that carries its own mystique, warranting the longest entry in Eugenio Barba's *Dictionary of Theatre Anthropology*. Barba measures the English word against Chinese, Indian, Japanese and Balinese equivalents to create a constellation of terms that draw in concepts of presence, power and the life force, whilst admitting that what all of these terms refer to is 'an intangible, indescribable, unmeasurable quality'.[8] Crossing to an Italian context, Barba considers the Latin terms *anima* and *animus* in relation to the qualities of energy that are produced by the breath:

> Boccacio commenting on Dante and summarising the attitudes of a millenarian culture, said that when *anima*, the

living and intimate wind, is drawn towards and desires
something, it becomes *animus* (in Latin, animus means air,
breath). Soft energy, *anima*, and vigorous energy, *animus*,
are terms which have nothing to do with the distinction
between masculine and feminine, nor with Jungian archetypes or projections. They describe a very perceptible
polarity, a complementary quality of energy difficult to
define with words, and therefore often difficult to analyse,
develop and transmit.[9]

This difficulty may be tackled, however, and in training performers
can learn to 'dilate their daily presence' through sensitive management of the energy fields produced from the breath. Their goal is to
achieve 'the presence of energy in action both in time and space',
an effect which Barba illustrates with three photographs of the
actress Iben Nagel Rasmussen performing in a village street in
Sardinia. Here, he points out, the presence of energy is evident in
both static and mobile sequences, and is expressed through the
dynamics of body posture: the set of the head, positions of the feet,
angles of the shoulders and arms.[10]

Going by the entry in the *Oxford English Dictionary*, the genealogy of the term *presence* in English does not include any definitive
relationship to concepts of energy or dynamics but there is an
implicit relationship through the verb to *present*, which has distinct
theatrical connotations: to show, exhibit or display; to represent a
character on the stage; to act or play a scene. Barba's analysis alerts
us to the ways in which theatre tends to convert presence as a state
(and status) of being into presence as an act. As a state of being, its
associations are metaphysical and religious; as an act, it may be
associated with the practical work of performance and performance training. Both must work together, though, to produce the
kinds of reactions that have created the poetics of presence in the
western tradition. Energy itself must be seen as something at once
scientific and uncanny, a matter of both technique and mystique.

Most programmes of stage training, like Barba's, are concerned
with the training of energy, teaching the performer to filter out
tensions and impulses so as to convert the energies of everyday life
into something more potent and resolutely purposed. Julie Holledge
finds specific strategies for helping student actors to fill the space:

The first exercise I do... involves them walking onto a
stage from the wings, finding the strongest position on the

stage to stop, surveying the auditorium, and saying 'I own this space'. The rest of the class sits in the auditorium and responds... 'yes you do'... 'or no you don't'. The trick of the exercise is for the actor to control time, relax, and achieve perfect physical alignment.

From here, the detailed exploration of energy paths can begin:

> I think there is a lot to be said for the emphasis on counter-tensions in the performing body, contradictions: the overt and the hidden, inner and outer. These counter-tensions that flow through the body, that are never still but constantly in motion... I think it is these transitions and juxtapositions that hold our interest.[11]

At the level of physiological communication, this is coming close to Roach's identification of how paradox and opposition are at the heart of the matter, but how does it sit with the high valuation of harmony in western traditions? For Colley Cibber, Betterton's capacity to generate power is born of his extraordinary harmonic control:

> When any discourse receives force and life, not only from the propriety and graces of speaking agreeable to the subject, but from a proper action and gesture for it, it is truly touching, penetrating, transporting, it has a soul, it has life, it has vigour and energy not to be resisted.[12]

The crafts and disciplines of acting in our own time are very different, but Cibber's impression that the whole is more than the sum of the parts, that it has to do with orchestration and flow, is not so distant from the description given by Holledge. The cumulative effect of training and technique still cannot produce that 'vigour and energy not to be resisted', unless there is a quicksilver physical intelligence at work through the live unfolding of the performance on stage. Actors will talk of 'sparking' during the course of a performance, but sometimes the intelligence and spontaneous life are drawn from a molten quietness. Janet Suzman finds this in Marlon Brando:

> With acting at its best... there's a kind of inner burn which can't be taught, and which a talented performer will have,

where the detail with which you illuminate your character's life seems preordained and infinitely natural.[13]

Not all energies are equal, and if, as Patrice Pavis reports, presence is regarded in the profession as 'the supreme attribute', some
attention to the notion of supremacy is also called for. The energies
of electricity and magnetism provide an image repertoire for eighteenth and nineteenth century writers. In the twentieth century,
radium became the favoured metaphor. Jean-Paul Ryngaert claims
that presence exists 'not exactly in the physical characteristics of
the individual, but in a radiating energy whose effect one can sense
even before the actor has done anything or spoken, in the intensity
[*vigueur*] of his being-there.[14]

Julie Holledge recalls an interview with Canadian performer
Pol Pelletier, 'who swore that her performing energy had cracked
the back wall of the theatre'. This suggests a supernatural
force few would even attempt to wield, and Pelletier is an
unashamed absolutist in her philosophy of training. Her 'Six
Laws of Theatre' – the laws of exaggeration and imbalance, the
law of the spine, of the expense of energy, of no mind and, lastly,
the law of the link in which all is brought into flow – are
designed to be all-encompassing. As she avows in her solo work
Joie (1992): 'Changer le Monde. Oui, j'ai cette prétention'.
(*Change the world. Yes, that's my bid.*) In her off-stage persona
she is equally trenchant. 'My goal, really, is not only to give
people aesthetic emotions, but to chemically and energetically
transform them'.[15]

Michael Chekhov devised a series of physical and psychological
exercises to promote awareness of radiation. Typically, these
include expansive movements combined with mental images of
power emanating from a concentrated core within the body. 'Do
not cut short the stream of power generated from the center', he
urges, 'but let it flow and radiate for a while beyond the boundaries of your body and into the space around you'. The instruction
to 'let it flow' is alternated, however, with statements indicating
that a conscious act of will is involved: 'send the rays of your body
into the space around you' and 'while radiating strive to go out
and beyond the boundary of your body'. The power in the body is
inexhaustible, and accumulates through expenditure so that by
practising radiation as an active, decided process, the actor will
gradually 'experience more and more of that strong feeling which
may be called… presence on stage'.[16]

To an extent, then, the qualities of presence and even radiance can be developed through training, yet certain performers seem to explode beyond the reach of what training can do for other artists in their field. If we think of Olivier or Nijinsky or Bernhardt as supreme exemplars of theatrical presence, this is because their performances inspired reportage that enshrines a blazing after-image of their original impact. Nijinsky was the 'vivid, radiant boy', who in challenging the limits of human physical capability, also presented a metaphysical challenge to the limits of human being. Dancers before him had been described as etherial or tran-scendent, but Nijinsky set a precedent for the dancer in whom physical and metaphysical forcefields converged. Such a conver-gence is especially spectacular in dance, though the power that trig-gers it is often perceived as an inner stillness, as in Lincoln Kirstein's description of Suzanne Farrell during her time as a star of Balanchine's New York City Ballet:

> Like other powerful artists she invests her own mystery, an enclosed alchemy of power, vulnerability, the control and conscious manipulation of tension. When she dances it is not only a body in motion but an apparatus analysed and directed by operating intelligence. It is as if some sort of radium slumbers but is always present and ready in her corporeal centre; when ignited, it grows to white heat. It enables her to transcend occasions, patterns, appearances. It commands recognition but is not always easy to read. Balanchine has been able to provide a habitation in which this core is fired, or can activate itself.[17]

After his reference to an 'alchemy of power', Kirstein resists the temptation to push his imagery towards the mystical and supernat-ural, grounding it in an almost mechanistic terminology – 'appara-tus' and 'operating intelligence' – so that he can draw out the poetry through an evocation of how radium actually behaves.

There is something intrinsically mysterious about radium, so for a culture oriented towards scientific and technological modes of understanding, it seems the perfect successor to notions of magical agency. This may be partly because it is a more recent discovery than magnetism and electricity, which, while their powers were first being learned, seemed like realisations of the supernatural. Dialogue between the performing arts and the energy sciences has a long history, and the chapters to come will explore it further, but the balance between science and supernaturalism never stabilises. A strong inclination one way or the other will sometimes occur in surprising contexts. Brando may have impressed some with the mystique of his 'inner burn' but he himself insisted there was no mystery about acting; his interest was always focused on the technicalities. The American writer Robert Lindsey records a telling anecdote about him:

> Within twenty minutes of our first meeting, he had my shoes off, my belt loosened and my fingers wired to an instrument that measured my galvanic skin response, all the while explaining that it was a technique he sometimes used to get a personal profile of people by asking questions and observing the reaction of the meter. I was more puzzled than jittery. At our first meeting, I discovered that he was the most curious man I had ever met...[18]

An actor's energy may be extraordinary, but what of the characters he or she is called upon to play? Whilst energy radiating from the figure on stage may suggest power of a higher order, the modern dramatic actor's work will involve taking on a range of characters reflecting ordinary social types.

Mystique and instrumental science have an intimate relationship when it comes to investigating energies. Guy Brown, a research fellow in human bioenergetics with the Royal Society, writes of his subject in a way that links micro-measurement with cosmological drama:

> Our cells are energized by huge electric fields driving currents of charged particles through a myriad of tiny wires. Four different types of cellular electricity drive minute machines: motors, gates, latches, and chemical factories. The pace is unimaginably frantic, the electric forces are colossal and the flying sparks are life-threatening. This is the real secret of living energy and electricity is the true vital force.[19]

There is something about the image of Brando painstakingly listening into the vital force through a fussy arrangement of wires, that evokes a central paradox about the actor's art. Not Diderot's paradox of controlled abandon, but rather the ancient paradox of scale that sees the macrocosm in the microcosm. The energy in a flick of the wrist or a twitch of the mouth can be made to speak volumes by a skilled actor, through the holding power of a body invested with energies of greater magnitude, from a dynamic range not commonly accessed in everyday life. I find the image of Brando and his wiring kit oddly resonant with another image that seems at first to belong in an entirely different register. This appears in Peter Brook's autobiography, *The Shifting Point*:

> I have a little figure from Vera Cruz of a goddess with her head thrown back and her hands held up – all so right in conception, in proportion and form that the figure expresses a sort of inner radiance. To create it, the artist must have experienced this radiance. But he did not set out to describe radiance to us through a set of abstract symbols. He told us nothing: he only created an object that makes concrete this very quality. And this to me is the essence of great acting.[20]

A coda to this is recorded in Michael Kustow's 2005 biography of Brook:

> Until I came across this statue, I thought an actor was someone who constructed, in a very complicated way, his 'character'. And then I realised this 'character' wasn't true. The actor is someone who must empty himself. So although this statue is an empty object, in its attitude one can feel fullness. It really is an expression of pure joy. So from the 1960s, I started using this object, in workshops with actors. The actor with this object understands that it's through a shedding of skills that he achieves this. It's like a direct reference to what a living actor is.[21]

From the energy of a minute human nerve impulse to that of the gods, coursing through a living being that has converted itself into an open channel, there is some kind of continuity, and it has to do with the continuity between ancient and modern that so many commentators insist we have lost. It is a continuity Guy Brown emphasises in his book *The Energy of Life*, suggesting that the ancient Greek concept of *pneuma*, the vital energy of heat and breath, is developed through the doctrines of Aristotle and then Galen in ways that create the foundations for modern scientific understanding of energy in the body. 'The ghost of pneuma', he says, 'still haunts the modern idea of energy'.[22] It is curious, then, that the word *pneuma* does not make its appearance in rehearsal studios and writings on performance training in Europe and America when its equivalents from other traditions – the Chinese *chi*, Indian *prana*, of Japanese *ki-hai* – are honoured adoptions. If we go in quest of the cultural energy sources of the western dramatic tradition, these are well documented and reveal much about the relationship between *pneuma* and presence.

Mysteries

Behind the two Renaissance models of the dignitary and the magus stands the Greek duality of the Dionysian and the Apollonian. Apollo, the sun god envisaged as a beautiful youth, is representative of form and structure, music and light, grace and law; Dionysus is the intoxicated god of wine, associated with dance and abandonment, chaotic celebration, excess and animal power. The Apollonian/Dionysian binary has been reinterpreted by several important modern thinkers including Schopenhauer and Nietzsche, but the axis dividing the prototypes of the magus and the dignitary is set at a different angle, reflecting the changing principles of humanism in the modern world. The magus is essentially an archaic type but one that travels through time, combining the mental powers of Apollo with the dark and transformative energies of Dionysus. The dignitary has Apollo's grace and sense of order but reinterpreted for a developing modernity: he is of noble lineage, learned in the classics, has mastered rhetorical skills and courtly behaviour, and is politically intelligent. As social changes open out this model to include accomplished men and women across the social spectrum, the 'other' of the magus goes through some radical evolutions but the magus remains an avatar from an ancient world.

What forms does this take? Sometimes there are fears that the magus's power has been lost, or hopelessly downgraded. 'Over the centuries', according to Peter Brook, 'the Orphic rites turned into the Gala performance – slowly and imperceptibly the wine was adulterated drop by drop'. The complaint is made as part of his case for a return of what he calls the 'Holy Theatre', which he defines as one that 'not only presents the invisible but also offers conditions that make its perception possible'. The paradox here – that of aiming 'to comprehend the visibility of the invisible' – is one Brook finds in Zen tradition, but it also has an important history in the west, through the doctrines of neo-Platonism.[23]

An actor who in Hamlet's words 'holds as 'twere a mirror up to nature' may be reflecting the fashions and forms of the times but, in hermetic terms, mirroring nature involves something much more potent and esoteric, as expressed in the words of Plotinus, one of the philosophers through whom Renaissance hermeticists found a link with the deeper histories of occult cosmology.

> Those ancient sages, who sought to secure the presence of divine beings by the erection of shrines and statues, showed insight into the nature of the All; they perceived that, though this Soul (of the world) is everywhere tractable, its presence will be secured all the more readily when an appropriate receptacle is elaborated, a place especially capable of receiving some portion or phase of it, something reproducing it and serving like a mirror to catch an image of it.[24]

This evocation of the 'place or receptacle' with a special capacity for receiving the presence of the All, in association with the idea of the divine being mirrored in a sacred object, harks back to the ancient mysteries. Rituals of invocation were an early form of theatre practised in the Mediterranean world before modern distinctions between 'eastern' and 'western' cultures arose; Egyptian, Greek, Persian and Roman mythical traditions were amongst those that gave rise to mystery cults. The mysteries offered something more encompassing than the numinous shrines and statues to which Plotinus alludes, and were certainly associated with the creation of a specially appointed place designed as a reflection of the cosmos. This was usually a cave or underground chamber adorned with symbolic markings to indicate the canopy of the heavens and the zodiac.[25] Sometimes the orientation of it was chosen so that rays from the sun would strike through the entrance to the heart of the chamber at the equinox or the solstice. Dio of Prusa described 'a mystic recess, overwhelming by its beauty and size', in which the *mystai* (initiates) 'would behold many mystic views and hear many sounds ... with darkness and light appearing in sudden changes and other innumerable things happening'.[26]

Sometimes the 'things happening' were violent. Mithraic rites climaxed in the sacrifice of a bull on a slatted board placed over the heads of the *mystai* so that they would be drenched in the hot blood. The abandoned dancing associated with Dionysian festivals evoked the mythical event in which the young god was captured by a group of crazed revellers and torn to pieces. An association between violence and revelation, with sacred value being accorded to the blood of the slain god, is part of Christian ritual. Acts of violence lend themselves to dramatic structure. There are sequenced preparations, parallelled with a graduated build-up of fear and anticipation in the spectators, and the act itself can be made spectacular. Some twentieth-century performers, notably the Vienna Action movement of the 1960s, have tried to regenerate primordial energies through works of performance art involving the killing of animals, or the display of freshly killed carcases. Such adventures typically fail to engage with the symbolic language of mystery dramas, and with the different levels on which they work as human experiences.

Terror may be a powerfully effective way of opening up the psyche, but the magus knows many ways of conjuring terror. In the mysteries of Eleusis, 'the most frightening and the most resplendent of all that is divine for men' was brought into the chamber where the *mystai* were participants in a sequence comprising *legomena* (spoken), *dromena* (enacted) and *deiknymena* (shown) elements.[27] The climactic moment was the revelation of the great secret. Some accounts inevitably leaked out, though what could be told did little to communicate the significance or effect of what was experienced. Details are sparse: a single head of grain was held aloft by the hierophant, and was beheld in silence 'as a simple manifestation of the life in the grain and in all things'.[28]

We can add some contextual information. The Eleusinian mysteries were based on the story of Demeter, goddess of the harvest, and her daughter Kore (Persephone), whose journey to the underworld expresses the cyclic death and rebirth of nature. Demeter's emblem was the head of grain, symbolic of the whole life cycle from conception through birth, growth, the traumas of cutting and threshing, incorporation into other life forms, and return to the earth for regeneration. Participants in the mystery were taken through phases of darkness and disorientation after which this vision of the grain shining in the light, framed by the star-embossed walls of the cavern, would have acquired greatly enhanced impact. For participants, according to Walter Burkert, the experience was 'patterned by antithesis, by moving between the extremes of terror and happiness, darkness and light'.[29]

The heart of the mystery lay not in any immaterial secret but in corporeality itself, with its capacity to encompass the divine and the magical. So it was that the most potently esoteric moment of the Eleusinian rituals was the showing of the grain of corn. In this were contained all the elements of the cycle, culminating in a renewed experience of being alive to the corporeal world. Human life was situated at the intersection of the natural and the divine. Natural and astrological lines of force converged in the figure of the hierophant holding the emblem of the grain. One of the central paradoxes of presence in the theatre is epitomised here: although a strong stage presence brings a heightened sense of the here and now, it is also resonant of the expanded life cycle which moves through the realms of the dead, links up with ghosts and immortals, then returns to the natural world with renewed vital force.

In one of the surviving accounts, it is stated: 'I came out of the mystery hall feeling like a stranger to myself'. Plutarch associated the mysteries with the experience of death itself:

> Wanderings astray in the beginning, tiresome walkings in circles, some frightening paths in darkness that lead nowhere; then immediately before the end all the terrible things, panic and shivering and sweat, and amazement. And then some wonderful light comes to meet you, pure regions and meadows are there to greet you, with sounds and dances and solemn, sacred words and holy views.[30]

The fact that people who had been through an experience like death and returned to the realms of the living marked them out from other mortals, who would only make the journey one way. To complete the cycle was a privilege originally reserved for the gods. 'Just how initiates into the mysteries appropriated this power, we do not know', as Marvin Meyer writes:

> Kore returned from the realm of Hades; Dionysus vivified his devotees; Adonis rose from the dead, Attis gave an intimation of new life; Osiris reigned as king of the underworld; and the bull provided life for the world. Hence, if human beings could assimilate the power that made life triumphant in the world of nature, they too might live in a more complete way.[31]

Eliphas Levi, a nineteenth-century historian of magic, interpreted the experience of the mysteries as a dramatic journey:

The candidate descended through dark subterranean regions, wherein he traversed successively among flaming pyres, passed through deep and rapid floods, over bridges thrown across abysses, holding in his hand a lamp which must not be extinguished. He who trembled, he whom fear overcame, never returned to the light; but he who surmounted every obstacle intrepidly was received among the mystae.[32]

The power of the magus who had learned to move between the realms of light and darkness, life and death, matter and spirit, was immense:

Length and even perpetuity of life, the field of air and its storms, the earth and it metallic veins, light and its wondrous illusions, darkness and the realms thereof, death and its ghosts – all these do therefore obey the royal sceptre of the magi... The adept becomes king of the elements, transmuter of metals, interpreter of visions, controller of oracles, master of life in fine, according to the mathematical order of Nature.[33]

Such descriptions invoke Presence with the capital letter, and have echoes in the accounts of great stage performances throughout the modern era. According to the eighteenth-century tragedian David Garrick, the distinction between a great genius and a good actor was that the former was 'transported beyond himself' and worked upon the audience like a magus.[34] Garrick's contemporary Sarah Siddons inspired something close to idolatry in her admirers, of whom William Hazlitt was the most eloquent. 'She was regarded less with admiration than with wonder', he wrote, 'as if a being of a superior order had dropped from another sphere, to awe the world with the majesty of her appearance'.[35]

A century later the French tragedienne Rachel was exuding an aura of supernaturalism so potent that the novelist Charlotte Brontë felt she was witnessing the rise of 'a great and new planet'. Amongst the numerous testimonials she inspired was an unlikely tribute from someone later to become a pillar of the English establishment as the Dean of Westminster:

It is difficult to describe it. She had seemed to be a woman – she became a 'being' – sublime irony, prophetic enthusiasm, demoniacal fierceness, succeeded each other in flashes like lightning.[36]

Henry Irving, the greatest stage mesmerist of the late Victorian era and the model for Bram Stoker's Dracula, was renowned for his uncanny evocations of the diabolic and the divine. 'In the course of his overwheening career', writes Nina Auerbach, 'he played not only Mephistopheles and Napoleon, but a mystic Dante, reconceiving the cosmos'.[37] In a lighter register is Geoffrey Whitworth's impression of the young Nijinsky:

> The vivid radiant boy is also the hierophant of mysteries, and in the glamour of his presence 'Armide' comes to seem not merely a matchless display of lovely form in motion, but also a type of the supreme functioning of a state of being most strange and utterly alien to our own.[38]

After the funeral of Maria Callas in 1977, the director of the Paris Opera declared, 'Goddesses do not die'.[39]

Those who exude this kind of supernaturalism are also those who experience the stage itself as an arena charged with power. Here one may think again of the young Simon Callow, stepping out before a vacant auditorium onto a bare stage and finding it 'throbbing with energy'. Ian McKellan, of whom Harold Hobson wrote 'no player of similar age... has such lustre, such interior excitement, such spiritual grace', recalls following a group of variety theatre performers backstage in his youth. 'I stood in the dust and dark backstage, comparing the tawdry reality with the glamorous illusion onstage. It's a contrast that still absorbs me. It holds a secret and a mystery that I never hope to solve'.[40]

Laurence Olivier woke up a whole generation of theatre-goers to new levels of excitement with his capacity to take the stage and generate a forcefield of his own. Kenneth Tynan's description of a climactic moment in his 1945 performance as Oedipus could be an account of something experienced by one of the *mystai* at the crisis point of an ancient ritual:

> Olivier's famous 'Oh! Oh!' when the full catalogue of his sin is unfolded must still be resounding in some high recess of the New Theatre's dome: some stick of wood must still, I feel, be throbbing from it. The two cries were torn from beyond tears or shame or guilt: they came from the

stomach, with all the ecstatic grief and fright of a new-born baby's wail... A man seeing the horrors of infinity in a trance might make such a sound: a man waking from a nightmare to find it truth might make such a sound; but no other man, and no other actor.[41]

Tynan found something profoundly ritual in Olivier's Oedipus, and something alchemical in his Richard III. 'Olivier's Richard eats into the memory like acid into metal, but the overall impression was of lightness and deftness'. This was 'active, energetic evil' in the tradition of Blake. There was animal ferocity and 'vulgar nastiness' yet they were drawn from an element of another kind 'in the same way an obscene statue can be made of pure gold'.[42]

I have argued that the magus is a continuing prototype in western theatre, and one that is resurgent even in cultural environments permeated with science and technology. But Peter Brook is not alone in his concern that the theatre has lost its hieratic powers. One of the fiercest voices calling for the return of the magus is that of Antonin Artaud, writing in the 1930s. Artaud presents a vision for an 'alchemical theatre' of transfusions and transformations, in which the mystery of creation can be re-staged as it was in the Orphic and the Eleusinian mysteries. The actor as alchemist had a mission of the highest order: to be the centre of orchestrated sounds, colours and forms capable of producing in the spectator a 'complete, sonorous, streaming, naked realisation'. What was to be conjured here was the dissolution of all opposites 'into one unique expression which must have been the equivalent of spiritualized gold'.[43] This may be a reference to the great Eleusinian secret, the manifestation of the ear of corn. There is a fiercely committed atavism in Artaud's call to presence. Vitalisation means *re*vitalisation; the birth is also a rebirth, and to bring it about there must be recourse to what is archaic and original in dramatic tradition. For Artaud, the 'religious and mystical bearings' from which modern consciousness has come adrift may be traced back to the ancient mysteries.[44]

To what extent, though, is alchemy in the eye of the beholder? Every so often the rhetoric of a commentator takes off into the stratosphere – Colley Cibber writing on Betterton, Hazlitt on Sarah Siddons, Jules Janin on Rachel, Geoffrey Whitworth on Nijinsky – and, if the writing is good enough, manages to communicate a vision that is absolutely convincing. But as the mythologising moves down the line, inflating itself through the processes of repetition and exchange, it acquires a certain amount of hot air. Perhaps there really was an experience of mystery somewhere at its source, but what begins to circulate is simply the exercise of myth-making, as when the Countess Ann de Noailles said of one of Nijinsky's performances, 'it was as if the creation of the world had added something to its seventh day... I understood that I was witnessing a miracle'.[45]

Many performers who are the subject of this kind of glorification are wary of it. In a 1967 interview with Tynan, Olivier spoke of the actor as 'the illuminator of the human heart', but also offered a somewhat embarrassed apology for using 'high-faluting' terms. 'At the opposite end of the pole', he said, 'you've got to find, in the actor, a man who will not be too proud to scavenge the tiniest little bit of human circumstance, observe it, find it, use it some time or another'.[46] Attention to detail, process and technique is an antidote to the more loaded expectations of an exhilarated public. Brando is an insistent de-mystifier of acting, offering such provocations as 'if a studio offered to pay me as much to sweep the floor as it did to act, I'd sweep the floor'. With his widely known commitment to method acting, and his acknowledgement of Stella Adler's training as the foundation to his approach, he maintained throughout his career a repertoire of tricks and techniques ranging from the apparently cavalier (cutting up the script and leaving pieces of it taped to the objects around him, so as to provide an impression of spontaneity when he delivered the lines he had not learned) to the obsessive:

> If I can't figure somebody out, I'll follow him like a weasel with persistence until I find out what his nature is and how he functions... I am endlessly absorbed by human motivations. How is it that we behave the way we do? What are those compulsions within us that drive us one way or another? It is my lifelong preoccupation.

He writes compellingly about studying the behaviour of a chimp, is aware that the human face has 155 muscles in it and trains himself in biofeedback techniques as an aid to controlling his emotions.[47]

Brando's distaste for myth making comes out strongly in a passage describing his responses to Leni Riefenstahl's films of the Nazi rallies:

> The Germans in the stadium at Nuremberg didn't know that Hitler was an unstable, maniacal personality, and that the people around him were thugs, liars and murderers.

> They were creating myths about him in the theatre of their minds... There is theatre in everything we see or do during the day. As Hitler demonstrated, one of the basic characteristics of the human psyche is that it is easily swayed by suggestion. Our susceptibility to it is phenomenal, and it is the job of the actor to manipulate this suggestibility.[48]

The figure of Hitler has come to epitomise the dangers of allowing any human personality to be trusted as the bearer of Presence in its mythological sense, but cautions about this were being expressed in the modern theatre before Hitler appeared on the scene.

They are the basis of Edward Gordon Craig's case for the replacement of the actor by the über-marionette. Craig distrusts the very process of acting, to which he denies the status of an art form on the grounds that the actor is the slave of the passions, a mere vehicle for forces that are chaotic and inimical to aesthetic form. Craig's problem is not with any inflationary response to the actor's presence, but with its primordial and Dionysian affiliations. The über-marionette is the best substitute for the actor, in Craig's view, because it is a blank-faced and evacuated substitute for the human, free of the taints of human expression. 'There is something more than a flash of genius in the marionette, and there is something in him more than the flashiness of displayed personality'.[49]

'The flashiness of displayed personality' is a telling phrase, resonant of anti-theatrical prejudice through the ages. Distaste for exhibitionism is part of this, and when what is being exhibited is the personality, there is an offence against deep-seated principles of humility and social dignity. A lack of discipline at some profoundly psychological level is being manifested, a kind of vulgar eroticism of the psyche. Commercial entertainments through the twentieth century seized on this and embraced it, reinventing it as a new kind of ideal and in the process inventing a new kind of stage presence. This will be further considered in Chapter 4. But for Craig, writing in 1907, the prospect of a personality-driven theatre meant the loss of connection to the sacred and mythic bedrock of drama, whereas the marionette is 'the last echo of some noble and beautiful art of a past civilization'.[50] Other theatrical visionaries with equally strong commitments to the archetypal forms of dramatic presence do not fight shy of human actors, but they do demand of them a special order of discipline.

Disciplines

In his short treatise on the Holy Theatre in *The Empty Space*, Peter Brook cites Merce Cunningham, Jerzy Grotowski and Samuel Beckett as exemplars. They have several things in common, he says: 'small means, intense work, rigorous discipline, absolute precision'. Theirs are theatres that explore life, 'yet what counts as life is restricted'.[51] The actors' work is accordingly set about with cautions and refusals, a kind of *via negativa* of unlearning. Brook's biographer Michael Kustow records his address to his Paris company in 1970 as they prepared to begin work on *Orghast*, a work Brook created in 1971 in collaboration with the poet Ted Hughes for performance in the ruins of the temple of Persepolis. 'Inside the group one should recognize that all everyday emotions have to be kept out', Brook announced, 'and – this is the prime discipline – one should rigorously prevent them from ever creeping into the work'.[52] It is as if this kind of work is driven by a mistrust of all the lesser things an actor can become and, more crucially, of the actor's propensity to become a counterfeit presence:

> In the theatre, the tendency for centuries has been to put the actor at a remote distance, on a platform, framed, decorated, lit, painted, in high shoes – so as to help to persuade the ignorant that he is holy, that his art is sacred. Did this express reverence? Or was there behind it a fear that something would be exposed if the light were too bright, the meetings too near? Today, we have exposed the sham. But we are rediscovering that a holy theatre is still what we need.[53]

One of the techniques Brook used in training was to strip away the repertoire of physical and verbal behaviour the performers had built up through past experience. He describes an exercise in which one actor was to direct the actions of another who had his face to the wall and could not receive any visual signals. Words were also banned, so the communication could only happen through impro- vised sounds. The idea that sound can be a source of primordial dramatic energy was explored more systematically in *Orghast*, which was a version of the Prometheus myth, about the original theft of fire from the gods and its introduction to human life. Hughes waxed eloquent – and esoteric – in his account of the prin- ciples on which the vocal experiment was based:

When we hear it we understand what a strange thing is
living in this Universe, and somewhere at the core of us –
strange, beautiful, pathetic, terrible. Some animals express
this being pure and without effort, and then you hear the
whole desolate, final actuality in a voice, a tone. Then we
really do recognize a spirit, a truth under all the truths. Far
beyond words.[54]

One can recognise here an evocation of presence in its most archaic
manifestation. It was a particular challenge to the individual
performer. 'What you hear in a person's voice', Hughes told Tom
Stoppard in an interview, 'is what is going on at the centre of
gravity in his consciousness at that moment'. In everyday communication, the kind Brook sought to eliminate from the rehearsal
process, 'the attention is scrambled' and 'the voice loses its anchor,
or its roothold rather, in what is really going on in the man'.[55]
    The demands on modern actors seeking to interpret the most
ancient dramatic traditions are stringent and comprehensive.
Grotowski's training regime includes advanced yoga exercises,
gymnastics, contrary co-ordinations based on Dalcroze, and vocal
work focused on the production of non-human sounds like dripping
water or the revving of a motor. None of these in themselves is
unusual in actor training, but they are taken to levels of difficulty
and endurance few training programmes would attempt. In Brook's
view, Grotowski shows the way towards acting as 'an art of
absolute dedication, monastic and total'.[56] Grotowski himself has
an imagery for this that dramatises the distinction between personal
presence and the archetypal Presence required for the holy theatre.
'If he [the actor] does not exhibit his body, but annihilates it, burns
it, frees it from every resistance to psychic impulse, then he does not
sell his body but sacrifices it'.[57] He talks of imposing 'the sort of
shock needed to peel off the layers behind the life-mask' and
pushing his company 'to overstep every conceivable limit'.[58]
Theatre itself must be stripped of its riches – its sets and costumes,
technologies and complex buildings; it must become poor.
    It seems that in being asked to undo all familiar patterns of reac-
tion and behaviour, actors in this kind of theatre are being asked to
undo modernity itself. Is there some essential qualitative difference
between the forms of humanity modelled in post-Renaissance civilisation, and the human experience expressed through the ancient
mysteries? Are the cultures of modernity nothing but an excres-
cence around the vital core of being? Grotowski insists that his

holy theatre is contemporary 'in that it confronts our very roots with our current behaviour and stereotypes and in this way shows us our "today" in perspective with our "yesterday"'. And, he adds, 'it is a sincere and absolute search into our historical ego'.[59] The kind of ecstatic presence achieved by his leading interpreter, Richard Cieslak, may be claimed for the modern world, then, but where in history do we go in order to get the bearings for it? Brook returns to the Greek myths in *Orghast*, but he is also a passionate advocate of Shakespeare as the supreme creator of holy theatre, and his own productions of *Lear*, *Titus Andronicus* and *Midsummer Night's Dream* bring out the spectrum of horror, confusion, strangeness, rediscovery, communal reorientation and vital exuberance that belongs to the mystery dramas of the expanded life cycle. One of the landmark theatre works Grotoswski created in the 1960s was *The Constant Prince*, based on the seventeenth-century Spanish play by Calderon de la Barca.

This was the production in which Cieslak gave his most extraordinary performance, as the figure at the centre of a modernised passion play in which stages of torture and death were mimed with a conviction that communicated extreme anguish. The Polish critic Josef Kelera, after confessing himself quite sceptical of the portentous talk about 'holy theatre', reported:

A sort of psychic illumination emanates from the actor. I cannot find any other defnition. In the culminating moments of the role, everything that is technique is as though illuminated from within, light, literally imponderable. At any moment the actor will levitate... He is in a state of grace.[60]

There is no question that Cieslak's impact was born out of discipline. Franz Marijnen describes his physical capabilities in some notes from a workshop given by Grotowski and Cieslak in Brussels in 1966:

All the exercises that were practiced in detail and separately during the former lessons, are now executed by Cieslak in one co-ordinated movement. He links them up in one complete cycle. His entire body adapts itself to each movement, to the slightest detail. With unbroken concentration and control of all his muscles – and there are many – he works through the whole cycle, improvising around it.[61]

Grotowski has interesting views on the balance between mystique and technique. Not only does he avoid buying into the dichotomy, he presents a surprising take on the matter of precedence:

> I am frequently asked whether certain 'mediaeval' effects indicate an intentional return to 'ritual roots'. There is no single answer. At our present point of artistic awareness, the problem of 'mythic roots', of the elementary human situation, has definite meaning. However, this is not a product of a 'philosophy of art' but comes from the practical discovery and use of the rules of theatre. That is, the productions do not spring from *a priori* aesthetic postulates; rather, as Sartre has said: 'Each technique leads to metaphysics'.[62]

There is no suggestion here that the techniques are being devised *in order to* lead to metaphysics, rather that the discipline imposed by the 'rules of the theatre' is an end in itself, but one that culminates in a massive opening out. The only programmatic intention Grotowski admits to is that of the *via negativa* – a stripping away and cutting back.

Eugenio Barba, who worked closely with Grotowski in the 1960s and edited the documents that comprise his influential work *Towards a Poor Theatre*, concentrates on the opening out and is interested explicitly in cultivating presence, which he explains as the outcome of preparatory work. By turning presence into an act, Barba's analysis renders it available to conscious cultivation, yet it is evident that there is no formula approach that will work. The principles are subtle and their application requires fine intuition. His training regime aims to help performers achieve a state of dilation in body and mind, what he calls 'the pre-expressive level'. This is a state of readiness in which stage presence is constructed in advance of any appearance on the scene. Franco Ruffini compares the technical and conceptual approach here to that of Stanislavski. 'By means of the system, the actor learns to be organically present on stage, before and apart from the roles which he will have to perform'.[63] It seems that *prae-sentia*, presentiment, the most nebulous and esoteric connotation of presence, actually provides the line of approach by which it may be captured and controlled.

Stanislavski is the chameleon figure behind the most radically different actor training experiments of the twentieth century. Stella

Adler adopted and adapted his 'method' to create a programme for American actors that suited the demands of a growing film industry. This meant an essentially naturalistic foundation. Grotowski, for whom Stanislavski is 'a personal ideal', sees the 'bag of tricks' approach so often associated with method acting as the first thing he must take away.[64] Yet Grotowski's recognition that technique leads to metaphysics is curiously analogous to Stanislavski's view of how one can work with the human psyche. Creative inspiration, according to Stanislavski, arises from the subconscious, the 'inner life of the human spirit', which alone can manifest on stage as the true expression of presence or, as Stanislavski puts it, the state of *I am*. But the subconscious is inaccessible to consciousness. 'We cannot enter into that realm. If for any reason we do penetrate into it, then the subconscious becomes conscious and dies'. This is the predicament from which his director alter-ego Todorov derives his most subtle principle:

> Fortunately there is a way out. We find the solution in an oblique instead of a direct approach. In the soul of a human being there are certain elements which are subject to consciousness and will. These accessible parts are capable in turn of acting on psychic processes that are involuntary... Therefore our art teaches us first of all to create consciously and rightly, because that will best prepare the way for the blossoming of the subconscious, which is inspiration.[65]

As with Grotowski's working process, the potent dramatic core of the work can only be approached with peripheral vision, and is only accessed by means of displaced operations whose connection with it is never fully comprehensible. This is a discipline of the will, which is continually frustrated in its untrained manifestations.

Under the direction of Stanislavski, Grotowski, Barba or Brook, the actor is remade from the outside in and the inside out, in preparation for the act of being on stage, with all its vibrant aliveness and dangerous mythic resonances. What is dangerous, fundamentally, is not the violent purport of any particular enactment, but this act of being on stage. As Simon Callow sees it, 'Standing on stage is an aggressive act. It says: "Look at me. Listen to me". It says: "I'm interesting, I'm talented, I'm remarkable". "Oh yeah?" Says the audience. You'd better prove it'.[66] Anthony Sher makes a similar point. 'It *is* a dangerous business, standing in front of several hundred of your fellow human beings and saying, "*I* am interesting enough to watch". The good ones keep danger in the air'.[67]

The danger and the power are one and the same thing, as Norman Mailer brings out in a confronting analysis of the distinction between stage and film presence. He begins by proposing that 'existentially, theatre and film were in different dominions'. And he, too, goes back to archaic origins for his point of reference in elucidating the special conditions of live performance:

> ... anyone who has ever experienced a moment of unmistakable balance between the audience, the cast, the theatre, and the *manifest* balance of the play, an awe usually remarked by a silence palpable as the theatrical velvet of an unvoiced echo, knows that the foundation of the theatre is in the church and in the power of kings, or at least knows (if theatre goes back to blood sacrifices performed in a cave – which is about where the most advanced theatre seems ready to go) that the more recent foundations were ecclesiastical and royal.

Mailer's allusion to blood sacrifice, secreted here in a double parenthesis, haunts the next step of the argument. Aside from any drama to be enacted, a dangerous power-play is engaged between performer and spectator, an engagement that is on one level about the establishment of hierarchy, but on another is sudden, instinctual and always potentially violent:

> Theatre, at all of its massive best, can be seen as equal to a ceremony, performed by noblemen who have power to chastise an audience, savage them, dignify them, warm them, marry their humours and even create a magical forest where each human on his seat is a tree and every sense is vibrating to the rustle of other leaves.

But the modern actor faces the audience as neither a nobleman nor a priest, with discipline as his only armour:

> ... he cannot know in advance if his effort will succeed or not. In turn, the audience must respect him. For he is at least brave enough to dare their displeasure. And if he is bad enough... well, how can he forget old nightmares

where audiences kill actors? ... His presence is the real truth: He is at once the royal centre of all eyes, and a Christian up before the lions.[68]

It is in the context of an essay on film, in a book on writing, that Mailer launches into this virtuoso account of the live art of theatre. As a contribution to the poetics of presence, it is somewhere in a league of its own – not because it is unmatched as a piece of commentary (though it certainly has a unique kind of verbal bravado) – but because it comes from outside the domain of theatre writing, and is bowled onto the page with a surprisingly fierce aim.

When Mailer turns his attention back to film, he gives an account of the film actor as engaging in a performance far removed from the ritual mysteries, but it is also an enactment of death and the return of the life cycle. If there is something dangerous about theatre, 'there is something sinister about film', says Mailer. The actor 'must work into a focus of will. The real face he speaks to, whether a step or ten steps to the side of the director, is a circle of glass'. In this process, life is being lost. 'An emotion produced from the churn of the flesh is delivered to a machine and its connections manage to produce a flow of images which will allow some related sentiment in those who watch'. This is the point at which the vital spark re-enters. 'The living emotion has passed through a burial ground – and has been resurrected'.[69]

Returning from an existential to a practical view of the matter, actors can and do cross between theatre and film (in both directions) all the time, but in doing so they answer to very different technical demands. Some of the same kinds of talent may be called for, but the skills are not the same at all and their cultivation requires quite distinct principles in training. Julie Holledge puts it this way:

> The screen actor is engaged in one on one communication. The stage actor projects performance energy into the auditorium where it mingles and hopefully coalesces the collective energies of the audience; a screen actor uses magnetic introjected energy to draw individual viewers inside the character's mind through the aperture of the eyes.[70]

Mailer's death-dealing camera is effaced here with the image of direct eye contact between spectator and actor, an illusion, of course, but in an art form centred on illusion, not such a stretch from the actor's perspective. Janet Suzman tells a story about Brando's technique for preserving the film artifice around eye contact:

> I did a film called *A Dry White Season*, and we were doing a court scene and the great Marlon Brando arrived. There was Donald Sutherland, and Susan Sarandon, me, Michael Gambon, and Ronald Pickup, and all kinds of people sitting in the courtroom waiting for the great man to appear, and he did. But what was most notable was – and he's obviously picked this up from way back in his career – he never looked up, he kept his eyes down.

The effect, Suzman notes, was to give him an immunity to the distractions of the film set, with its endless parade of specialists to adjust hair and make-up, or cater to the actor's whims: 'he had a ring round him of concentration and he preserved it'.[71]

This is an identifiable technique, with a specific genealogy in the training system of Stanislavski and its offshoot in the American Method school. Ian Richardson gives an account of how he used the image and its associated training technique in preparing for the role of Francis Urquhart, an imaginary political leader on the Thatcherite model:

> I studied a book about people in power, and how they needn't necessarily be like the film stars that the girls swoon over, but they have this incredible aura of power about them. I thought, 'How do I establish this aura, so that when I'm on camera, it is a measurable chemistry? Stanislavski talks about the circle of concentration: you imagine a band around your head, which you expand outward and outward until it touches the audience.[72]

Here concentration – as the internalisation and accumulation of intensity – may be seen as the inverse of radiance, but also as its precondition. As an originally mental or psychological process (albeit one with physiological effects), this contrasts with Barba's prioritisation of a somatic approach to the generation of energised presence for the stage. However, the two systems also resonate in some interesting ways, especially in their emphasis on preparation and the necessity of conjuring a state of intensified alertness before appearing in front of an audience. Barba acknowledges the compatibility: 'By means of the system, the actor learns to be organically present on the stage, before or apart from the roles which he will have to perform'.[73]

Stanislavski's own way of explaining the method of concentration provides some clear indications as to why it transferred so readily from the stage to the screen. His wording brings out a sense of the close-up in which the camera moves in on the inner life of the character:

> But whatever may be the sphere of the actor's attention, whether it confines him at some moments to public solitude, or whether it grips the faces of all those before the stage, dramatic artistic genius, as in the preparation of the part so in its repeated performance, requires a full concentration of all the mental and physical talents of the actor, and the participation of the whole of his physical and psychic capacity. It takes hold of his sight and hearing, all his external senses; it draws out not only the periphery but also the essential depth of his existence, and it evokes to activity his memory, imagination, emotions, intelligence and will. The whole mental being of the actor must be directed to that which is derived from his facial expression.[74]

If the Method is, as Christine Gledhill states, 'the contemporary performance mode most able to deliver "presence"', this is because it trains the actor to be 'the face as window to the soul'.[75]

The stage actor radiates, the film actor concentrates; but some caution is needed with any formulaic differentiation. Since radiation is dependent on concentration, we are only talking about a difference in the order and priority of approach. Most obviously, presence cannot mean the same thing on screen as on the stage. On the screen, the drama of transient immediacy takes place at one remove, but concentration can produce a displaced sense of present-ness, as Carole Zucker affirms. Those actors who 'fill the screen with their intense concentration', she says, can 'achieve a complete engagement and integration with moment to moment reality'.[76] Sometimes, curiously, this entails a strategic avoidance of acting. Dustin Hoffman tells the story of how he got the limp right for Ratso Rizzo in *Midnight Cowboy* by following a suggestion that he put rocks in his shoe. A more dramatic example of the same kind of strategy was Brando's approach to playing a death scene in *Mutiny on the Bounty*:

Brando went out and did research... and found out that when you die from burns you die from shock, and he found out what shock was like. It was like being encased in water. So when he came to do the shot, he put himself in a bathtub on the ship. When it got time for the close-up, he was in the bathtub filled with ice. So he didn't have to 'act' it.[77]

Many such stories are told of and about Method actors who ground their screen performances in immediate physical reality to achieve a presence effect before the camera, but presence on screen can only be virtual, with the camera as intermediary in the divorced timeframes of acting and viewing.

Since the advent of cinema, stage acting has itself been strongly influenced by the techniques of performance that work best on the screen. Audiences move between film, television and live theatre, as actors do, influenced by the probing observations of the camera and accordingly carrying with them expectations about what makes a performance convincing. Live performances that are too 'big' quickly provoke scepticism and so fail to engage us, and images of pre-twentieth-century actors may appear to us rather absurd, with over-stated attitudes and expressions. A sense of scale is created on very different terms in a mass media environment, where actors who achieve celebrity are known in globally multiplied close-up and the most high profile film actors are also stars, whose personal lives are of more interest to the media than anything they do in their professional capacity. 'Star quality' has much to do with talent for creating and manipulating oneself as an image, and its relationship to presence is tenuous. Nor is it to be directly equated with charisma, a term uneasily situated between 'presence' and 'star quality'.

Charisma

'Charisma' and 'charismatic' are words whose usage has escalated in conjunction with the growth of mass media culture, but they have a long history. In spite of the plethora of websites now offering courses in 'instant charisma' as a product for purchase (in the form of short courses in easily acquired techniques), the prerogative of bestowing *charisma* in the original meaning of the term was exclusively divine. The Greek word χαρισμα means a favour specially vouchsafed by God, and may take the form of a grace or talent, including, for example, a gift of healing or prophecy. Through the influence of the German philosopher Max Weber, charisma is associated in twentieth-century usage with a kind of leadership that responds to a prevailing disenchantment with the world, by offering a vision of life enlarged beyond the parameters of an economic and administrative system. In Weber's analysis, charisma is expressed through the whole person, so that it becomes an attribute of personality – or personhood – rather than a specific talent:

> The term charisma will be applied to a certain quality of an individual personality by virtue of which he is set apart from ordinary men and treated as endowed with supernatural, superhuman, or at least specifically exceptional powers or qualities.[78]

Charles Lindholm, in a more recent sociological study of charisma, sees two key precursors to Weber's interpretation of it: in J.S. Mill's view of genius and Nietzsche's doctrine of the *Übermensch*. Mill's genius 'stands outside the realm of ordinary people as a kind of magic beacon, a unique and inexplicable phenomenon', and is associated with the imagery of elemental force. A genius is 'like the "Niagra River" and cannot be constrained by the "Dutch canals" of ordinary rules and norms'.[79] Energy, illumination and uniqueness are the factors in Mills's characterisation of the genius that readily translate in terms of stage charisma. They are also the qualities shared with Nietzsche's superman, whose virtue is an overwhelming vitality. As he wrote in *Twilight of the Idols*, 'great men, like great epochs, are explosive material in whom tremendous energy has been accumulated'.[80] And great women, too, one might add, with the image in mind of Rachel epitomising the force of a Revolution, or Sarah Siddons, Sarah Bernhardt and Maria Callas, of whom more will be said later.

The notion of the charismatic individual, as distinct from that of a person endowed with a particular gift, may be strictly speaking a twentieth-century interpretation of the term. Charles Lindholm says that it was 'virtually unknown a generation ago'.[81] Lindholm's book was published in 1990, and even since then the word has spun out and diversified in general usage, changing its applications particularly in response to a celebrity culture, which seeks its leadership through fashion and style, or in the 'role modelling' associated with almost any form of globally publicised success. In this sense, any actor or performer who has the eyes of the world turned upon them through enough camera lenses might be regarded as charismatic, and charisma might be seen as the media alternative to live presence, but such a picture is oversimplified. If charisma is a gift, the gift of compelling attraction is especially highly prized in the live theatre, as it is in the media spotlight; and compelling attraction may be not so much a gift in itself as a sign of other qualities that are sought out instinctively by large numbers of people.

A more relevant distinction to make between presence and charisma is that charisma needs to be understood in a longitudinal sense, as a heightened life force that animates a whole career and fuels the trajectory of a sustained mission in the world. Presence is an expression of life force in the moment, so that the moment itself is transformed in a way that has an impact on all who witness it. Its very transience is a factor in its uncanny potency. Clearly, there is also an area of overlap here: the charismatic will almost inevitably be someone with presence, someone who can 'turn it on' for an assembled crowd, but the reverse is not always the case. There are actors with the most powerful stage presence who might attract no attention whatsoever outside the framework of a performance and would have no wish to be a personal force in the world. Yet the charismatic leader and the actor with presence have in common a capacity to communicate with a peculiar intimacy to the individuals massed as their audience. In order to explore this interweave, I will consider two cases, one who crosses between the theatre and the public stages of the political world, and one who is a political figure drawing on specific theatrical techniques.

Adolf Hitler is a figure who haunts all post-war discussions of charisma. Weber died in 1920, before Hitler's rise to power, but he offered something like a prognosis of the Hitler phenomenon through his vision of the charismatic as an epoch-changing but also potentially chaotic influence. Hitler's skills as a political and military leader were uneven at best, and what continues to haunt us about his rise to power is the way he communicated with such hypnotic levels of will and energy in public gatherings. No-one who has watched filmed scenes from the Nuremberg rallies can be in any doubt that the massed reactions are being triggered and controlled by the figure on the podium. How this control was achieved is a matter upon which speculation is rife, but Ian Kershaw, one of Hilter's recent biographers, takes the view that performance skills had much to do with it:

> He was above all a consummate actor. This certainly
> applied to the stage-managed occasions – the delayed entry

to the packed hall, the careful construction of his speeches, the choice of colourful phrases, the gestures and body language... theatrical use of the hands as the speech rose to a crescendo; sarcastic wit aimed at opponents: all were devices nurtured to maximize effect.[82]

Then there are the personal qualities. Those Kershaw lists are conducive to the build-up of an extraordinary will-power: 'Single-mindedness, inflexibility, ruthlessness in discarding all hindrances, cynical adroitness, the all-or-nothing gambler's instinct for the highest stakes'.[83] When these qualities came into play before an audience, they were fed and galvanised by the live responses. Starting in the Munich beer halls in the early 1920s, Hitler gained rapid momentum in a sequence of largely impromptu addresses from a table drawn into the midst of the crowd so that he could speak literally and psychologically from amongst them. As one eye witness recorded:

> He spoke for two and a half hours, often interrupted by frenetic torrents of applause – and one could have listened to him for much, much longer. Everything came from the heart, and he struck a chord with all of us... He uttered what was in the consciousness of all those present.[84]

This is an especially arresting example of co-presence: the future of 'modern man' hangs in the balance during these marathon engagements over a wooden table in the beer hall. Events in Russia and France had demonstrated the revolutionary potential in massed groups of ordinary people, but perhaps it was only the exceptional individual who was truly capable of harbouring the vital energies and experiencing the larger emotional registers. A mood Nietzsche would have labelled *ressentiment* was dominant in the consciousness Hitler was speaking to: a sense of national inferiority, simmering fury about 'interest slavery', frustration with a political leadership that was seen to be placating foreign powers. At a public gathering in a Festival Hall in Munich in 1920, 'the atmosphere suddenly livened when Hitler came to speak'. Contrasting with previous speakers, 'his tone was harsher, more aggressive, less academic... his sentences short and punchy'. He whipped up the crowd with invective against the Centre party leadership then drove them to hysteria with a sustained verbal onslaught against the Jews, as if heralding the enactment of a revenge drama.[85]

One of the paradoxes about Hitler is how the off-stage person known as the 'little corporal' acquired such magnitude before the public. Much of what was going on could be explained in performance terms, as the concentration, control and release of energy, with especially galvanic effects achieved through shifts in the pitch and register of the voice. Crescendo and climax were the governing shape of his presentations, and he could sustain both for inordinate amounts of time. But Hitler was not fundamentally an actor or a performer, because he took himself literally and played only one role. His grasp of dramatic narrative was one-dimensional and paranoid. He had locked himself into his Wagner-inspired platform theatre, which could offer nothing, ultimately, but implosion. There was a presence here, but not one that could have thrived in any other kind of theatrical context.

An effective stage presence can manifest itself through an infinite variety of moods and guises, but behind it is a very different order of control from that which Hitler was exercising, because it begins with control of the performer's own bio-energetic fields. In most cases (there are exceptions), there is a calmness at the centre of all the sound and fury that adds to the dramatic power while it is raging. It is through return to this centre that new impulses can be generated, changes in role and mood can be managed. Perhaps some form of emptiness is indeed required of the actor, if not the facial blankness Edward Gordon Craig sought with his prescription of the puppet mask.

Hitler was at the opposite end of the political and human spectrum from another charismatic orator who, by the end of the 1920s, was establishing a stage career whilst also becoming the figurehead for the civil rights movement in America. Paul Robeson, dubbed 'Ol' man charisma' by *Time* magazine in an article published to mark his centenary, brought to the world stage a prodigious range of qualities and abilities. The journalist in *Time* also calls him a 'Promethean figure' who, as an actor, was unmatched for the breadth of his talents.[86] Another centenary tribute describes him as 'four-sport athlete and Phi Beta-Kappa valedictorian of Rutgers University, Columbia School Law graduate, stage and screen star, renowned singer, civil rights militant, left-wing activist'. This writer fills out the profile with a personal memory:

> From my childhood I was drawn to Robeson. I remember sitting, at age 8, in the living room of my parents' home in Noristown, pa., listening, mesmerized, to his full and

resonant voice. With depth and perfect enunciation, he was singing 'Jacob's ladder' and 'Amazing Grace'. As the old RCA Victor phonograph record rotated slowly, Robeson's voice exhibited a tone of richness and durability that matched the antique record player'.[87]

Perverse as it may seem to offer comparisons with Hitler, there is some parallel in their capacity to translate a flair for communicative intimacy into an effective delivery before a massed audience (Robeson at the zenith of his career spoke and sang before crowds of 25,000 and more.) With Robeson, though, there was a calm centre. Antonio Salemmé, who tried to capture something of this in his sculpture of Robeson as a young actor, commented on his easy command of time and space, both on and off stage. 'He spoke slowly and took his time about everything. He never looked at his watch. Paul had this air of not going anywhere, and yet he travelled fast'.[88] The impression of intimacy was created through this ease, which allowed for an opening out of simple emotions. Robeson was an unashamed idealist, whose genius lay partly in an ability to give the ring of searing truth to pronouncements that might have sounded naïve or simplistic from the mouth of anyone else. With him, co-presence meant commonality of the simplest kind, and there was no place for ressentiment in his identification of the human common denominators. 'When I sang my American folk melodies in Budapest, Prague, Tiflis, Moscow, Oslo, or the Hebrides or on the Spanish front', he said, 'the people understood and wept or rejoiced with the spirit of the songs'. And this understanding arose through 'the common language of work, suffering and protest'.[89]

As an African American and a graduate of Rutgers, Robeson spanned two social worlds and two orders of human experience that were separated by deeply determined forms of violence. At Rutgers he distinguished himself as a scholar of languages, and as an athlete: he was twice selected for the All-American football team. Even here, though, he had to fight back from assaults by his team-mates in order to claim his place in the game. During his student years he also made his name as a fine bass singer, giving concert performances of Negro spirituals to supplement his scholarship income. Having gained his degree, he went on to study at Columbia Law School but his stage career began to take precedence in the early 1920s, when he drew critical attention for some performances with a Harlem-based African American amateur theatre group. From there he took off into professional theatre, with roles in two plays by Eugene O'Neill. After *The Emperor Jones* had its première in London in 1925, Robeson's dual profile as an actor and concert singer gained international momentum. There was a Paris concert attended by a celebrity audience in 1927, and a sell-out concert at the Albert Hall in 1929. The ovations, multiple encores and press adulation had by this time reached the proportions of legend.

Everything about Robeson was larger than life, as is reflected in the epithets he drew from critics: 'gigantic', 'magnificent', 'superb', 'great'. He was a Renaissance man with nothing of the magus about him and everything of the dignitary, represented in a modernised form and identified with a social world where nobility had to be claimed by those who had been denied even the standing of ordinary citizenship. A charismatic in the original sense of the term, he expressed a bemused detachment about the gift he had for performance: 'I don't know what it is, that all my life has caused me to succeed whenever I appeared before the public, far beyond what my experience, training or knowledge deserved'.[90] The performances themselves created an impression that something was being given:

> Paul Robeson's voice is all honey and persuasion, yearning and searching, and probing the heart of the listener in every tiniest phrase. A rich, generous, mellow, tender, booming voice that you think couldn't say a bitter word or a biting sentence with a whole lifetime of practice.[91]

As a civil rights campaigner, Robeson also demonstrated charisma as Weber interpreted it. His impact was associated with a breach of the established social order, a vision for a new kind of life, and a systemic upheaval. As one witness reported of his appearance at a training camp in Tarazoa during the Spanish civil war, 'the whole place lit up. It was like a magnet drawing you... as if somebody was reaching out to grasp you and draw you in'.[92] Like all love affairs, those conducted with the public at large are prone to break-up. The Robeson legend splintered on the shifting edge of a dangerous reality when towards the end of the 1940s he began to attract the attention of the House Un-American Activities Committee. By the mid 1950s, when he was confined to the United States because his passport had been revoked, the pressure began to tell on him. He suffered a breakdown from which he emerged permanently scarred, prone to clinical depression and suicidal outbursts.

Robeson is a rare example of someone who demonstrates charisma and stage presence in equal measure, but it is as if he had two careers – as a stage performer and a civil rights leader – and the two qualities ran in parallel through them. If, as Mailer and others have suggested, presence on stage is dangerous, charisma is arguably more so, because it eats into the personality of the one who harbours it, and can generate a level of public excitement that becomes intolerable. Presence may be the supreme attribute of the performer, but the lure of charisma carries with it the insidious idea that it is a supreme attribute of human being. Thereby hangs the ancient tale of hubris, around which so many of the great dramas of western tradition were composed. The job of the actor is not to fall into it, but to evoke its powers and its hazards, while remaining in control of the live communicative event of the performance.

2

DRAWING POWER

L'attraction: voilà la loi de l'univers.

Jean-Antoine Roucher[1]

During the Renaissance, the actor was a paradoxical figure in the social hierarchy. Someone of low birth might make their name playing monarchs and emperors. As a member of a generally disreputable profession, the player might still hold sway over the crowds with his oratorical command. There was power on the stage of the Globe Theatre, power which could lend to the actor the authority of the magus or the compelling attraction of the lodestone. In metaphysical terms, the actor was an equaliser, a channel for presence and authority of many kinds but also someone in whom the condition of human mortality was epitomised, as in Shakespeare's line:

> All the world's a stage,
> And all the men and women merely players.[2]

The metaphor of which this may be the best-known expression was widely current in the Elizabethan era. Sir Walter Raleigh drew together a circle of intellectuals who called themselves The School of Night and wore black costume for their gatherings, where they shared a view of 'the grand theatre of the world' through the melancholy perspective of truth seekers prepared to acknowledge:

> Our graves that hide us from the searching sun
> Are like drawn curtains when the play is done.[3]

Theirs was not the drama of the expanded life cycle, but it was not without its mysteries. The Earl of Northumberland, a prominent member of the School known as the 'Wizard Earl', was painted by the miniaturist Nicholas Hilliard beside the esoteric symbol of a set of scales balancing the globe on one end with a feather on the other.

Such an image was an incitement to interpretations of many kinds, but there was a scientific trick to it: the fulcrum was moved so far to the heavier end of the balance beam as to compensate for the extreme differential in the weights. As Frederick Turner comments in his classic study of the School of Night, 'we are presented with the vertiginous idea of the whole universe in one pan of the scales, and nothing in the other: with the implication that if we can inhabit that nothingness ... we shall gain magical control over the world'. Figuratively, the emblem conveyed the more esoteric point that the microcosm could balance the macrocosm, but this too was a matter for experimental study.[4] William Gilbert, court physician to Queen Elizabeth and Northumberland's contemporary, went out of his way to avoid being associated with wizardry but there were similarities in the mysteries the two men were exploring. Gilbert investigated the microcosm/macrocosm equivalence through experiments in magnetism that began 'by forming a little loadstone into the shape of the earth':

> By which means he compassed a wonderful designe, which was, to make the whole globe of the earth maniable, for he found the properties of the whole earth, in that little body; which he therefore called a terrella, or little earth; and which he could manage and try experience upon, at his will.[5]

The name and design of the Shakespearian Globe conveyed the idea that the theatre, too, was a microcosm that could balance 'the great stage of the world'. In *The Tempest*, Prospero harps on the ambiguities of a world that is all and nothing, ready to be converted in an instant from one end of the balance scale to the other:

> These our actors,
> As I foretold you, were all spirits, and
> Are melted into air, into thin air:
> And, like the baseless fabric of this vision,
> The cloud-capped towers, the gorgeous palaces,
> The solemn temples, the great globe itself,
> Yea, all which it inherit, shall dissolve,
> And, like this insubstantial pageant faded,
> Leave not a rack behind.[6]

In Shakespeare's theatre, this power is not directly attributed to the actor playing the magus in the drama; it is only implied, if that.

With the escalation of puritan attacks on the theatres, leading to their closure during the civil war (1649–60), the status of the actor reached what was probably an all-time low. Yet the turbulence of the period gave rise to more mobile hierarchies that were in the long run to favour those who made the stage their profession. In the mid seventeenth century, when England was going through one of the worst periods of chaos in its history, new ideas were arising of what it meant to be a powerful human being.

'Natural power', wrote Thomas Hobbes, 'is the eminence of the faculties of body or mind, as extraordinary strength, form, prudence, arts, eloquence, liberality, nobility'. Power was diversifying, operating according to changing dynamics and finding new bases. Hobbes continues his line of thought about human power by focusing on power itself, much as a physicist might, seeking out its 'means and instruments' and its laws. Natural power combines with instrumental power – manifested as wealth, friends, reputation and 'the secret working of God, which men call good luck' – with the effect of augmenting itself:

> For the nature of power is in this point like to fame, increasing as it proceeds; or like the motion of heavy bodies, which, the further they go, make still the more haste.[7]

Such a view would be encouraging to those who sought to acquire power, or cultivate it in their own spheres of operation. In the statement above, Hobbes draws an analogy between power and fame, which at the time meant rumour or reputation. But fame too was changing its meanings. To be much rumoured or talked about was to have one's reputation in the public eye, to be 'famous'. 'Famous' was not necessarily a flattering epithet – it could equally mean infamous or defamed – but power and fame were becoming associated. 'The public worth of man, which is the value set on him by the commonwealth, is that which men commonly call dignity', as Hobbes pronounces. Birth and lineage were no longer the *sine qua non* of individual power, and here the interpretation of 'commonwealth' is telling:

> The greatest of human powers is that which is compounded of the powers of most men united by consent

in one person, natural or civil, that has the use of all their powers depending on his will.[8]

It might not have occurred to Hobbes that the actor on the stage could exercise this kind of drawing power, though a century later David Garrick was demonstrating it to extraordinary effect. If power in the Hobbesian mode was set to favour the actor and to give a new lease of life to the mysterious phenomenon of presence, it did not do so immediately or without recurrent, sometimes violent struggle.

When the theatres were officially re-established in 1660 after the restoration of the monarchy, the social status of the actor was volatile and those who led the new companies did so under the pressures of social stigma. Colley Cibber tells stories of the abusive behaviour of audiences towards actors on stage, and records that 'disgrace and prejudice' surrounded the profession when he started out as a young actor in 1690. In 1698, Jeremy Collier's pamphlet on 'the immorality and profaneness of the English stage' was a renewed onslaught, proclaiming with heavy-handed sarcasm that 'the stage test for quality' was an inversion of everything that constituted public decency:

> A fine gentleman is a fine whoring, swearing, smutty, athe-
> istical man. These qualifications, it seems, complete the
> idea of honor. They are the top improvements of fortune
> and the distinguishing glories of birth and breeding.[9]

So much for the dignitary. Collier's primary target was the dramatists and the characters they created, though the flow-on of contempt to the actors who impersonated them was part of the picture, and it was they who had to front up to the rowdy audiences.

Respect was hard won, through the work of prominent figures like Betterton, Charles Hart, Edward Kynaston, Mrs Barry, Mrs Bracegirdle, William Mountfort and the manager Aaron Hill, who wrote a treatise on acting and established a training academy. The case was made through an emphasis on aesthetic technique and fine judgement in performances, and on the personal dignity of the actor. Cibber's praise of Betterton reflects the enlightenment values of proportion, harmony and symmetry:

> The person of this excellent actor was suitable to his voice;
> more manly than sweet; not exceeding the middle stature;

inclining to the corpulent; of a serious and penetrating aspect; his limbs nearer the athletic than the delicate proportion; yet however formed, there arose from the harmony of the whole, a commanding mien of majesty.

By all accounts (and there are many excellent accounts of his impact), Betterton's aesthetic was itself a revelation; for a country in recovery from civil war, proportion and harmony meant more than a dilettante's preferences, and he made them into a living experience, so becoming a leading influence on taste. James Thomas Kirkman, looking back on the era in a memoir, captured this in appropriately full-blown cadence:

> The strength and melody of his voice, the majesty of his deportment, the skill and force of his enunciations, the expression of his countenance, and the general harmony of the whole, has such an effect upon his auditors, that judgement was disarmed, and lead captive in transport and admiration.[10]

An actor with an established reputation might be on sure enough ground to challenge taste, as when Charles Macklin as Shylock defied expectations with an unconventional approach to the role and was rewarded with 'the tremendous silence of a brilliant and crowded audience'.[11]

As David Garrick came to dominate the London stage in the mid eighteenth century, the status of the player was heading towards a new zenith. Increasingly it was the actor, not the play, who drew audiences to the theatre and a star system was taking hold in commercial terms. Samuel Johnson, always a little grudging in his praise of his celebrated contemporary, conceded:

> Then, Sir, Garrick had under him a numerous body of people; who, from fear of his power, and hopes of his favour, and admiration of his talents, were constantly submissive to him. And here is a man who has advanced the dignity of his profession. Garrick has made a player a higher character.[12]

So here was a dignitary; but what of the other side of the equation, the capacity of the magus to draw in the powers of the universe? Hobbes was no subscriber to the model of the magus, nor were the free thinkers who had come to the fore during the interregnum and introduced an ongoing strain of scepticism to English culture. During the Restoration the role of the genius, strongly identified with the leading figures in the scientific academy, became an alternative to that of the Renaissance magus, providing a new set of images and paradigms through which the power of the actor could be interpreted.

Genius

Following the restoration of the monarchy, royal patronage was granted to other institutions than the theatre. The foundation of the Royal Society coincided with the re-establishment of a theatrical tradition, and the term 'genius' was being applied to great men of knowledge and ideas as it was to leading players. If Newton was the genius of his age, Betterton was a genius in his own sphere and the solar imagery associated with the two men has distinct echoes. Cibber proclaimed: 'This genius was so strong in Betterton that it shone out in every speech and motion of him'.[13]

There are differences, though, in the way this metaphor is used. Newton's sun is circling and encompassing, suggestive of the workings of a great mind. The poetry in which he was celebrated evoked a sun rising in the sky, its light breaking across a darkened world. The actor's sun is a stable point at the centre of its own universe, and here the imagery is a development of descriptions from the Shakespearian era, such as the widely quoted portrait of 'An Excellent Actor':

> ... By a full and significant action of the body he charms our attention: sit in a full theatre and you will think many lines drawn from the circumference of so many ears, whiles the actor is the centre.[14]

With Newton there was no concern about the full and significant action of the body: he was proclaimed 'a celestial intelligence entirely disengaged from matter'.[15] As the imaginative language surrounding the actor develops further, planetary evocations accord both light and gravity to the figure who commands the stage. There is a presence that shines and illuminates, but there is also an intelligent physicality, in which speech and motion are earthed, and towards which all others present are drawn.

In the theatre as in science, 'genius' was the term used to mark out the exceptional or inspired individual from others working in the same field whose abilities were conventional and studied. As the concept developed over the eighteenth and into the nineteenth century, it inspired rhetorical elaborations that stretched the distance between ordinary capacity and extraordinary talent. As Thomas Carlyle wrote in 1827:

> Genius has privileges of its own; it selects an orbit for itself; and be this never so eccentric, if it is indeed a celestial orbit, we mere star-gazers must at last compose ourselves; must cease to cavil at, and begin to observe, and calculate its laws.[16]

But where the scientist with genius had to contend with adversarial reactions from the guardians of received wisdom, the genius of the stage was identified by the very capacity to gain the adulation of the crowds. The drawing power was immediate and explicit, with direct economic returns. It took over a generation for Newton to become widely celebrated as the herald of transition to a new era, but Garrick's reception was instantaneous, as Richard Cumberland recalled:

> ... when after long and eager expectation I first beheld little Garrick, then young and light and alive in every muscle and in every feature, come bounding on the stage, and pointing at the wittol Altamont and heavy-paced Horatio – heavens, what a transition! – it seemed as if a whole century had been stept over in the transition of a single scene; old things were done away, and a new order at once brought forward, bright and luminous, and clearly destined to dispel the barbarisms and bigotry of a tasteless age.[17]

William Hazlitt laments that 'the genius of the great actor perishes with him', but also relishes the contemporaneity of stage genius, which must always be living and present. Although there is a void produced when a great actor dies, it will not be long before another comes to fill it.[18] The great scientist, though, is a genius for posterity, and after his death is celebrated in language that accords quasi-divine status. The eighteenth-century architect Etienne Boullée wanted to place Newton 'in the abode of immortality, in the heavens'.[19] Patricia Fara, who cites this description in her study *Newton: The Making of Genius*, points to the divergence between artistic and scientific genius through the work of Immanuel Kant.

In his *Critique of Judgement* (1790), Kant focuses on originality as the primary quality of genius, defined as 'a talent for producing that for which no rule can be given'. The work displaying this quality is arrived at by steps that cannot be replicated because its creator 'does not to himself know how the ideas for it have entered into his head'.[20] Some of the mystique surrounding stage presence derives from this mystique surrounding genius. From the 1660s onwards, there was a growing literature on the actor's art, but the increasingly sophisticated fascination with its technical components was typically accompanied by insistence on what could not be learned. 'What talents shall we say infallibly form an actor?' asks Colley Cibber. 'This, I confess, is one of nature's secrets, too deep for me to dive into'.[21] Garrick's comment on the great French actress Clairon in a letter written in 1769 prefigures the terms of Kant's analysis:

> Madam Clairon is so conscious and certain of what she can do, that she never... had the feelings of an instant come upon her unexpectedly. – but I pronounce that the greatest strokes of Genius, have been unknown to the Actor himself, 'till Circumstances, and the warmth of the Scene has sprung the Mine as it were, as much to his own Surprize, as that of the Audience – thus I make a great difference between a great Genius and a good Actor.[22]

One of the stranger manifestations of genius, though, was the way it could transmit its effects through those who shared its arena, creating the illusion that they, too, were possessed of it. Kitty Clive, whose own stage career lasted the best part of forty years, wrote from her retirement to congratulate Garrick on contradicting the old proverb that you cannot make bricks out of straw. He had done, she said, what was 'infinitely more difficult', in passing off the actors and actresses of his company as if they were possessed of a genius they sadly lacked. On his own retirement, she warned, they would be exposed. 'They think themselves very great', but 'now let them go on in their new parts without your leading strings, and they will soon convince the world what genius is'.[23]

The genius may have been successor to the magus in the world of scientific modernity, but the sense of working magic through incommunicable processes is retained, as is the capacity to tap into the wider forcefields of the universe.

> ... the ever-shifting forms of an eternal principle, that
> which is seen but for a moment, but dwells in the heart
> always, and is only seized as it passes by strong and secret
> sympathy, must be taught by nature and genius, not by
> rules or study.[24]

This is Hazlitt, writing in the Romantic period when the idea of
genius had a full-blown flowering, taking it into much bolder
poetic formulations than were attempted in the more constrained
intellectual climate of the Restoration. Amongst the acting profession,
Hazlitt singles out Mrs Siddons as the supreme exemplar
of the qualities he is identifying. With her exception he is
ambivalent about the attribution of genius to actors, yet his way
of characterising its operations evokes the theatrical model
because of the stress on public impact: 'It is not enough that a
man has great power in himself, he must shew it to all the world
in a way that cannot be hid or gainsaid'. Those impressed with
this power must also be made to feel it, and the one who holds
the power is set on an imaginative journey that may overawe
lesser spirits:

> It is after we enter upon that enchanted ground that the
> human mind begins to droop and flag as in a strange road,
> or in a thick mist, benighted and making little way with
> many attempts and many failures... The undefined and the
> imaginary are regions that we must pass like Satan, difficult
> and doubtful, 'half flying, half on foot'.[25]

Genius, however scientific, continually beckons across the
enchanted ground and the leading players of the Restoration were
most potent in Shakespearian roles that shared nerve connections
with satanic and supernatural realms. Stage presence could never
lose the atavistic resonances of the ancient mysteries, with their
traumatic disruption of rational understanding. The natural world
and all reasoned ways of knowing it were cracked open when
Betterton confronted the ghost in Hamlet with a 'tremor inexpressible',
or Garrick's 'sublimely horrible' Richard III gripped an audience
with sympathetic terror, or Sarah Siddons as Lady Macbeth
displayed the horrors of the mind 'flitting in frightful succession
over her countenance'.[26] At the same time, the figure of the lead
actor was being accorded powers that belonged to the new order of
scientific understanding.

'The paradigm of attraction'

In Hazlitt's descriptions, echoes of Milton alternate with language more properly belonging to physics. It is in the nature of greatness, he says, 'to propagate an idea of itself, as wave impels wave, circle without circle'.[27] Such language was being called for in response to some of the extraordinary things that were happening in the theatres.

Sceptical as he was about the cult of blind admiration surrounding leading actors, Hazlitt could not resist a story of waves, impulsion and circles when there was a human genius at the centre of it:

> I have heard... that once, when Garrick was acting Lear, the spectators in the front row of the pit, not being able to see him well in the kneeling scene, where he utters the curse, rose up, when those behind them, not willing to interrupt the scene by remonstrating, immediately rose up too, and in this manner, the whole pit rose up, without uttering a syllable, and so that you might hear a pin drop.[28]

The connections between genius, physical force and human power were being suggested with varying degrees of explicitness through the eighteenth century. One of the more explicit attempts to chart them is to be found in an essay by an unnamed writer published in the *Occasional Paper* in 1719. The writer employs mechanical imagery to support his insistence that genius should be diligently cultivated, and supplied with 'proper materials' to fuel it. Thus it will be set for 'going through the World with Wind and Tide'. And 'as Gravitation in a Body... doth not barely imply a determination of its Motion towards a certain Center, but the *Vis* or Force, with which it is carried forward', so the English word *genius* incorporates the Latin terms *ingenium* or *Vis ingenita*, the natural force or power with which every Being is invested.[29]

Part of the context for this statement is the scientific debate between mechanists and those interested in the phenomenon of attraction: the drawing power of magnetism and gravity. The writer in the *Occasional Paper* is treating gravity as a force contained in the body falling towards the centre rather than in the centre itself. It is this second interpretation, of gravity as attractive power, which comes to provide the principle source of metaphor for modern stage presence. It is not until the nineteenth century that we see the uninhibited use of this metaphor, as it also begins to appear in the rhetorics surrounding powerful figures in the political arena. Napoleon, in particular, inspired new adventures in verbal expression. One writer remembered being held up by his nanny to watch the great man ride by and claimed: 'Perhaps by some chance he cast a glance at me, and with that glance took my spirit into magnetic slavery'.[30] This was in 1810, and by this time the ideas of Anton Mesmer had taken hold and the craze for personal magnetism had spread widely in Britain and Europe. This is the subject of the next chapter, but it is worth taking a forward glimpse at how the poetic imagination would come to feed on these associations. In her novel *Villette*, Charlotte Brontë includes a scene featuring the great tragedienne Vashti (a thinly disguised portrait of the Parisian stage star Rachel):

> The strong magnetism of genius drew my heart out of its wonted orbit; the sunflower turned from the south to a fierce light, not solar – a rushing, red, cometary light – hot on vision and to sensation. I had seen acting before, but never anything like this: never anything which astonished Hope and hushed Desire.[31]

Here the planetary imagery from the poetics of genius combines with the metaphor of magnetism to create an image of drawing power that is more intensely physical than anything that would have been articulated in the time of Betterton or Garrick. For over a century following the Restoration there is an inhibition on applying such overt imagery of drawing power to the actor.

When Newton began his researches into magnetism, it was a controversial subject and regarded as occult. This did not mean necessarily that it was identified with magic, simply that it was concerned with hidden causes. Magnetism and gravity were examples of forces that operated on bodies across distance. Attraction and repulsion, unlike mechanical pushing and pulling, could be effected by agents not in contact with the moving objects and 'the paradigm of attractions' had mystified scholars in Europe since the middle ages As J.L. Heilbron explains in his classic history of electrical research, 'a literal attraction, an action at a distance, exceeds the power of creatures which ... can produce local motion only by pushing. Hence it implies either a perpetual miracle or a spiritual, non-mechanical agency'. Thus the physicist, who 'must have nothing to do with occult qualities ... must reject action at a distance, attractions understood as a primitive force'.[32]

William Gilbert is concerned to dissociate his researches into magnetism from those of writers who 'treat the subject esoterically, miracle-mongeringly, abstrusely, reconditely, mystically'. He rejects the term 'attraction' as one that 'has wrongfully crept into magnetic philosophy' and blames some of the lesser Greek thinkers for the category error that attributes drawing power to material bodies rather than to circulating forces.[33] Many of the key researchers in the later sixteenth and early seventeenth century were Jesuits who frowned upon any meddling with intangible causality. The French scientist Desaguliers insisted that gravity, gravitation and attraction were phenomena to be studied only as effects. The cause was beyond the business of mortal intelligence.[34] Descartes condemned outright any enquiry into magnetism and concentrated on the challenge of formulating a theory that would account for the apparent phenomenon of attraction by demonstrating that all action depends on contact through the movement of minute particles invisible to the naked eye.[35]

Newton became caught up in this double-bind that proscribed enquiry into the hidden causes of an observable phenomenon. Endeavouring to bring the subject of attraction out of the domain of the occult, he began to develop a hypothesis of 'several distinct aethers' that confused the distinction between material and immaterial phenomena. The aethers were 'each very subtle and elastic' and possessed of 'a principle of unsociableness' or its opposite, which could account for their visible impact upon the motion of solid entities.[36] The strong attractive properties of substances such as amber or glass could be accounted for by the presence of 'effluvia' that permeated all matter but might be more concentrated in those particular forms of it. Here he is in line with Gilbert, for whom the circulation of 'electrical effluvia' is related to a macrocosmic arrangement of forces:

> The matter of the earth's globe is brought together and held together by itself electrically. The earth's globe is directed and revolves magnetically; it both coheres and, to the end it may be solid, is in its interior fast joined.[37]

The significance of this approach was that it avoided according the attractive power to any particular natural body, and maintained the principle that all motive agency was a manifestation of divine influence. As is now well known, Newton was also interested in alchemy and devoted to a more esoteric search for the indicators of divine presence in the material world through the animating spirit of the aethers. George Cheyne, one of his disciples, wrote about divine presence as the magnetic core towards which all beings were oriented, and condemned 'earthly and sensual Attractions' for disrupting 'the beautiful progress of spiritual Beings, towards the Centre and End of their being'.[38]

What we see here is that attraction and magnetism were associated with divine presence before they became by-words for stage presence. To suggest that an actor had a drawing power as an agent in his or her own right might have been to risk the charge of occultism being levelled against the writer – or worse, the charge of sacrilegious agency against the actor. Such references certainly do not appear where one would expect to encounter them: in writings that set out to capture the distinctive impact of the most lauded players. In some cases, we have the image of magnetism without the word. Cibber writes of Betterton that, 'upon his entrance into every scene, he seemed to seize upon the eyes and ears of the giddy and inadvertent'.[39] Or we see the displacement of the power centre from the actor to the theatre itself, as when Alexander Carlyle recorded that 'the theatres were not very attractive this season, as Garrick had gone over to Dublin'.[40] A more striking example of this kind of displacement onto an abstract principle can be seen in the prologue Samuel Johnson wrote for Garrick's 1747 season in *The Merchant of Venice*:

> 'Tis yours this night to bid the reign commence
> Of rescued Nature, and reviving Sense;
> To chase the charms of Sound, the pomp of show,
> For useful mirth, and salutary woe;
> Bid scenic virtue form the rising age,
> And Truth diffuse her radiance from the stage.[41]

It is as if the actor's role here is that of mediator, responsible for keeping vulgar energies at bay and allowing true powers to shine through, but without any of these powers being attributed to himself.

To us the inhibition may seem quite perverse, especially when Garrick could draw a response like that of the young Hannah More:

> Yes I have seen him! I have heard him! – and the music of
> his voice, and the lightening of his eyes still act so forcibly
> on my imagination that I see and hear him still.[42]

The term 'attractive' could, however, be applied to women on the stage. Colley Cibber refers to Mrs Bracegirdle's 'attractions' and writes that she 'threw out such a glow of health and cheerfulness, that, on the stage, few spectators that were not past it, could behold her without desire'.[43] The association of sexual attraction with magnetism was becoming an established convention. William Gilbert had written of 'magnetic coition' in his 1600 treatise *De Magnete*, avoiding explicit reference to sexuality yet unmistakably evoking it, as in this passage drawing on the ancient authority of Pythagoras:

> A breath, then, proceeding from a body that is a concretion of moisture or aqueous fluid, reaches the body that is to be attracted, and as soon as it is reached it is united to the attracting electric; and a body in touch with another body by the peculiar radiation of effluvia makes of the two one: united, the two come into most intimate harmony, and that is what is meant by attraction.[44]

During the Restoration scientific ideas about magnetism began to gain popular currency and there was a growing trade in erotic magnets. A magnet attached to one of the posts of the marriage bed was also supposed to assist in maintaining the sexual bond – if it moved, this was a bad sign.[45] Rings with chips of lodestone incorporated into them were bought by lovers or those who wanted to sustain a strong friendship. Newton himself wore one of these rings. Mutual attraction confused the issue of where between the two lovers the motive power resided, and whether it was a drawing power or an active inclination. Perhaps this is why the notion of sexual attractiveness was not controversial in the same way as the idea of personal magnetism. The sexual attractions of the actress prepare the way for a wider use of the metaphor, though Sarah Siddons, in an epilogue to her 1782 farewell performance in Bath, made curious use of it. Her three small children, the excuse offered to the audience for her departure, were called onto the stage near the end of the recitation:

> Stand forth, you elves, and plead your mother's cause:
> Ye little magnets, whose soft influence draws
> Me from a point where every gentle breeze
> Wafted my bark to happiness and ease.[46]

That the power of these small magnets should draw a celebrated actress away from the stage at the height of her popularity is an unexpected reversal of what had yet to become conventional imagery.

The leaking of vocabulary from magnetism into theatrical parlance is difficult to trace in definitive stages. We can, though, see tendencies shifting, both through changes in scientific understanding and through an expanding confidence in the social and cultural power of theatre. By the mid eighteenth century, Newtonian ideas about the principle of attraction had firmed up, and there were aggressive counter-challenges to the mechanists for their arrogant sense of certainty about how the world worked. Cultural change also freed up the imaginative range of the actor, allowing performers in the nineteenth century to experiment at the boundaries of the magical and the occult, even the diabolic. Certainly the properties of magnetism and magnetic attractiveness did not lose the frisson of sorcery. 'Wickedness is a myth invented by good people to account for the curious attractiveness of others' became one of Oscar Wilde's most widely quoted aphorisms.[47]

Motive power

Because of the controversies surrounding magnetism and the paradigm of attraction, writers in the Restoration period were in need of some explanatory model for the phenomenon of action at a distance in the theatre. Somehow the singular presence of the actor on the stage had an impact upon the massed people in the audience. The reactive effects were palpable: from the social reactions of laughter and applause through to the deeper physiological sympathy that caused tears to flow, or the spectator's blood to run cold when the actor encountered a ghost. We talk freely now of 'being moved', but in the Restoration there were literal questions about the causality of emotion as motion, involving the motility of nerves and the flow of sensibilities. As changes in theatre design removed the spectators from the stage and created a marked gap between stage and auditorium, and as the size of audiences grew, there was increasing fascination with the question of how to account for the impact of the lone figure acting at a distance upon the entire 'house' so as to effect and orchestrate a collective play of emotions.

This fascination was not new in itself, but there was a new intensity about it and an added complexity arising from the influence of scientific speculation about magnetism and attraction. Influence from the explanatory approaches favoured by Gilbert and Newton, with their emphasis on the agency of aethers or effluvia, inhibited a direct focus on the 'attraction' or drawing power of the figure on stage, and deflected concentration onto what was circulating between stage and auditorium. Of course the actor was implicated in this, not least because he or she was an impersonator of compelling figures. Through the revival and reinterpretation of Greek and Roman dramas, actors took on the roles of emperors, heroes and orators whose power over the crowds was legendary:

> When Caesar would appear,
> And on the stage at half-sword parley were
> Brutus and Cassius; O, how the audience
> Were ravished, with what wonder they went hence ...[48]

Was the performer the source, the repository or the channel for the energy circulating between the stage and the auditorium? In some of Newton's descriptions, the performance is in the thing attracted. In his account of the behaviour of paper fragments inside a glass dome, he might be describing a virtuoso display of acrobatics:

> ... after I had done rubbing the Glass the papers would continue a pretty while in various motions, sometimes leaping up to the glass and resting there a while, then leaping down and resting there, then leaping up and perhaps down againe, and this sometimes in lines seeming perpendicular to the Table, Sometimes in oblique ones, Sometimes also they would leap up in one Arch and downe in another, divers times together, without Sensible resting between; sometimes Skip in a bow from one part of the Glasse to another without touching the table, & Sometimes hang by a corner and turn often about very nimbly as if they had been carried about in the midst of a whirlwind, & be otherwise variously moved, every paper with a divers motion.[49]

The passage is suggestive of an elegant lightness in the dancing fragments, but the spectacle of humans dancing crazily was less likely to meet with aesthetic approval. Clowns and acrobats had their detractors because of their tendency to exhibit too much energy, so as to produce a kind of hyperactivity without any sense of generative power. This sarcastic passage appears in a 1603 playscript:

> Why, what an ass art thou! Dost thou not know a play
> cannot be without a clown? Clowns have been thrust into
> plays by head and shoulders ever since Kempe could make
> a scurvey face... Why, if thou canst but draw thy mouth
> awrye, lay thy leg over they staff, saw a piece of cheese
> asunder with they dagger, lap up drink on earth, I warrant
> thee they'll laugh mightily.[50]

The audience, laughing mightily, are themselves taken up in the
wave of vacuous reactivity, to be carried on the current like
Newton's flighty scraps of matter, without any interior sense of
gravity. Hamlet warns the players to rein in their clowns and
prevent 'barren spectators' from falling for the drug of instant
laughter. And the player's worst offence is the habit of generating
forced energies that will catch at the lower levels of the auditorium:

> O, it offends me to the soul to hear a robustuous periwig-
> pated fellow tear a passion to tatters, to very rags, to split
> the ears of the groundlings, who for the most part are
> capable of nothing but inexplicable dumb shows and noise.

True acting requires more managed forms of energy, a holding
back so that the forcefield is contained: 'for in the very torrent,
tempest, and, as I may say, whirlwind of your passion, you must
acquire and beget a temperance that may give it smoothness'.[51]

Hamlet's advice to the players was constantly alluded to in
Restoration discussions of acting, and it is the focus on energetics
that seems to resonate most strongly. The vulgar sensibilities of
those who demand all noise and antics remain a touchstone for
what must be resisted by the genuine actor. David Garrick, writing
to an aspiring young player in 1764, echoes the cadences and the
substance of Hamlet's lines:

> Guard against the splitting the ears of the Groundlings
> who are capable of nothing but dumb show and noise ... a
> true Genius will convert an Audience to his Manner. Be
> not too tame neither.[52]

But it was not only the groundlings in Garrick's time who lured the
players into bad habits: King George II was one of those who hated
anything on stage that distracted him from the hilarities of his
favourite clowns. Of the two monarchs, though, Garrick was the

one with most enduring public impact, combining in his person the regal authority of so many kings and princes.

Garrick's long reign over the eighteenth-century stage was attributed variously to his naturalism, his diversity and his emotional power, but above all to his energy. It is evident both from his own writings and from the comments of his contemporaries that Garrick was exceptionally intelligent about the management of energy in performance, though this emerges from what are often quite laboured attempts to describe it. George Christoph Lichtenberg, a German visitor to Drury Lane who left some of the fullest descriptions of Garrick's late career performances, offered this rather clunky analysis:

> ... where other players in the movements of their arms and legs allow themselves six inches or more in scope in every direction farther than the canon's beauty would permit, he hits the mark with admirable certainty and firmness.

Such an adherence to the Enlightenment values of proportion, harmony and symmetry might win the approval of the connoisseur, but how did it account for the adulation stirred up by this actor across the social spectrum? Lichtenberg also described, rather more memorably, the impact of Garrick's Hamlet on a full house:

> The whole audience of some thousands are as quiet, and their faces as motionless, as though they were painted on the walls of the theatre.

Lichtenberg, besides being a keen observer of acting, was one of the foremost electrical researchers of the time but he does not make the metaphorical connections that would now seem obvious to us.

Although technique and mystique seem far apart in Lichtenberg's account, in Garrick's own statements they are oddly blended as he focuses on subtle points about the control and release of energy. Advising a young actor on how to play Macbeth at the moment of Duncan's murder, he presents a complex picture of how forces that are retained and allowed to vibrate within the body can multiply their compelling power over the auditorium:

> He should at that time be a moving statue, or indeed a petrified man; his eyes must speak, and his tongue be metaphorically silent; his ears must be sensible of

imaginary noises, and deaf to the present and audible voice of his wife; his attitudes must be quick and permanent; his voice articulately trembling, and confusedly intelligible.

But as the energies are held in, they force the presence on stage into uncanny dispersal.

The murderer should be seen in every limb, and yet every member, at that instant, should seem separated from his body, and his body from his soul. This is the picture of complete regicide, and at this time the orb below should be hush as death.[53]

These are the words of someone who knew what it was to have total command over the attention and reactions of a large assembly, so much so that he was able to slip out of the quasi-supernatural aura he created to focus on absurd little stratagems that helped him sustain the illusion. The advice quoted above is immediately followed by the suggestion that the actor 'wear cork heels to his shoes, as in this scene he should seem to tread on air'.[54]

Garrick's *Essay on Acting* (1744) opens with a denunciation of the 'little fashionable actor' who captures attention like an *ignis fatuus* and lacks 'real substantial light'. The definition of acting that follows places emphasis on the controlled techniques of expression while pointing towards a central concern with what is expressed:

Acting is an entertainment of the stage, which by calling in the aid and assistance of articulation, corporeal motion, and ocular expression, imitates, assumes, or puts on the various mental and bodily emotions arising from the various humors, virtues and vices, incident to human nature.

The word missing here is 'passions', but that is the topic of his next paragraph. 'Now in some cases the passions are humors, and humors passions', he says, but in general it is the passions that belong to tragedy and the humours to comedy. A haberdasher and a Greek hero may both be motivated by the passion of revenge, but the physical expression of this must be qualitatively different – a matter of technique upon which Garrick provides all the particulars. The crucial issue is the appropriate management of physiological interpretation, a skill that arises from the more mysterious endeavour to 'discover the workings of spirit... upon the different modifications of matter'. Here we are getting closer to the *je ne sais quoi* component of the actor's genius, the motive force behind the gestural and facial movements he specifies. What are these 'workings of spirit'?[55]

Seventeenth-century debate on the passions was linked with philosophical enquiry into the relationship between body and soul, matter and spirit. As Descartes says, 'what is a passion in the soul is usually an action in the body. Hence, there is no better way of coming to know about our passions than by examining the difference between the soul and the body'.[56] From here he builds an argument about different kinds of movement: he explains 'the mechanism of the body' with its internal flows of blood and muscular hydraulics, describes the filtering of the blood so that only its 'very fine parts' or 'animal spirits' pass through the brain, and considers the 'actions and passions of the soul' which operate as a governing will over the actions of the body. Perceptions come to the soul by means of the nerves, creating sensations or 'passions' in the soul itself. The passions of the soul are defined as 'those perceptions, sensations or emotions of the soul which we refer particularly to it, and which are caused, maintained and strengthened by some movement of the spirits'.[57] The 'spirits' referred to here being the circulating molecular animal spirits that Descartes associates with brain activity, what we have is an attempt at a dynamic model of soul/body communication in which the passions are centrally implicated.

In Garrick's time, scientific and aesthetic enquiries converged on this recognition that something was in circulation, something invisible and intangible in itself, yet palpable in its effects. It was a catalytic agent in the world, operating on physical bodies and also at work in mental operations and emotional reactions. In science it was called 'aether', 'pneuma' or 'effluvium'; in the domain of the arts it was called 'sensibility' and manifested through the passions. The domains of the arts and sciences, though, were not distinct in the way that they became in the nineteenth century, and vocabulary leaked across from one to the other.

Empirical knowledge was a matter of sensibility, defined by Denis Diderot as the receptiveness of the soul to the impressions of the created world.[58] In the mid eighteenth century, at the time when Garrick published his essay on acting and John Hill

71

Many things come together in this extraordinary statement. It is one of the first references to electricity as a way of describing the powers of the actor; the allusions to sensibility and fire link it with an influential French treatise on acting by Sainte-Albine (which had been translated into English by John Hill); the imagery creates an analogy between the circulation of the blood, of electricity and of the communication between actor and audience. What we can see happening in the language is the shift towards a view of the actor as repository and generative source of the circulating power.

Electrical fire

Garrick's description of the electrical fire that 'shoots through the veins, marrow, bones and all, of every spectator' reflects the fascination of eighteenth-century researchers (in whose work he took an active interest) with electricity in bodies, especially human bodies. Newton linked the principle of attraction with the flow of electrical effluvia, and in his notes for the *Opticks* he posed the question: 'Do not all bodies therefore abound with a very subtile, but active, potent, electric spirit by which light is emitted, refracted and reflected?'[69]

Experiments conducted at the Royal Society by Francis Hauksbee and by Stephen Gray focused attention on the transmission of electricity between bodies, using balls, sticks, corks, feathers and paper fragments to track reactions, but in 1729 Gray raised the stakes by incorporating the body of a child into one of his demonstrations. A charity boy from the Charterhouse school was suspended on ropes in a horizontal position, and electrified with a glass tube, so that feathers and paper fragments flew upwards towards his hands. The spectacle was repeated for gatherings of curious ladies and gentlemen, and soon inspired a range of new social games and popular entertainments. One experimenter took the boy's place and substituted gold leaf for the fragments of paper, so that he appeared with his limbs coated in glowing gold. Boys were installed in more dangerous and imaginative fit-ups, including one promoted as 'the beatification', which involved standing on resin blocks while the entire body was electrified so that it was surrounded by a glowing aura. A conductor attached to a swing seat enabled ladies to try the experience of literally scintillating: emitting sparks for the amusement of the company. G.M. Bose, who took up a professorship at the University of Wittenberg in 1738, devised a way of insulating a dining table – and one chair, for the experimenter – then connecting a circuit running through the other chairs so that the guests would simultaneously leap in the air. Electrified knives and forks were another favourite dinner party trick. As techniques were refined so that current could be isolated in parts of the body, electrified kisses became a new experience for daring lovers. Not all metaphors are born in the poetic imagination.[70]

If the topic of magnetism was occult and led to arcane debates about causality, electricity lent itself to entertainment and display. The same issues of causality arose, but by the 1740s they were becoming less fraught and it was possible to speculate freely about electricity as attractive power. No doubt, too, the spirit of mischievous play in popular experiments took some of the tension out of the process of interpreting them. When beatification could be treated as a satirical game, using a human guinea pig as an illuminated presence, the cultural climate was evidently loosening up. The vogue for electrical researches crossed between the realms of science and performance, with travelling lecturers cashing in on the more spectacular and mystifying aspects of electricity. Advertisements for one 1752 entertainment on 'Electrical Fire' claimed 'that our Bodies at all Times contain enough of it to set a house on Fire' and promised demonstrations including:

A Battery of eleven Guns discharged by Fire issuing out of a Person's Finger
Spirits kindled by Fire darting from a Lady's eyes
Electrified money, which scarce any Body will take when offered to them.[71]

Much of the spectacle hinged on the association between electricity and lightning. Benjamin Franklin's letters on this were read out at the Royal Society on a regular basis from 1747, and in portraits he was typically presented against a background of forked lightning. One of these was by Benjamin Wilson, a painter whose own electrical researches were significant enough to get him elected to the Royal Society in 1751, and who acknowledged that the more he learned about electricity, the more mystified he was:

Experience, which is our best guide in all physical enquiries, but particularly in electrical ones, every day convinces me, that we know but little of that subtile fluid, which operates so secretly, and at the same time so powerfully, upon earth, and its atmosphere. I confess that I am even now less acquainted with the principle of its action, than I thought I was twenty years ago.[72]

Lightning was one of Wilson's obsessions. There is a story of him racing out of a theatre performance during a thunderstorm, snatching a curtain rod with which to direct the electrical fluid from the lightning into a bottle.[73] The idea that lightning might be triggered inside the theatre doesn't seem to have occurred to him at this point. Garrick himself was alert to the idea of lightning issuing from human presence, and applied the image to a charismatic audience member – Alexander Pope:

> I saw our little poetical hero, dressed in black, seated in a sidebox near the stage; and viewing me with a serious, and earnest attention. His look shot, and thrilled, like lightning through my frame; and I had some hesitation in proceeding, from anxiety, and from joy.[74]

Some kind of displacement is going on here: Garrick, only 24 years old at this time and in his debut season as Richard III, may be sensing his own presence, suddenly reflected back to him as he takes the stage for his first scene.

It soon became something of a convention to paint dramatic scenes from Shakespeare showing the impassioned actor against a backdrop of lightning, as if there were some direct relationship between the two kinds of power. Valentine Green's painting of Garrick in *Macbeth* (1776) may have inspired future renditions of the dagger scene with an electric sky seen through the window. In Thomas Beach's portrait of Kemble and Mrs Siddons in this scene (1786), it is Siddons who is the energetic focus, and the lightning forks directly above her head. Joshua Reynolds paints Garrick in *Lear* (1776), echoing the composition of an earlier mezzotint by Benjamin Wilson, where the whole dynamic of the scene is organised by shafts of storm light and spears of lightning that shoot diagonally across the illuminated figure of the actor.[75]

Garrick was aware of scientific researches into electricity. He and Benjamin Wilson remained in correspondence over twenty years, and Garrick went to see demonstrations of Wilson's research.[76] Through Wilson he met Franklin in 1772, at a time when his own experiments with stage lighting were becoming more adventurous. Too much so for some tastes. Thomas Gainsborough wrote to him, concerned that 'when eyes and ears are thoroughly debauched by glare and noise, the returning to modest truth will seem very gloomy for a time'.[77] But the debauchery was taken further when the following year de Loutherbourg joined Garrick at Drury Lane as a scene designer. Lighting effects were de Loutherbourg's speciality. It was the inner fire of the actor's performances, though, that suggested all this.

After sensibility and understanding, fire was the third of the qualities identified by Hill/ Saint-Albine as essential for the player. Hill was insistent that the 'invigorating flame' could not be faked. He was also insistent that an actor could never have too much fire. For the actor to feel the passions strongly, he says, may be enough to make an impression on a small gathering of people, but

> when a numerous audience is to be moved in the strongest
> and most pathetic manner, much more is required. In this
> case there is necessity for a due portion of fire, but even of
> vehemence. Both these are requisite here, to the affecting
> the audience, as agitation of the air is to flame. A fire may
> be sufficient to warm, nay to burn the neighboring objects,
> while it smothers within its bounds; but it will never take
> place upon more distant things, unless it have the assis-
> tance of a strong mind to promote and carry on its
> ravages.[78]

The imagery here is an odd composition. How can there be such a thing as 'due proportion of fire'? When fire is used to burn things, its quantity and intensity have more to do with what is being burned, and the conditions of the burning than with the degree of fire itself when it is first applied. A candle flame will serve to set fire to a building, as many pre-twentieth-century theatre practi- tioners learned from experience. Hill's references to quantity, to a mass of people being moved, to agitation of the air and transmis- sion across distances are more commensurate with the workings of electricity, and the way the fire is supposed to work upon audi- ences is suggestive of what researchers were discovering in their games with charges and current.

Some of the most ambitious and widely reported experiments involved testing the passage of current between human bodies. The French researchers Jean Antoine Nollet and Guillaume Le Monnier sought to discover just how many people could be involved in the transmission of a current from the Leyden jar: Monnier began in

1746 with 140 courtiers, Nollet responded with 200 Carthusian monks, and a truce seems to have been called at the point where Monnier demonstrated that the population of an entire Carthusian monastry, stretching out for more than a mile, could all be connected in a synchronised jump.[79]

Being 'moved and affected' (to use Hill's words) in the theatre was not quite such a directly physical experience, but it was a physiological process, set in train by forces whose impact must be the quintessence of the spectacle. Whether the keyword in the explanatory model for this was passion, sensibility or electrical fire, the dynamics were the same, and carried essentially the same implications when applied to the analysis of acting: whatever the force, the actor served as its repository and the agent of its transmission, achieving the still mysterious feat of sending it out across the footlights so that it passed through the assembled crowd, causing them to be visibly moved. However, a new conceptual dimension was introduced through advancements in scientific understanding about electricity. The scientific mind was not content with the knowledge that a force was in motion. There were questions to be answered about the nature and origin of the force, how it was directed, how its quantity and strength could be measured and what conditions would cause it to be intensified or dissipated. These questions were also relevant to the art of the actor. Benjamin Wilson was interested in 'the different degrees of power with which the electric fluid endeavours to enter a body', and John Hill was responding to a debate about whether the actor could have 'too much fire', arguing that the issue was rather in the intelligence governing its direction.[80]

Quantity, intensity and direction were the main investigative concerns in electrical research from the mid 1700s and the enabling factor in Nollet's famous experiment with the leaping Carthusians was the Leyden jar. This was a receptacle for the collection and storage of electricity, which also enabled its concentration. An electrical machine was used to charge a horizontally suspended metal rod, connected to the jar with a wire at one end. Once the charge was accumulated, it could be stored for use as required, and on its release, as Nollet and Monnier demonstrated, its reach could be prodigious. Analogies with what an actor could do, especially when it came to transmitting the fire through a large assembled crowd, are easy enough to draw but they crept slowly into theatrical parlance. Tracy C. Davis remarks that electricity prevails in the metaphoric language used to describe Edmund

Kean, and she links this with the transformation in conditions of viewing brought about through the introduction of gas and electricity in stage lighting.[81] Kean did not rise to fame until 1814, and it is much harder to track the electrical metaphor from this date back into the second half of the eighteenth century. References are thin on the ground.

Even so, Garrick was described as 'electrifying' early in his career. Charles Macklin, an actor twenty years his senior who was understably sceptical about the adulation with which the new star was being received, gave some stern advice on Garrick's performance as Lear, then was gracious enough to acknowledge: 'the curse had such an effect that it seemed to electrify the audience with horror'.[82] This use of the word, arresting as it was, did not immediately catch on, although it is quite evident from contemporary accounts that his power operated in ways that challenged the descriptive talents of those who came under its spell. A contemporary memoir by Thomas Davies shows the author doing his best with a limited stock of descriptive strategies, recording that 'several shouts of approbation proclaimed the triumph of the actor and satisfaction of the audience', and that 'the death of Richard was accompanied by the loudest gratulations of applause'. Many accounts of the performances that remain to us fall sadly short in their attempts to communicate Garrick's impact, typically resorting to the default comment that this or that was 'much applauded'. Occasionally, Davies strikes out with a more avant-garde statement: 'Mr. Garrick shone forth like a theatrical Newton'. But the boldness of the comparison is not sustained. This Newton 'threw new light on elocution and action; he banished ranting, bombast and grimace; and restored nature, ease and simplicity, and genuine humour'.[83] We are back to the conservative aesthetics of proportion, harmony and symmetry, and the claim by the rival actor Quin that 'Garrick was a new religion' still lacks a convincing eyewitness chronicler.[84]

The tragedian Lekain, Garrick's contemporary in France, was the subject of an extensive commentary by Talma, whose range of expression reflects a transition in the way the impact of great acting was being interpreted. Talma uses Lekain as the exemplar of the principles set out by Saint-Albine. 'To form a great actor like Lekain', he pronounces, 'the union of sensibility and intelligence is required'. When it comes to fire, though, Talma starts to hedge. Sensibility and intelligence alone will not suffice, he says, but instead of naming the third principle, he departs at a tangent with some remarks about voice and memory. Fire is alluded to indirectly: the tragic actor requires 'force and intensity', and Lekain exhibits 'the movement of an ardent and impassioned soul'.[85] There is mention of how an innovative interpretation of a role was received 'by an electrical movement which manifested itself in long and loud applause', but there is no analysis of this electricity between the player and the public. It is here that the greatest challenge seems to have presented itself to those trying to document the success of actors and actresses.

It was easier to focus on theory, or to generalise about strengths and weaknesses in technique, especially when even the most lauded players were rather erratic in their performances. The presence of the actor, recognised pervasively and immediately by those in the auditorium and manifested through the strength of connection with them, somehow kept escaping the commentators' grasp. There are occasional exceptions, though, in the accounts left to us. Abraham Fleury, defending Marie-Françoise Dumesnil against her detractors, succeeds in capturing some sense of her power in operation:

> One evening, when Dumesnil had thrown into the character of Cleopatra a more than usual degree of that fiery energy for which she was so distinguished, the persons who occupied the front rows of the pit, instinctively drew back, shrinking, as it were, from her terrific glance. An empty space was thus left between the spectators in the pit and the orchestra.[86]

Those used to observing the behaviour of positive and negative magnetic effects might have found ways to account for this phenomenon, and those who had been witness to the more spectacular shock effects of the Leyden jar might have made an association between the movement in the front rows of the pit and the capacity to build up and store the fiery energy for release on cue. That association remains latent in James Ballentyne's description of Sarah Siddons as Queen Katherine in Shakespeare's *Henry VIII*, delivering her climactic rejoinder in the trial scene:

> And no language can possibly convey a picture of her immediate re-assumption of the fullness of majesty, glowing with scorn, contempt, anger and the terrific pride of innocence, when she turns round to Wolsey, and

exclaims, 'To you I speak!' Her form seems to expand, and her eye to burn with a fire beyond human.[87]

The impact of Siddons on her audiences was not consistent, but there are many testimonials to the fact that when it was at its strongest the effect was hypnotic. Recalling the audience reaction to a particular a speech, James Boaden uses words that echo Talma's account of Lekain: 'At the last line, there was a triumphant hurry and enjoyment in her scorn, which the audience caught as electrical, and applauded in rapture for at least a minute'. It takes Siddons herself, though, to capture the connection between the electrical current and the cumulative psychical power behind it. Concentration was her own first principle, and in her capacity for total absorption in the role she generated an effect of self hypnosis. In Shakespeare's King John, she recorded, 'the spirit of the whole drama took possession of my mind and frame, by my attention being incessantly riveted to the passing scenes'. Lady Macbeth was the part with which she was most famously identified, and on the night before her 1775 debut in it she went over the script in a private preparation:

> I went on with tolerable composure in the silence of the night, (a night I never can forget,) till I came to the assassination scene, when the horrors of the scene rose to a degree that made it impossible for me to get farther. I snatched up my candle, and hurried out of the room, in a paroxysm of terror. My dress was of silk, and the rustling of it, as I ascended the stairs to go to bed, seemed to my panic-struck fancy like the movement of a spectre pursuing me.[88]

Siddons may be seen as a precursor of Mesmer. In her determination to maximise the intensity of the absorption by optimising the conditions for concentration, on and off stage, she also prefigures Stanislavsky. From this concentration she generated her power over the attention of the audience, commanding the auditorium with the fire in her eyes.

Presence in an actor was equivalent to the phenomenon of accumulated charge. Franklin's attention to issues of discharge and balance in electricity also provided the basis for an elaboration of this idea. He divided bodies into those 'wanting' electrical fluid and those 'abounding' with it. Where too much electricity was present, it pooled to form a charged electrical atmosphere.[89] The image of the feather and the globe on the balance beam returns in a new guise: some bodies are full, and some are empty, and the electrical fire acts purposefully, seeking transmission from the one to the other. All those anonymous members of the audience were drawn to the source of power that was set to transmit itself so that they too would become present in it.

By the time Edmund Kean began his main stage career in 1814, it had already become something of a cliché to refer to a performance as having 'an electric effect' on the audience. As a stock in trade remark, this at least had a little more style than the old standby 'much applauded', but as a descriptor it was double edged. Electricity may have connected large assemblies of people through an energy current, but it gave shocks that were sudden, violent and intermittent. Without the sustained concentration Siddons brought to her roles, the electrical effect was transient. Kean's identification with it was set in perpetuity by Coleridge's remark that to watch him on stage 'was like reading Shakespeare by flashes of lightning'.

In a challenging reappraisal of this influential one liner (and it is one of the most influential one liners in theatre history), Tracy C. Davis traces its source in Coleridge's *Table Talk*, where, as she points out, it appears in the context of a quite negative appraisal of Kean's capacities as an actor: he was original but 'copied from himself', producing a set of trademark effects such as his 'rapid descents from the hyper-tragical to the infra colloquial' that were sometimes impressive but often unreasonable.[90] Add to this, Davis suggests, the knowledge that a 'flash of lightning' was code for a dash of gin in common talk, and that Kean was a notorious drinker, and the myth of the romantic actor is on very shaky foundations. She points out that Kean's performances created very different impressions on spectators depending on where they were seated. To view him from the pit, where the light showed up the rapid transitions of facial expression for which he was celebrated, was one thing; to see him without the advantages of light and proximity was another, as Hazlitt recorded:

> That which had been so lately nothing but flesh and blood, a living fibre, 'instinct with fire' and spirit, was no better than a little fantoccini figure, darting backwards and forwards on the stage, starting, screaming, and playing a number of fantastic tricks before the audience.

'It is in the working of his face', Hazlitt specifies, 'that you see the writhing and coiling up of the passions before they make their serpent-sting; the lightning of his eye precedes the hoarse bursts of thunder from his voice'.[91]

There is no suggestion that 'lightning' here means anything other than the electrical kind. When Garrick wrote that a glance from the great Alexander Pope 'thrilled, like lightning through my frame', he was not thinking about downing a tot of gin. Electricity and lightning were being applied as theatrical metaphors fifty years before Coleridge coined his phrase, and it is significant that Garrick was not only one of the first to use them (albeit in isolated instances), but one of the few pre-nineteenth-century writers who could make the figurative language resonate with a genuine understanding of what the actor's power could mean.

Coleridge's remark does not just describe Kean. It focuses a new tradition of rhetoric around stage presence, a rhetoric with modernised imaging and vocabulary. It would perhaps be wrong to take Kean's lightning from him altogether, though Davis with her dissenting reading is making a vital intervention by alerting us to the fact that the lightning metaphor is double edged. That Talma avoids directly adopting the 'fire' principle in his account of the model actor also signals this. Perhaps a performer could have too much fire, or fire of the wrong kind, and whilst lightning might be associated with awesome elementary power, it is no compliment to call an actor 'flashy'. What Garrick understood and Siddons demonstrated was that real drawing power depended on concentration and sustained management. But this, too, could have dubious manifestations. When the influence of Anton Mesmer began to spread towards the end of the eighteenth century, introducing an idea of magnetism that was overtly personalised, the dual nature of this kind of power came to the fore.

3

MESMERISM

'I shall never forget her... She will come to me in sleepless
nights again and yet again'.[1]

Charlotte Brontë, on Rachel Felix

'I am truly horrified by modern man', wrote the Russian socialist
Alexander Herzen in 1849. 'Such absence of feeling, such
narrowness of outlook, such lack of passion and indignation,
such feebleness of thought'.[2] In Paris, where Herzen's impressions
of his enfeebled species were painfully intensified, the rapid
expansion of the city produced 'a seething, sweating population',
whose motivation was being tested.[3] In February 1848, as revolution began to foment in the streets for a second time, Herzen
rushed to the scene in the hopes of being witness to the start of a
seismic political shift.

What he saw disappointed him in complex ways, not least with a
sense that modern man as a collective was devoid of charisma, of
the kind of passionate energy that was displayed by a lone individual on the stage of the Comédie Française, where the tragedienne
Rachel, carrying the tricolour and dressed in a simple Roman
tunic, delivered her own rendition of the people's anthem. She did
not actually sing the Marseillaise, she recited it: commencing in her
inimitable low-toned chant of 'agonising sorrow' and rising to
deliver the call to arms as 'a scream – full of fury and passion'. It
was passion driven by 'the heartlessness of a hangman'.[4] Herzen,
with his commitment to the revolutionary movement in Russia,
was someone with a vested interest in how power might be put to
work in a public assembly, and Rachel 'the she-Napoleon of the
stage', had in the eyes of Parisian audiences become revolution
personified. She had more than drawing power. She had holding
power, an uncanny capacity to 'enchain' the attention of her audiences, to take possession of them so that 'a profound silence'
reigned from the moment of her appearance until she ended the
performance, leaving them held as if in suspended animation
before they broke out into hysterical acclamation.[5]

The writer Jules Janin, who had appointed himself Rachel's critical patron, also recognised what was at stake in this extraordinary performance of hers. The Marseillaise was itself fraught with dangerous resonances, echoes of the terrors unleashed during Robespierre's reign in the first revolution. But the evocation of terrors from the past was Madame Rachel's speciality:

> She was a Muse, a Fury. She came out of the Helicon, from the Field of Mars. Erynnis the violent, the implacable, was surpassed in that moment and you could have seen all the people dumbfounded and agog, listening to the maledictions pronounced by that same voice upon which were born so divinely the romances of Racine and grandeurs of Corneille... How beautiful she was, how bold, and how dangerous![6]

It was, Janin wrote, as if she held concealed in the folds of her mantle the fate of the world – war or peace. Herzen sensed only that she spread despair, but in Janin's account her influence on the assembly was catalytic: 'the fever of heroism seized upon all their souls'. Was she supplying what Herzen felt they lacked? More specifically, was she transmitting to them a force and passion of which they were empty but of which she held concentrated supplies?

Benjamin Franklin's theories of electricity were related to a larger view of the earth as a composite of energies held in balance. Where these energies built up into powerful forces, they were compelled to seek release through transmission to forms or substances deficient in energy. He may not have envisaged cultural or psychological applications of this principle, but others did. Moving backwards a little over half a century, to the period leading up to the first French Revolution, another experimentalist was exploring the principle in just these ways, and attracting a great deal of popular attention in the process.

Anton Mesmer, who set up his training programme for a select group of initiates in Paris in 1783, advertised a healing programme based on the channelling of 'universal fluid'. He soon captured the imagination of the press and the public. Over the following two years, the *Journal de Paris* devoted more of its coverage to his exploits than to any other topic. By the early 1780s, the hold of mesmerism on the popular imagination was such that it was being referred to as an epidemic.[7] Jean-Sylvain Bailly, an important

French astronomer with Newtonian sympathies who was part of an official commission of enquiry into Mesmer's work, was disturbed at the political and cultural potential of his influence:

> When imagination speaks to the multitude, the multitude no longer knows either dangers or obstacles... Nations follow sovereigns, and armies their Generals.[8]

And a multitude deficient in passion, vision and ideas was especially vulnerable to the transfusion of dangerous energies. Bailly's diagnosis was prophetic, made as it was in 1784, before the rise of Robespierre and Danton, and while Napoleon – later to be hailed as 'the world spirit on horseback' – was still at military school in Paris.[9]

It takes two sides to created a mesmerising experience: the mesmeriser and the mesmerised. But whilst we have an extensive social and psychological literature about the effects of mesmerism or hypnotism from the subject's point of view, there has been more circumspection about analysing the qualities of the mesmerist. It is much easier in scientific terms to offer an explanation for the phenomenon of collective hysteria than it is to account for the qualities in particular individuals who are able to arouse it. With the benefit of hindsight and some Freudian understanding of hysteria, we can see that imagination and projection account for much of what is going on, but Freud and Mesmer occupy very different frameworks of understanding, and it is Mesmer who brings us closest to what is happening when the multitude hails a political leader, or when a player with Rachel's magnetic potency takes the stage.

As the child of a vagrant family, Rachel tested her earning capacities at an early age, singing on the streets to collect coins. And like Edith Piaf, that other Parisian waif turned superstar a century later, she was marked for life with the diminutive stature of an undernourished child, an attribute that ultimately served to strengthen her uncanny command over her public. Charlotte Brontë's entranced fictional portrayal of Rachel as 'Vashti' in her novel *Villette* has helped to commemorate her as the prototype of the mesmeric performer. Her successors would include Henry Irving, Sarah Bernhardt, Vaslav Nijinsky, Maria Callas and Piaf, all of whom are distinguished by the depths of their psychical hold over an audience and by an aura of otherworldliness. All of them have had their detractors, people who were not bound by the spell and remained coldly aware only of unreliable technique, overused mannerisms, bizarre emotive registers. Mesmerism itself is a practice that creates sharp divisions between different kinds of human intelligence: at one end of the spectrum are those who succumb to its influence, and at the other the dissenters and sceptics, who may seek to expose it as fraud.

In the quality of compelling power often referred to as 'mesmeric', stage performers have something in common with charismatic political leaders. They convert a mass of individuals into a highly charged unity; they erase the everyday thoughts and mundane reactions of their audiences by transporting them to another plane of feeling; they create a sense of expanded destiny and heightened meaning that seems common to all who wish to embrace it.

It has now become something of a cliché to refer to an impressive theatrical experience as 'mesmerising', but this tells us little or nothing about the quality of the performance. Indeed, the cultural mythologies spawned by mesmerism have tended to portray it as a means of faking performative talent. The character of Svengali in George du Maurier's novel *Trilby* (1894) is the genius in the story. He is the magus with nothing of the dignitary, a caricature Victorian Jew of Dickensian ugliness whose musical genius is thwarted by his personal inability to appeal to an audience. He therefore rechannels his gifts by hypnotising a young woman, Trilby O'Ferrall, who is 'wistful and sweet' yet provocative in her own naïve way, and endowed with the kind of face and figure that will grace the stage. Trilby is tone deaf, but under hypnosis she is transformed into a singer of heart-stopping power and brilliance. Again we have the principle of fullness and emptiness: on her first appearance in the story, Trilby's rendition of a popular song is 'too grotesque and too funny for laughter', but Svengali follows her performance with one of his own, delivered on a penny whistle. Of this it is said:

> ... it would be impossible to render in any words the deftness, the distinction, the grace, power, pathos, and passion with which this truly phenomenal artist executed the poor old twopenny tune.[10]

The story taps into deep-seated cultural anxieties about the performer as automaton, a mere puppet whose sounds and movements are produced through the determination of a hidden agent. E.T.A. Hoffmann's story 'The Sandman' (1814), later to be adapted into the ballet *Coppelia*, is one of the influences behind Du Maurier's *Trilby*. Here the hypnotist is Dr Coppelius, who lures young men into his power by persuading them to dance with his beautiful daughter Olympia, but, as it turns out, she is a mere animated doll. Just as Trilby is the prototype of the opera singer as automaton, Olympia is the model for the dancer and, paradoxically, the role of Coppelia has become one in which ballerinas may get their first opportunity to play a lead. The most troubling implication of these stories is that the performer is a channel not for genius or passion or even universal fluid, but rather for an alien will.

And what of the audience? In the case of *Trilby*, they are hypnotic subjects at one remove, empty vessels waiting to be filled with the vital energy they lack, all too readily entranced by a stage star who is herself in a trance. Du Maurier's character sketch of the theatre-going public offers us a middle class version of the vacuity Herzen complained of in a previous generation of 'modern man'. They are 'carriage people' who cruise aimlessly about the city with 'nothing to say to each other, as though the vibration of so many wheels all rolling home the same way every afternoon had hypnotised them into silence, idiocy, and melancholia'.[11]

Mesmerists who present stage acts in their own right often create the entertainment by getting audience members to perform under hypnosis, with the conviction that they are stellar singers or dancers. Why create entertainment the hard way when it can be made available with a meaningful glance and a snap of the fingers? The absurdist reduction point of this logic is tested in a *Little Britain* sketch featuring Kenny Craig, Matt Lucas's suburban hypnotist. Kenny has an audience gathered in a local community hall, and addresses them with his usual cursory prelude: 'Look into my eyes, look into my eyes... Snap! You're under'. When he snaps them out of their trance, he instructs, they will be convinced that they have just spent two hours watching a fabulously entertaining show, and will report as much to all their friends. He then draws up a seat on the stage and reads a book.

The equation of mesmerism with charlatanism goes back to 1780, when Anton Mesmer's own career was at its zenith, though it is based on a view of the mesmerist as a quack doctor rather than a quack entertainer. *Little Britain* has given the tradition a nice twist, and one that has a perverse validity. Is the figure on stage who mesmerises an audience doing so out of consummate skill or as a manifestation of some personal power that is not, fundamentally, associated with any legitimate stage talent? Here the Kantian rationale that divorces genius from skill threatens to backfire: when mystique is valued so decisively over technique, the way is open for those who seek to exploit the potency of mystique in itself. With Mesmer, the role of the magus returned to the cultural main stage, modernised and rescripted under the influence of an extensive repertoire of concepts taken from the experimental sciences.

Mesmer's secret

Anton Mesmer began his career with degrees in astronomy from the University of Ingolstadt (whose most famous student was the fictional Victor Frankenstein) and in medicine from Vienna. At Vienna, he completed his course with a dissertation about the astrological influences on human anatomy, relating the circulation of bodily fluids and nerve signals to tidal and gravitational movements. Following his graduation in 1760, he continued to elaborate this thesis.

The idea that human physiology was subject to the influence of gravitational forces came from Richard Mead, Newton's physician. Mead developed Newton's concept of circulating aethers into a hypothesis about 'universal fluid' that circulated through the macrocosm as well as the anatomy of individual bodies. In embracing the hypothesis and seeking to extend its explanatory range, Mesmer was following in the tracks of some of the most respected scientists of the era. The experiments of Nollet, Franklin and others had explored the circulation of electrical 'effluvia' in ways that suggested some universal principle at work. At around the time of Mesmer's first public demonstrations in Paris, Luigi Galvani was testing specific applications of electrical current to show how it could trigger muscular action in humans and animals – even dead ones. He proposed that 'animal electricity' was stored in all living creatures. Mesmer's preferred term was 'animal magnetism', since he was interested in forms of transmission involving the experimenter as a repository of drawing power, and therefore able to act upon the bodies of others in ways that altered the gravitational flows to which they were normally subject.

By the 1780s, when revolution was brewing in Paris, expanded ideas of human power were in vogue. An anonymous poem inspired by the first manned balloon flights proclaimed:

Le feu, la terre et l'eau soumis à tes lois:
Tu domptes la nature entière.
[Fire, earth and water made subject to your laws,
You tame all nature.][12]

When such sentiments were being freely expressed and widely embraced, there were no longer any generalised inhibitions around the idea that magnetic power might be invested in a person, though Mesmer chose not to advertise himself in those terms. Rather, he focused the attention of his patients on an elaborate and rather cumbersome piece of apparatus, the *baquet* or magnetic bath. Based on the model of the Leyden jar, this was a device for storing electrical charge. Bottles of magnetised water were arranged with iron rods projecting out from the fluid as conductors, so those assembled for treatment would grasp them, then hold each other's hands to form a human chain (as Nollet's Carthusian monks had done) to promote the magnetic circulation.

Given their foundation in some of the most widely accepted theories of the day, where did these experiments depart from what was scientifically sanctioned? Mesmer's critics sought to draw the distinction, beginning with the fluid itself:

It is not like the electrical fluid, luminous and visible; its action is not like the attraction of the loadstone, the object of one's sight; it has neither taste nor smell, its process is silent, and surrounds you or penetrates your frame, without your being informed of it by the sense of touch.[13]

The last point is an odd one, since tactile contact – with the *baquet*, between patients and above all with the mesmerist – was essential to the treatment system. But the rest of the complaint here is also on dubious ground. Joseph Priestley in a recently published work on *The History and Present State of Electricity*, had emphasised that 'the imagination may have full play, in conceiving of the manner in which an invisible agent produces an almost infinite variety of visible effects'.[14] Priestley's own term for the circulating principle was *phlogiston*: an element breathed into the air by living beings, so requiring the air thus polluted to cleanse itself through the filtering agencies of water and plants.

A number of factors in Mesmer's practice, especially the power attributed to the experimenter himself, served to arouse the suspicion of professional men of science. Mesmer purported to be acting as a physician, effecting cures for complaints that were sometimes extreme: paralysis, fever, degenerative diseases, acute pain. His patients were in a condition of dependency exacerbated by his manner of treatment, which involved the laying on of hands and some distinctly theatrical scenarios. In Paris, he set up a private establishment at the Hotel de Coigny, where society patients entered to an ambience of strange light reflected from mirrors, and music played on the glass harmonica (an instrument of uncanny resonance, as its name implies). The mesmerist greeted them wearing a purple cloak. In the treatment rooms, they were encouraged to go into trances, and thence into states of crisis, at which point they were taken aside into specially appointed 'crisis rooms'. Cartoonists portrayed the scene as one of decadent abandon, with the mesmerist in the ass's head of a charlatan.

If what went on inside the hotel bore the signs of a contagious delirium, there was the added concern that Mesmer's ideas were catching on like wildfire amongst the general population. Mesmer himself was a complex character and, as Robert Darnton suggests in his classic study, somewhat elusive:

> One cannot even get close enough to the man to determine whether or not he was a charlatan; if he was, he certainly dwarfed his fellow quacks. A friend and patron of Mozart, a personage of the first order in Paris, he exerted an influence on his age that testifies to the power of the personality hidden in his robes and rituals, the power that we appropriately acknowledge in expressions such as a 'mesmerised' audience or a 'magnetic' personality.[15]

'Magnetic personality' has become something of a cliché, but when we return to Mesmer as its original example, the term has nuances and implications that we have lost sight of. The magnetism is to be taken literally, as is the exceptional capacity to concentrate it in his person so it can be released at will. Undoubtedly Mesmer used techniques of theatricality in manipulative ways, and much of the effect on his patients can be attributed to their own susceptibility to this kind of manipulation. But if the *baquet* was a piece of theatre, an elaborate prop, the rationale of creating an accumulated power source and using it for targeted transmissions was founded in Mesmer's absolute conviction about his own gift for mind control.

For all his debt to current ideas in physics and chemistry, Mesmer had brought the magus back with a vengeance.

Astrological symbols featured as prominently in his thinking as anatomical knowledge, and the occult principle of balancing the microcosm against the macrocosm was at the heart of his practice along with Franklin's theory of how electrical currents sought to balance abundance against deficit. When he called his foundation 'The Society of Universal Harmony' he was harking back to Hermetic cosmologies, and he was to become a key figure for later exponents of magic, such as Eliphas Levi, who wrote in his 1860 *History of Magic*:

> Let us now have the courage to affirm one truth which will be acknowledged hereafter. The great thing of the eighteenth century is not the Encyclopaedia, not the sneering and derisive philosophy of Voltaire, not the negative metaphysics of Diderot and D'Alembert, not the malignant philanthropy of Rousseau: it is the sympathetic and miraculous physics of Mesmer. Mesmer is grand as Prometheus; he has given men that fire from heaven which Franklin could only direct.[16]

Magnetism, according to Levi, was the great secret of the Magi, the key alike to the celestial fire and the molten energies of the earth.[17] It was 'the wand of miracles', though only in the hands of initiates.

The training regime of the Society of Universal Harmony began with a vow of silence, which it seems was most solemnly enforced around one particular essential truth at the heart of the practice. Its revelation now seems something of an anti-climax, since the 'secret' is familiar to us from countless motivational gurus. This is how it was expressed by one of the most high profile members of Mesmer's inner circle, the Marquis de Puységur, who made the decision to go public with it in his lectures:

> The entire doctrine of Animal Magnetism is contained in two words: Believe and Want. I believe that I have the power to set into action the vital principle of my fellow-man; I want to make use of it; this is all my science and all my means. Believe and want, Sirs, and you will do as much as I.[18]

A commission of investigation presided over by Benjamin Franklin came to a different conclusion about the hidden dynamic underlying the dramatic treatments. Having tried out for themselves the *baquet* and various other extravagances Mesmer laid on for his clients, they could confirm that there was nothing at all to experience without the assistance of willful self delusion. The secret was in the imagination of participants.

Here we see the beginnings of the tradition of sceptical enquiry that has focused primarily on the hypnotic subject and his or her predispositions to mesmeric influence. In this kind of enquiry the powers of the mesmerist remain unexplained, other than to the extent that they can simply be attributed to fraud or imposition. Those on the occult side of the picture, though, are keen to provide an analysis of the powers of the mesmerist, whilst maintaining, as A.E. Waite does in his introduction to Levi's work, that such enquiries are part of 'the exact and absolute science of Nature and her laws'. In Waite's account of it, this science is a kind of physics plus. Franklin's law of equilibrium and its relationship to the behaviour of electricity is a belated rediscovery of the 'universal agent' known to the alchemists. 'It has been said that this agent is a light of life by which animated beings are rendered magnetic, electricity being only its accident and transient perturbation'.[19] Levi finds the authority for this view in a statement from the Zohar: 'The science of equilibrium is the key of occult science'. He interprets Mesmer's doctrine accordingly:

> He recognised ... the existence of a first matter which is fluidic, universal, capable of fixity and motion ... In virtue of this matter the world and those who dwell therein attract and repel; it passes through all by a circulation comparable to that of the blood. It maintains and renews the life of all beings, is the agent of their force and may become the instrument of their will. Prodigies are results of exceptional wills and energies. [20]

By this account, Mesmer and others who have been able to demonstrate hypnotic hold over gatherings of people are acting as human Leyden jars, concentrating and storing energy which they then release to lesser individuals who have massed together in their craving to be charged up. The mistake of the commissioners was to succumb to the theatrical ruse of the *baquet*, when they should rather have been testing their susceptibility to Mesmer's personal magnetism. As we have seen, the Leyden jar was beginning to serve as an implied metaphor for the actor's power in Garrick's time but Mesmer, exploiting the opportunities of a new cultural climate, introduces an additional dimension with his focus on the will.

At the same time, he is taking the concept of circulating fluids or energies and exploiting it to potentially sinister effect: if there are powers in circulation, powers which can be concentrated and directed towards particular ends, then they can be personalised and turned to one's own ends. 'In the pre-scientific conception of the body of the late classical and medieval periods', Stephen Connor observes, 'the body is seen as both open to and in complex interchange with manifold external influences, agencies and energies, natural, divine, and demonic'.[21] Mesmerism was a revival of this conception, laced with some of the newest scientific ideas. The taboo placed on the concept of attraction by thinkers of the late Renaissance perhaps had some justification if personal magnetism was to be deployed in order to invade the physical and mental being of others.

The figure of the mesmerist in literature and drama was almost guaranteed to be compelling, and was nearly always sinister. Svengali, Dracula and Caligari became prototypes for the modern story of the fatal mesmerist, and all have something about them that is not quite human – or, more specifically, not quite mortal (though Svengali, in a somewhat creaky twist of the plot, does actually die.) As the craze for mesmerism spread and more practitioners began to experiment with their own powers, somnambulism became one of its more occult developments. Subjects were put to sleep in the hopes of opening them up as channels of communication with the dead, or – as in vampire legends – the undead. Supernaturalism and the drama of the expanded life cycle had found their way back into the heart of cultural modernity, feeding off exactly those scientific ideas that should have banished them.

Supernaturalists

Voltaire advised Marie-Françoise Dumesnil that in order to achieve the degree of fiery passion required for one of her roles, she must have *'le diable au corps'*.[22] This was to become a catchphrase amongst actors and directors. Passions that involved a violent breach of the bounds of proportion, harmony and symmetry could stir up ancient and disorderly forces, and to embody them was to open oneself up to possession. One of the archetypes for possession in the western tradition is the priestess at Delphi who channelled the voices of gods and demons from deep within the chasm in the earth over which her throne was set. Some of the most striking descriptions of Rachel (in particular those by Jules Janin and Charlotte Brontë) portray her as modern Europe's reincarnation of the Delphic priestess, with her oracular voice pitched to a low, uncanny frequency and driven by a breath too powerful to have issued from her own weak lungs.

Rachel made her debut at the Comédie Française in 1837, at the age of seventeen. 'There were four people in the stalls', one witness recalled, 'I made a fifth. My attention was suddenly attracted to the stage by a strange and expressive countenance. The brow was prominent, the eye dark, deep set and full of fire; while a certain elegance and dignity in movement and attitude saved the fragile body from insignificance'.[23] She had come from nowhere: the child of vagrant Jewish parents, she had survived by singing in the streets of Paris with her sister until she was spotted by a music teacher who offered to take her into his school. By her early teens, she had earned the nickname 'la petite Diablesse' ('the little devil') and this was no casual epithet. Élisa Rachel Félix had more than a little of the devil about her.

Edwin Forrest, a prominent American actor who saw her early performances, described her as 'that little bag of bones, with the marble face and the flaming eyes' and declared, 'there is demoniacal power in her'.[24] Charlotte Brontë, recording her impressions of Rachel at the zenith of her career thirteen years later, put it more strongly:

> On Saturday I went to hear and see Rachel – a wonderful sight – terrible as if the earth had cracked deep at your feet and revealed a glimpse of hell – I shall never forget it – she made me shudder to the marrow of my bones: in her some fiend has certainly taken up an incarnate home. She is not a woman – she is a snake.[25]

The oracle at Delphi had her origins in the myth of Apollo's battle with the Python, the 'primeval, chaotic monster', at the foot of Mount Parnassus on the spot where there was a deep chasm marking the navel of Gaia, the earth goddess.[26] His priestess took her seat upon a tripod spanning the chasm and, although in her prophecies she was supposed to be the mouthpiece of Apollo as 'god of patriarchal law and moral order', her breath issued from the depths where the residue of the Python's energies still churned.[27] Here, then, was one of those myths focused on the darker mysteries of female sexuality. The priestess was known as 'the Pythia' or Pythonness and, whether or not her powers were demonic, they were certainly demonised by early Christian writers. Saint John Chrysostom gives this account of her:

> This same Pythoness... is said, being a female, to sit at times upon the tripod of Apollo astride, and thus the evil spirit ascending from beneath and entering the lower part of her body, fills the woman with madness, and she with disheveled hair begins to play the bacchanal and to foam at the mouth, and thus being in a frenzy to utter the words of her madness.[28]

As Steven Connor comments:

> The pythia is important because she stands on the threshold of the pagan and the Christian worlds. She is meant to stand as the image of an inheritance from or throwback to foul, forgotten, chthonic beginnings: she provides the vent or doorway through which the dark, demonic, imperfectly superseded world of magic may creep back.[29]

In the sixth book of Virgil's *Aeneid*, Aeneas and his men are led to the cave of the oracle where they are witness to the transformation of the priestess as she is possessed:

> ... her breast heaved, her wild heart
> Grew large with passion. Taller to their eyes
> And sounding no longer mortal
> Since she had felt the god's power breathing near.[30]

Jules Janin describes Rachel's stage transformation in just this way. Upon entering the theatre, the diminutive figure appears to grow immediately in stature. As she takes the stage her head becomes erect and her chest opens out; her eye brightens, her foot strikes the ground with a sovereign authority and her words 'vibrate across the distance'.[31] Sometimes she suffers badly from nerves in the lead-up to a performance, but once in front of her audience, all she has to do is wait for the spirit to enter her. And soon the wild passions come, 'those sudden movements drawn from the heart, that rugged energy, and the abandon...' In such moments he sees her as the pythoness seated over the abyss, breathing vapours from the depths, attending to the voices she will channel.[32] As she channels, physically diminutive Rachel also becomes sexualised, with a swelling breast and fiery, predatory eye. The effect upon her audience is overwhelming: 'It is an inspiration that crushes and kills; she compels you, she presses upon you, she obsesses you'.[33]

There is no doubt that Rachel was an obsession for Janin. Not contented with reviewing all her performances at length in his regular columns, he wrote a book about her that runs to over 500 pages and nearly 200,000 words. *Rachel et la tragédie* has a tendency to be repetitive, as one might expect, but the ways in which it is repetitive are telling: Janin has his particular themes and motifs, which are indicators of his own investment in the living myth of Madame Rachel. Certainly his dominant theme is that of Rachel as the pythoness, the Delphic priestess revisited on the modern world, an image that relates curiously to his view of the actress as the harbinger of revolution. One of his very first impressions of her – a decade before the episode of the Marseillaise, and in an entirely different context – was that the spirit of tragedy had found a new incarnation, 'its phantoms were being resuscitated by some unforeseen power and coming back to life'.[34] A poetic revolution was imminent. This was not the revolution of political rationalists, though it carried some of the terrifying moods of the Robespierre era. There was something atavistic and deeply uncanny about it and, as its leader, Rachel derived her powers through descent into the empire of the dead.

Yet, Janin insistently reminds his readers, the 'supernatural gift' was borne by a mere child, a figure so physically insignificant and so culturally unprepared that it was hard to see how she could sustain it.[35] The mythology of genius is always at its most captivating when the one on whom it is bestowed seems to have come from nowhere, a kind of foundling in the domain of the arts or sciences, and, as many fairy tales warn, the foundling may be a creature of dark and dangerous origins.

Reading Janin's account now, it is tempting to think that this Rachel was largely a product of his own imagination, a means of glamourising himself as her discoverer and critical patron. In the early stages of her career, he was evidently responsible for creating her reputation with his extensive and compelling testimonies. Was he anticipating Svengali, with this drama of the street girl who under his gaze so unaccountably took greatness upon herself? One way to test his own influence in the situation was to withdraw it, which he did when she took on her first major tragic role as

Roxane in Racine's *Bajazet*. His verdict was devastating: she was unequal to the task, inadequate in voice, carriage and stature. Her audience reception froze accordingly and she is supposed to have sought him out to acknowledge the truth of his verdict, begged his advice and support.[36] But if Janin had a touch of the Svengali, Rachel was no Trilby. As with all performers who arouse public adulation, there was no doubt an element of collective delusion in her impact, but it takes more than collective delusion to sustain a career over twenty years, across a wide range of demanding roles. Rachel was a force in her own right, and, by many accounts other than Janin's, one of extraordinary intensity.

George Henry Lewes, a prominent English critic who included a chapter on Rachel in his book *On Actors and the Art of Acting*, called her 'the panther of the stage' and wrote of her 'thin nervous frame... aflame with genius'. As in Janin's account, the overwhelming impression is that she is in some way possessed, and that in her physical frailty she is under threat from the 'irresistible power' she harbours:

> You felt that she was wasting away under the fire within, that she was standing on the verge of the grave with pallid face, hot eyes, emaciated frame – an awful ghastly apparition.[37]

One might ask, then, what is the source of the perceived power? Is it contained within the figure on the stage who magnetises the attention, or is the aura surrounding this figure a mere projection of the already formed fantasies, associations and drives the audience bring with them? Rachel provides an especially interesting test case for this question. Her recent biographer, Rachel Brownstein, admits she finds herself 'unable and unwilling' to resolve it, after years of sifting through the traces, but that it was Charlotte Brontë's portrayal of the actress in a chapter of her novel *Villette* that set the quest in train.[38]

The narrative persona in *Villette* is Lucy Snowe, a woman so deeply trained in self-denial that all her desires are turned back on her to create a morass of repressed sexuality and imploded psychic power. She suffers from a chronic sense of social isolation, thinks herself haunted by the ghost of a nun who was buried alive, and is obsessively counselled by a voice of 'Reason' that will not cease until she is 'altogether crushed, cowed, broken-in and broken-down'.[39] Here is a subject ripe for hypnotism, or at least an episode of delusory projection, and a visit to the theatre to see the celebrated tragedienne Vashti (a figure closely based on Brontë's own impressions of Rachel) provides the opportunity. On her first entry, Vashti impresses Lucy Snowe as an ominous cosmic vision:

> ... a great and new planet, she was: but in what shape? I waited her rising. She rose at nine that December night: above the horizon I saw her come. She could shine yet with pale grandeur and steady might; but that star verged already on its judgement-day. Seen near, it was a chaos – hollow, half-consumed: an orb perished or perishing – half lava, half glow.

Lucy responds with hysterical ambivalence, ridden by her own polarised voices of desire and reason:

> It was a marvellous sight: a mighty revelation
> It was a spectacle low, horrible, immoral.[40]

The vision generates an 'uttermost frenzy of energy' into which she is inevitably drawn. She notices, however, that the spell is not working in the same way on her male companion, who remains a 'cool young Briton', watching with curiosity and evidently immune to the alternating currents of wonder, worship and dismay by which Lucy herself is shaken.

When the performance is interrupted by an outbreak of fire, the Freudian scenario is complete, and so is one version of the case for a rationalised, sceptical account of Rachel's legendary power. She is a cultural construct, a figure upon whom the fantasies of her age converge, invested with heightened significance through the feedback loop of an inflated reputation; a phenomenon telling us more about sublimation than sublimity.

It is a far more challenging task to interpret the power as genuine, because this entails raising questions about the limits of human nature and human experience. The impact of the ancient mysteries lay in their capacity to deliver an experience of such cognitive and sensory magnitude that it seemed to take the *mystai* (initiands) to another plane of being. Even the most stringent rationalist can surely acknowledge that human beings develop habitual ways of life characterised by repetitive thought patterns, restricted sensory response and narrow emotional range. Herzen's view of 'modern man' implies that the inhabitants of an industrialised world are especially susceptible to this contraction of lived experience. Brontë had painful knowledge of the ways in which women could be forced into suffocatingly confined life styles and her Lucy Snowe is at least capable of acutely sensing the deprivation.

There was an especial poignancy about this at a time when scientific advances were presenting dizzying challenges to previously assumed limitations on human power. The nineteenth century saw the human race empowered as never before, whilst the majority of individuals lived under extreme social and economic constraint. As the young Frankenstein is taught in his student years, the modern masters of physics and chemistry could achieve startling effects without carrying any of the old baggage of magical belief into their researches:

> They ascend into the heavens; they have discovered how the blood circulates, and the nature of the air we breathe. They have acquired new and almost unlimited powers; they can command the thunders of heaven, mimic the earthquake, and even mock the invisible world with its own shadows.[41]

The poets of the Romantic movement made a hero of Prometheus for his refusal to accept divine veto on the human use of fire and all its derivatives.

In such a cultural climate, why was it necessary to resort to supernatural explanations for the kind of highly charged presence Rachel manifested? And why the demonisation of her powers? Certainly a perennial tendency to demonise female sexuality was in operation, but the Rachel legend also has characteristics that are not entirely gender-specific. In it, we begin to see an essential paradox in the discourse surrounding stage presence in western modernity, an ambivalent relationship between the cultures of science and poetics. Even as commentators draw on the spectacular imagery of electricity, magnetism and chemical reaction, they also persistently invoke the occult. Amongst the things at issue are the different ways in which science and poetics employ our intelligence: science works through continually renewing understanding and altering its bases, whilst the poetic imagination is embedded in deep histories of language, narrative and imagery. The Romantic period is one of fierce internal conflict over the cultural accommodation of new human powers over nature, and every Promethean triumph carries an undercurrent of misgiving. Frankenstein became embroiled in a horror story of his own making. Prometheus incurred terrible punishment from the gods for his audacity. Faust – another of the great mythical reference points of the era – gained his powers through a bargain with the devil. Female power had always been associated with sorcery and possession, and the Delphic priestess was reasserting her validity as an archetype.

The figure of the mesmerist reflects this ambivalence about tapping into the greater energies of the universe and crossing the boundary between the fatally limited humanity of tragic drama and a new superhuman status. But part of the yearning for an expanded sense of being was a desire to escape the realms of the known and rediscover mystery for its own sake.

Charles Dickens took an interest in mesmerism and attended public demonstrations frequently. When John Elliotson, a professor at University College Hospital, came under intense professional attack for his involvement in these demonstrations and was forced to resign, Dickens offered his friendship and support. Further than this, he attempted to learn the techniques himself and is said to have put friends and members of his family into trance states through the exercise of his 'Visual Ray'. In his public readings, where he created levels of tension and attention that could only be described as hypnotic, he insisted on performance conditions that always allowed him direct eye contact with his audience. Peter Ackroyd's biography of Dickens points to his overt fascination with 'what a thing it is to have Power'.[42] This highlights the difference between an interest in power as it is held in the natural energies of the world, and psychological power: the latter can be personalised and turned into power over others in potentially sinister ways.

One of Mesmer's unintentional legacies was the injection of a new kind of significance into the relationship between performer and audience. The actor had never been so powerful, and the later nineteenth century was a period in which the stage star acquired an aura of supernatural energy. There was also a growing interest in psychological power as a subject for dramatic exploration. Some dramatists took a strictly rationalist view of this and some offered a quasi-occult interpretation, but, whatever the approach, they were creating opportunities for actors to take on roles with special opportunities for exploiting their personal magnetism. Henry Irving, who had mixed success in his early career, reached a turning point when he decided to acknowledge his physical limitations and rely more fully on force of personality. According to his grandson Laurence Irving, author of a key work on the actor's life, the realisation occurred following his appearance at the Comédie Française in 1867: 'The perfection of dialogue, of situation, of diction, of gesture and of movement revealed to him an academic development of the actor's art which laid bare the weaknesses of his own blundering and untutored apprenticeship'. To compensate for this, though, 'he knew that within him smouldered the lightning of animal magnetism which, leaping the gap in the proscenium, sent its vital current through the audience, until, returning to its dynamic source, it held actor and audience in the grip of its mystical circuit'.[43]

It would be hard to find a more vivid or definitive statement about the actor as mesmerist, and the parallels with Rachel are immediately apparent: inadequacies of physique and training, combined with a stage concentration so potent it was transformative. Mesmerism in dramatic acting begins with the transformative self-hypnosis of the player. And here we may think again of Sarah Siddons, her imagination possessed by the terrors of Lady Macbeth, frightened out of her wits by the rustling of her own gown on the stairs. Irving, a century later, was more conscious of what he was doing in creating the hypnotic state and was able to take it further. Unlike Rachel, he did not always require a stage event or the context of a dramatic setting in order to arouse the possessing forces. His first overt experiment with them occurred at a benefit night in March 1871, when he decided to offer an interval recitation of Thomas Hood's poem 'The Dream of Eugene Aram' as a bonus for his audience:

> Then, without scenery or properties to help in creating atmosphere or illusion, he began, not to recite, but to act the ghastly story of the conscience-stricken schoolmaster. He soon had the audience in his power, sweeping them along with the irresistible fury of the poem. He forced them to witness the brutal killing, the panic-stricken attempts of the murderer to hide the body of his victim and to share with him the haunting terror of inescapable justice.[44]

This is Laurence Irving's narrative, but it is corroborated by Bram Stoker in what is perhaps the most extraordinary eye-witness testimony to the actor's power.

Stoker had seen a number of Henry Irving's performances, but did not meet him in person until 1876, when they had a long conversation over dinner. Irving, sensing that he had encountered someone with a special understanding of his gifts, proposed an after-dinner recitation of 'Eugene Aram'. Stoker recalled:

> That experience I shall never – can never – forget. Such was Irving's commanding force, so great was the magnetism of his genius, so profound was the sense of his dominance that I sat spellbound. Outwardly I was of stone; nought quick in me but receptivity and imagination. Here was incarnate power, incarnate passion... the surroundings became non-existent.

Following the dramatic climax, in which Stoker felt he was present at the unfolding of the 'awful horror', Irving collapsed physically, and Stoker, 'after a few seconds of stony silence ... burst into something like a violent fit of hysterics'. Stoker is then quick to point out: 'I was no hysterical subject. I was no green youth; no weak individual yielding to a superior emotional force'.[45] Undoubtedly this was true. He was an exceptionally fit middle-aged man with extensive experience of the world and a hard-headed entrepreneur's capacity for business. But he was also the future author of *Dracula*, who wrote: 'I am all in a sea of wonders. I doubt; I fear; I think strange things'.[46] According to Stoker's biographer Barbara Belford, *Dracula* began in this first personal encounter with Irving.[47] There was inspiration here for the Vampire sleep of fast-moving scenes and blood-drenched visions with which he later intoxicated so many readers.

Dracula was published in 1897, but its central figure was in the making long before that. In 1878, Stoker wrote a review of Irving's performance in *Vanderecken* (a drama based on the myth of the Flying Dutchman), describing it as 'a wonderful impression of a dead man fictitiously alive'. He did not stop there:

> It was marvellous that any living man should show such eyes. They really seemed to shine like cinders of glowing red from out the marble face... in his every tone and action is the stamp of death. Herein lies the terror – we can call it by no other name – of the play. The chief actor is not quick but dead.[48]

Irving developed a talent for finding suitable dramatic vehicles for his power, but Stoker's Prince of Darkness seems to be based on a presence that moved between roles rather than grew from within them. As with Rachel, it is as if all the power this actor exercised over audiences skews to the demonic. Charlotte Brontë's descriptions of Vashti are echoed and equalled by Stoker's evocations of Dracula:

> Never did I imagine such wrath and fury, even to the demons of the pit. His eyes were positively blazing. The red light in them was lurid, as if the flame of hell-fire blazed behind them. His face was deathly pale, and the lines of it were like drawn wires; the thick eyebrows met over the nose now seemed like a heaving bar of white-hot metal.

Dracula is always the seducer, driven by a feral and primordial sexuality that puts all innocent souls in mortal danger.

> Suddenly with a single bound he leaped into the room, winning a way past us before any of us could raise a hand to stay him. There was something so panther-like in the movement – something so inhuman, that it seemed to sober us all from the shock of his coming... As the Count saw us, a horrible sort of snarl passed over his face, showing the eye-teeth long and pointed; but the evil smile as quickly passed into a cold stare of lion-like disdain.[49]

The movement, the energy, the fire in the eyes, the uncanny qualities of anticipation and dominance: all were displayed to greatest effect in *The Bells* (premièred in 1871). This was a melodrama set in an inn on the Alsace border, with strong echoes of 'Eugene Aram' in the plot. Mathias the innkeeper is prosperous and middle aged, with a daughter about to be married and a high reputation as a leading citizen of the village. He also has a seriously bad conscience, having in his youth committed a murder that was never solved. As the play unfolds, the suppressed horrors of his deed surface with redoubled intensity under the influence of a mesmerist. The wide popularity of mesmeric demonstrations in the 1870s no doubt contributed to the sense of anticipation surrounding Irving's performance at the Lyceum (where Stoker later joined him as manager).

In the later decades of the nineteenth century, mesmerism became associated with the popular craze for spiritualism, with mesmerists calling up spirits of the dead, and entranced mediums producing ectoplasmic phantoms. Eliphas Levi's extravagant views on Mesmer in *The History of Magic* (1860) were echoed by Madame Blavatsky, who established her Theosophical Society in New York in 1875. There she gave public demonstrations of clairvoyance and spirit materialisation, warning that the hypnotic state was a powerful tool in the hands of the occultist, whether to cause the revelation of secret crimes, or to inspire new ones. In Paris at the hospital of La Salpêtrière, Jean-Martin Charcot was offering a diametrically opposed but no less sensational view of the hysteric. A prominent neurologist, Charcot was fascinated by psychosomatic connections and worked with patients (especially female patients) to demonstrate the effects of hypnosis on their behaviour. His public demonstrations were photographed and widely attended, drawing the interest of Freud, who became a student of Charcot in the 1880s.

Supernaturalism, as Levi understood so well, always flourishes where it can be surrounded by an aura of science and experiment. Those who attended performances of *The Bells* evidently felt they were witnessing more than a fantastic narrative drama: Irving gave them the impression of being drawn into an extraordinary actuality. Edward Gordon Craig, his rhetorical suspicion of acting re-routed into advocacy for this new form of it, was a profound convert. Insisting that he could not describe the performance, he proceded to do so at length, focusing on the dynamics of interaction between actor and audience. Irving's entrance, Craig writes, is preceded by a 'hurricane of applause' whose quality is entirely different from that which conventionally anticipates the first appearance of a popular leading player. The hurricane, or 'torrent' as he also calls it, belongs to the elemental energies of the drama and is a demonstration of co-presence: 'power responded to power'. Irving is to be both the mesmeriser and the mesmerised but the audience, as his hypnotic subjects, are no mere ciphers. They are not the deficient, vacant receptors Herzen complained of. Craig portrays their involvement as intense, almost mimetic of the actor's every reactive move.

Once on stage, 'he relaxes his force all over, seems to turn it off to an almost dead calm'. This ratchets up the concentration in the auditorium, preparing for some intricate business with the changing of his shoes. Craig's account of this is a small tour de force in its own right:

> Irving was buckling his second shoe, seated, and leaning
> over it with his two long hands stretched down over

the buckles. We suddenly saw these fingers stop
their work; the crown of the head suddenly seemed to
glitter and become frozen – and then, at the pace of the
slowest and most terrified snail, the two hands, still
motionless and dead, were seen to be coming up the side
of the leg.[50]

Every gesture and half-move, we are told, is 'mesmeric in the
highest degree' – but Craig's way of telling it helps to realise the
stage meaning of 'mesmeric' in specific ways. There is an
absolute command over time and space. Time is stretched out, so
that all the senses are opened to the instant, then collapsed with a
shock effect as the focus shifts. The expanse of the stage, corre-
spondingly, disappears into a visual tunnel whilst some minute
action is executed, so that when its fullness is restored by a scenic
transition, the spectacular effect is magnified. But it is not all
violent swings from one sensory extreme to the other: the whole
performance is built on nuanced rhythms – rhythms that are 'irresistible', Craig says – building and relaxing tension so the entire
concentration of the spectator is drawn in and involvement is all
encompassing.

One of the staples of mesmeric practices is the power of eye
contact, and here Irving had a repertoire of techniques all his own.
Craig calls it a 'dance':

> He moves his head slowly from us – the eyes still somehow
> with us – and moves it to the right – taking as long as a
> long journey to discover a truth takes. He looks to the
> faces on the right – nothing. Slowly the head revolves back
> again, down, along the tunnels of thought and sorrow, and
> at the end the face and eyes are bent upon those to the left
> of him... utter stillness.[51]

The eyes are the means by which the mesmerist generates a contagious interiority, drawing others into an imagined scene he or she
has conjured.

If there was something of the supernatural, and especially of the
demonic supernatural, about the presence of both Henry Irving
and Rachel Félix this is because they were mesmerists who also
operated as trance mediums, appearing to channel forces too
powerful for human containment. What were they channelling?
One answer might be: all the passions, ideals and intensities

Herzen found wanting in 'modern man'. While I have suggested that Irving did not operate on the Leyden jar principle of dispensing powerful charges into empty repositories, something analogous but more subtle may have been going on.

Perhaps the metaphysical and mystical dimensions of human imagination that science had tried to excise were coming back with a vengeance, answering to a need for the greater energies to be manifested not just in technological spheres but also as part of individual life experience.

Superhumans and prodigies

This yearning for the greater energies created a heightened investment in the modern actor's presence, and a culture of criticism strongly invested in poetics and metaphysics was developing around it. There was a renewed commitment to the esoteric, epitomised in the writings of Edward Gordon Craig, on whom Irving was a defining influence. 'So in the science of life', wrote Craig, 'in the crowded street or market place or theatre, or wherever life is, there are partial tones, there are unseen presences. Side by side with the human crowd is a crowd of unseen forms. Principalities, and Powers and Possibilities'.[52]

Part of the new critical stance was an 'ultimatum' style of assessment carried through from previous eras: this or that performer would be proclaimed the greatest of their generation, a genius of the highest order, a figure of unprecedented brilliance and attraction. The German poet Rainer Maria Rilke endorsed the 'spirit of unchecked admiration' aroused by 'the few great individuals whom our time was unable to stifle'.[53] Something was being added to the ultimatum; there was more at stake now. If 'modern man' had not already lost touch with the grander passions and deeper meanings, connection with them was becoming precarious.

Each new generation of commentators was ready to declare that theirs was the lost tribe. James Agate, the *Sunday Times* critic who was born in 1877, the year Stoker joined Irving as manager of the Lyceum, was asked in the 1930s for a retrospective view of the actor's career and had this to say:

> In my considered view, great acting in this country died with Irving, and I haven't seen smell or sight or hearing or feel or taste of it since. If our young playgoers saw Irving they would burst like electric lightbulbs.[54]

Despite protests that a great actor once gone leaves nothing behind that is worth having, the romance of hindsight around Irving remained strong for two generations into the twentieth century.

He died in 1905, but in 1908 Sarah Bernhardt was inspiring superlatives of a similar order from the literary luminaries of the time, including Victor Hugo, Marcel Proust, Henry James, Lytton Strachey, Oscar Wilde, D.H. Lawrence and Agate himself. Evidently unconcerned about bursting lightbulbs in her case, Agate wrote that her art 'lit up a firmament'.[55] Lawrence, who saw Bernhardt perform in *La Dame aux Camelias* towards the end of her career, saw her power as animal power, an extraordinary but entirely natural phenomenon:

> Oh, to see her, and to hear her, a wild creature, a gazelle with a beautiful panther's fascination and fury, laughing in musical French, screaming with true panther cry, sobbing and sighing like a deer sobs, wounded to death... there she is, the incarnation of wild emotion which we share with all live things, but which is gathered in us in all complexity and inscrutable fury. She represents the primeval passions of woman, and she is fascinating to an extraordinary degree.[56]

When she appeared in London as Phèdre, one of Rachel's greatest roles, Lytton Strachey was moved to describe it in terms that suggested echoes of the ancient mysteries:

> To watch, in the culminating horror of crime and of remorse, of jealousy, of rage, of desire, and of despair, all the dark forces of destiny crowd down upon that great spirit, when the heavens and the earth reject her, and Hell opens, and the terrific urn of Minos thunders and crashes to the ground – that indeed is to come close to immortality, to plunge shuddering through infinite abysses, and to look, if only for a moment, upon eternal light.[57]

Arthur Symons was likewise inspired by the wild beast metaphor. 'She seems to abandon herself wholly, at times, to her *fureurs*', he wrote of the same performance. 'She tears the words with her teeth, and spits them out of her mouth, like a wild beast ravening on prey'. But the electrical metaphor is also to the fore in his account, where she is described as sending currents of electrifying vitality 'through all manner of winding ways'.[58]

In Bernhardt, two traditions of rhetoric converge: she is Rachel's successor as the enchantress, but she is also the icon of a potent naturalism. Bernhardt herself cultivated this ambiguity in the strategic approach she took to the creation of her own myth. She kept a photograph of Rachel on her wall, and developed a range of behaviours designed to intimidate, mystify and inspire awe in those around her. Her physical qualities – the ultra-slim, attenuated silhouette, large eyes and finely etched mouth – lent themselves to an ethereal image with an aura of the uncanny, captured exquisitely in Ellen Terry's verbal portrait:

> She was as transparent as an azalea, only more so; like a cloud, only not so thick. Smoke from a burning paper describes more nearly. She was hollow-eyed, thin, almost consumptive looking. Her body was not the prison of her soul, but its shadow.[59]

The press became obsessed with this image, so antithetical to that of the fleshy *demi-mondaines* who set the standards of female desirability, and when she took a balloon ride during the 1878 Paris Exposition reporters waxed lyrical: 'She is a goddess, aerial and ideal, a creature of dreams, a spirit who aspires to the azure... Her slenderness is the result of the dissolution of matter. She cannot breathe until she is above the towers of Notre Dame'. Seeing her refuse an umbrella as she stepped out into the rain on landing, another reporter remarked that 'she was so thin she could slip between the raindrops'.[60] Publicity gimmicks like this were her forte. She had herself photographed sleeping in a coffin, and frequently appeared in public accompanied by animals from her exotic private menagerie. If Rachel was the 'panther of the stage', Bernhardt kept house with a live cheetah.

The association with wild animals drew out the other side of her persona, the aspect that was fuelled by intense natural energies. The English critic Arthur Symons described the experience of watching her entry on stage:

> Two magics met and united, in the artists and the woman, each alone of its kind. There was an excitement going on in the theatre; one's pulses beat feverishly before the curtain had risen; there was almost a kind of obscure sensation of peril, such as one feels when the lioness leaps into the cage, on the other side of the bars. And the acting

was like a passionate declaration, offered to someone unknown; it was as if the whole nervous force of the audience were sucked out of it and flung back, intensified, upon itself, as it encountered the single, insatiable, indomitable nervous force of the woman.

This was vampirism, or the Leyden jar principle in reverse. Symons is not tempted to invoke supernatural associations. He sees her as 'the incomparable craftswoman' and insists that hers is 'a very conscious art', but also that it is the 'irresistible expression of a temperament'. The effect is of 'awakening the senses and sending the intelligence to sleep'.[61]

Testimonials to Bernhardt's energy and willpower are a generic element in the literature surrounding her. She is portrayed as maintaining a near round-the-clock schedule of activity, obsessively controlling the arrangements for her performances and keeping after-show appointments far into the night. The controlling style fed back into the mythos: essentially, Bernhardt was a phenomenon of her own making. She was a cut above the *demi-mondaines* in her repertoire and her talents, but she had learned much from them about how to feed audience anticipation with an imaginative repertoire of off-stage performances. In her, presence and charisma converge as the life spills into the art. In an age where the press were always circling, presence could be charged up through the feedback loop of constant reportage. Sarah Bernhardt recognised this and played her hand accordingly, stimulating public interest wherever she went and ensuring that her image was being continually re-enhanced through the eyes of the best painters and photographers. Even the operation to amputate her leg became something of a theatrical *tour de force*, as reported by her anaesthetist. 'One feels she is always acting, playing the role of someone who has undergone a grave operation. Later that day I found the patient exactly the same as the woman I admired on the stage. Her eyes were made up, her lips painted'.[62]

A consciousness of image was one of her great skills. Amongst the surviving photographs of actors from the late nineteenth and early twentieth century, hers are amongst the few that do not look absurd. There is a sharp contemporaneity about the face and the attitude, a natural elegance. Those who love attention as much as she did become adept at cultivating it. At the dawn of the media age, 'attraction' is already becoming more of a calculated activity than a mysteriously inherent attribute. Yet this is far from being the whole story where Sarah Bernhardt is concerned. The Bernhardt phenomenon may be best described in the words of Eliphas Levi: 'prodigies are results of exceptional wills and energies'.[63]

There is something Nietzschean about Bernhardt's willpower, channelled as it was into a driving force that shamelessly subordinated other wills and interests. She is one of the prototype charismatics of the modern stage. She defines the personality of the diva: imperious, narcissistic, volatile, greedy, but also commanding and tireless, vitally responsive, capable of accommodating a vast emotional spectrum ranging from nuanced pathos to the fiercest extremes of passion. This is not just about ego. The prodigy in the arts of performance is rather a constellation of alter-egos, roles he or she is possessed by or – in Bernhardt's case – has taken possession of. Bernhardt is the kleptomaniac of the grand repertoire. In her mid 40s she declared she would play Wilde's Salome. In her mid 50s she played Hamlet. Hers was what Nietzsche calls 'the genius of the heart'

> ...from whose touch everyone goes away richer... newer to himself than before, broken open, blown upon and sounded out by a thawing wind, more uncertain perhaps, more delicate, more fragile, more broken, but full of hopes that as yet have no names, full of new will and current, full of new ill will and counter current.[64]

Nietzsche reinvented the figure who had travelled through history as the magus, the prodigy and the genius: he named it the *Übermensch* or superman, though Bernhardt proved that it did not have to be male.

The superman is superhuman without being supernatural: a creature of the natural world, who does not channel the gods but rather brings to humanity a godlike stature, through a dedication to all that is most powerful in human nature. Nietzsche's writings were performances in themselves, voiced through the alter-ego of Zarathustra, whose driving determination was 'to have one foot beyond life'. This is a sharp twist on the image of 'calling from beyond the grave' that Betterton inspired. The superman performs a living encroachment on the world of spirits and immortals, rather than an invocation of their presence in ours. Nietzsche outprotested Herzen in his conviction that 'the man of the present' was devoid of the 'ravenous hunger in conscience and knowledge' that was needed for a vital response to the fullness of the world.

His superman was a reactive literary performance, and arrogance was its keynote:

> ... he who is related to me through loftiness of will experiences when he reads me real ecstasies of learning; for I come from heights no bird has ever soared to, I know abysses into which no foot has ever yet strayed.[65]

Zarathustra is anchored in the natural world, absorbing the energies of animal life but surpassing them, and he keeps around him a personal menagerie of wild animals (another propensity Bernhardt echoed).

Nietzsche's reconception of human power was overtly theatrical – here Wagner was his inspiration – and characterised by an intense physicality. 'The body is inspired', he proclaims, 'let us leave the "soul" out of it'. Zarathustra is a Dionysian, who has 'often been seen dancing' and whose superhuman vitality spurs him through seven hour mountain walks from which he emerges 'perfectly vigorous'.[66] In him, we see the emergence of a concept of presence that is founded in the body, a body that is energised and invigorated to levels of intensity that render it a compelling expression of the here and now.

Although his major works were written in the 1870s and 1880s, Nietzsche's ideas went through an expanding reverberation across the turn of the century. The expression '*fin de siècle*' conjures the nerve-driven sense of human and cultural transition so intensely conveyed in his works. The year 1900 approached with an aura of cataclysm: the future threatened to swallow the past. A world weary with excesses of knowledge and activity was nevertheless about to undergo a rebirth, so that youth and age seemed to be backed onto each other, or overlapping. Wilde's reaction to the idea of Bernhardt playing the teenaged Salome was that she was the only person who could do it. Salome was a figure at whose feet the centuries had heaped up dreams and visions, and Bernhardt, 'that serpent of old Nile', was 'older than the pyramids'.[67] She carried sufficient life force to wear this burden of deep history, unlike many of her contemporaries, who felt bowed down. As the nineteenth century drew to a close, fears of decadence – racial and cultural decline through the loss of nerve force – prompted a counter-active investment in heroes and heroines of vitality. Dancers were at a premium, especially those who broke the mould of the classical tradition: Loie Fuller, Isadora Duncan, Vaslav Nijinsky. Fuller and Duncan, like Bernhardt, became icons. They spawned a revolution in style and were surrounded by imitators and replicas. Fuller was an inspired technician and Duncan an inspiring role model, but Nijinsky was a catalyst of a different order, a performer who made himself into extraordinary and compelling images, then escaped them in a perpetual search for fresh engagements with the present.

Nijinsky's capacity to embody the changing times as they happened was realised through his catalytic association with Diaghilev, who came into public life with an agenda to bring on the new era, and a rhetoric to match. The first major occasion for this was his exhibition of Russian historical portraits in the Tauride Palace, St Petersburg, in 1905, only one month after the Bloody Sunday massacre. At the opening, Diaghilev pronounced:

> Here ending their lives are not only people, but pages of history. We are witnessses of the greatest moment of summing up in history, in the name of a new and unknown culture, which will be created by us, and which will also sweep us away.[68]

While Diaghilev, the confident impresario and innovator, was talking his way into the future like a born prophet, Nijinsky, still a teenager, was out in the streets, witnessing the chaos. On the night of Bloody Sunday he saw the violence break out and heard the extraordinary rhetorical outburst that followed it, when Father Gapon, the leader of the marchers, declared that henceforth there was no Tsar, no Church and no God.

On stage, Nijinsky impressed observers as a kind of portent, heralding rupture and the winds of change blowing at gale force. It was as if everything he was and everything he did was cutting a rift between what had been and what was to come. This was both exhilarating and disturbing. Exhilarating because there was such glorious spectacle and verve in the performances – disturbing because there was an energy here that was stretching outside the known registers.

His debut role on graduation from the Imperial ballet school was the slave in *Pavillion d'Armide*. Alexandre Benois described how this 'young, rather stocky man' was transformed as the rehearsals progressed, becoming 'nervous and capricious', then reincarnating himself as an exotic and seductive figure. Nijinsky's biographer Richard Buckle claims that the conquest of Europe by Russian dancing and the reign of Diaghilev can be said to begin at the moment Nijinsky takes the stage in *Armide*.

Definitive moments, though, were the story of Nijinsky's life. There was the moment when he found himself in the crowd in the 1905 uprising; the moment of his first public performance, when the audience were so astonished they refused to go home; the moment of his first Parisian appearance with the *Ballet Russes*; the moment of uproar at the premiere of *Le Sacre du printemps* (*The Rite of Spring*), which Richard Buckle calls 'the ballet of the century'. And there was the moment when he ended his own career in a performance so strange and fraught with tension, people literally ran away from it.

But in 1905, all this alien energy was still packed into the figure Geoffrey Whitworth described as 'the vivid radiant boy', whose extraordinary hold over an audience could be attributed to his virtuosity. This comes across in the accounts of Nijinsky's sister Bronislava, a star-struck witness but also a technically knowledgeable observer:

> Nijinsky appears onstage in a long prolonged leap, grand assemblé, and while he is still up in the air a rumble runs through the theatre. When Nijinsky descends slowly, barely touching the stage with his feet, a sudden burst of applause erupts... While he waits onstage holding his pose, his whole body is alive with an inner movement, his whole being radiant with inner joy – a slight smile on his lips... a light quivering of his small expressive hands among the lace cuffs.[69]

Le Spectre de la Rose provided him with the role that gave greatest scope to his classical virtuosity, but he confused the aesthetic codes even as he played to them. The flagrant femininity of the role, with its rose-petalled costume, combined with the flamboyant virility of the choreography, culminating in the celebrated exit leap, which gave the impression of flight through the open window. But as the audience exploded into applause at the apparently superhuman feat, Nijinsky landed in the wings gasping for air. 'As he stood beside me in his leotard sewn with damp purple petals', said Valentine Gross, 'he seemed a kind of St. Sebastian, flayed alive'. Jean Cocteau saw both sides of the illusion:

> He evaporates through the window in a jump so contrary to the laws of flight and balance that I shall never again smell a rose without this ineffable phantom appearing before me.

And
I still hear the thunder of the applause, still see that young man smeared with grease paint – sweating, panting, one hand pressing at his heart and the other clutching a stage brace.[70]

This fetish about catching Nijinsky in the moment of his switch back to mortality goes with the mythology of otherworldliness and supra-humanity that always surrounded him. Anatole Bourman, a fellow student at the Imperial School, recalled a sense of the uncanny about his work in mime classes: 'I have sat and watched Vaslav playing with such power and conviction in his gestures that the goose flesh crept over my whole body and fear itself invaded me'.[71]

He certainly had a mesmerising power equal to that of Rachel, Irving or Bernhardt but the adulation he aroused was never something he embraced. Rather, he was oddly estranged from it, set upon a course of experiment to which audiences seem to have been almost irrelevant. The alluring sense of otherness that characterised his early performances developed into an outright alienation, aggressive and confronting in its impact. Nijinsky is one of the first great presences of the modern stage to exercise power over the public imagination by refusing to deliver what it wanted, and so keeping expectation on edge.

The roles he is identified with play on a sense of otherness in various ways. The orientalism of the *Ballets Russes* was expressed through the images he created, but it also prompted him to explore unfamiliar configurations of the body: the hands, the fingers, the elbows and the ankles had never done such things in western dance. In *Petrouchka*, he broke up the accustomed forms further. Cyril Beaumont described 'a curiously fitful quality in his movements' as the creature on stage 'leapt or twisted or stamped like the reflex actions of limbs whose muscles have been subjected to an electric current'. Benois was surprised at the courage he showed 'in appearing as a horrible half doll, half-human grotesque'.[72] Nijinsky was challenging the parameters of description on all fronts, just as he was challenging the limits of technique. In *Scheherezade*, his performance concluded with an inverted pirouette that was a shocking development from the graceful control he exuded: as he received the death blow from a scimitar, the slave fell, his legs shooting upwards in a spasm that carried through his spine until he was balanced on the crown of his head, and so he spun to the point of collapse.

Stories of his social ineptitude and disorientation contributed further to the legend. Hilda Munnings – alias Lydia Sokolova – provides one of the most resonant verbal sketches of the superman who was also Noman:

> He moved on the balls of his feet and his nervous energy found an outlet in fidgeting: when he sat down he twisted his fingers or played with his shoes. He hardly spoke to anyone, and he seemed to exist on a different plane. Before dancing he was even more withdrawn, like a bewitched soul.[73]

It is as if Nijinksy did not know how to be a person; he was a highly charged nervous system in search of a persona, and whenever he found a new one the energy took shape and took over. The nervousness was bristling out of control by the end of the second Paris season in 1910. There are accounts of sudden rages and dangerous fits of caprice, such as that which prompted him to drop his sister Bronislava from a high lift because she was not up to speed (she was recovering from an illness at the time). His instability seems, however, only to have prompted him to enlarge his sphere of experiment with ventures into choreography that stretched the aesthetic range of Diaghilev's company to breaking point.

In *l'Après midi d'un faune* (1912), he converted the exotic animal energy used to such intoxicating effect in his earlier performances into an overtly sexual expression that caused a furore. A review in *Le Figaro* described the performance as 'filthy and bestial'.[74] If there was something primordial about it, this was paradoxically what made it so new and fraught with prognostic suggestions. Nijinsky was offering a ballet for the future, drawn from the deep past. This direction was more fully realised in *Le Sacre du printemps*, which he choreographed to Stravinsky's score. The production was strongly influenced by the designer Nicholas Roerich, who was also an archeologist specialising in the stone age. Roerich had done a sequence of paintings portraying the dawn of civilisation, under such titles as 'The Daughters of the Earth' and 'The Call of the Sun'.

At this point in his career, Nijinsky's placement as an artist moved to the outer edge of the accustomed field of vision, challenging audiences and peers to adjust the parameters of their own seeing. He was becoming prophetic, but in ways that communicated first and foremost through the body. The company recruited for *Le Sacre* were in for a thorough shake-up to the nervous system. According to one of his dancers:

> What he seemed to demand was a school of ordered fragmentation: quivering, shivering, spasms, ejaculations; a metaphorical hysteria which exhausted the patience, goodwill and attention of his troupe.[75]

Another cast member recorded: 'I went dizzy; clutching my head, I burst into tears, ran off the stage and collapsed'. Famously, the première triggered a commotion, in which the well-heeled audience began slapping about them, hissing insults in all directions, as if Nijinsky's way of splintering rhythms and rupturing co-ordination had a wider fallout. Valentine Gross insisted:

> Nothing that has been written about the battle of *le Sacre du printemps* has given even a faint idea of what actually took place. The theatre seemed to be shaken by an earthquake. It seemed to shudder. People howled and whistled, drowning the music.[76]

It says something for Diaghilev that he stood through all this in staunch defence of the production and its creators: he may have been instrumental in bringing the team together, but this was not his chemistry. His were the concoctions that brought the adulation and the accolades, and here was Nijinsky's work, shaking all that to pieces, driven by a new determination on a wholly other wavelength. Here was a future Diaghilev had never foreseen, a future arriving as a stranger attended by portents nobody seemed to know how to read.

The times could not have been more nervous. It was May 1913, and the preconditions for war were falling into place. In Jacques Rivière's extraordinary description of *Le Sacre*, Nijinsky had created a Darwinian world injected with the psychical chutzpah of esoteric prophesy:

> This is a biological ballet. It is not only the dance of the most primitive men, it is the dance before man... Stravinksy tells us that he wanted to portray the surge of spring. But this is not the usual spring sung by poets, with its breezes, its birdsong, its pale skies and tender greens. Here is nothing but the harsh struggle of growth, the panic

terror from the rising of the sap, the fearful regrouping of
the cells. Spring seen from inside with its violence, its
spasms and its fissions. We seem to be watching the drama
through a microscope.[77]

This is the future as the nerves encounter it, a future born not of
aesthetic visions and designs, but of cellular fission. The splitting of
the cell is the image for the macrocosm, and those who sensed that
in 1913 had a better sense of what was to come than any conventional forecasters.

It was also a prescient image for what was happening to the
course of Niinsky's own life. After the *furore* surrounding *Le Sacre
du printemps*, the arc of Nijinsky's career was breaking up, mental
illness was encroaching and the onset of the war meant a period of
exile and anonymity. 'One pays dearly for being immortal',
Nietzsche warned. 'To have something behind one that one ought
never to have willed, something within which the knot of destiny
of mankind is tied – and from then on to have it on one!... It
almost crushes'. This pronouncement is accompanied by perhaps
the least flattering of all portraits of the superman's counterpart:
ordinary modern man, who can harbour some ugly counter-
reactions to the phenomenon of a great presence: 'There is something I call the *rancune* of what is great: everything great, a work, a
deed, once it is completed forthwith turns against him who did it'.[78]

Nietzsche rails against a cultural pathology he calls 'Russian
fatalism', characterised by an incapacity 'to receive anything, to
take anything *into* oneself'. This is like the antithesis of Nijinsky's
self-declared 'nervousness', a condition of charged receptivity in
which every sound, sight or sensation makes its imprint. There is an
antithesis also to the molecular hyperactivity described by Rivière.
The fatalist, says Nietzsche, undergoes a 'reduction of the metabo-
lism... a kind of will to hibernation'.[79] Nijinsky's *Sacre* was an
onslaught on this condition, but the nervousness he communicated
became an increasingly isolated campaign against the growing tide
of *ressentiment*, Nietzsche's term for the mind-set produced by a
reduced and exhausted consciousness. 'Vexation, morbid susceptibility, incapacity for revenge, poison-brewing', the primary symp-
toms of *ressentiment*, were undoubtedly growing elements in
European culture during the first half of the twentieth century.

The two world wars produced cultural lesions that altered the
dynamics of theatrical communication. There were mood swings in
the cultural climate itself that one can see reflected in the cults

surrounding charismatic figures who captured the people's imagination. If the mesmeric qualities are generated through a process of exchange with an audience, these figures can also be seen as barometers of the cultural mood: they served as catalysts for its shifts and swings, but were also themselves galvanised by the collective energies with which they engaged. The great twentieth-century mesmerists seem more troubled and multi-dimensional figures than those of the nineteenth. No doubt this is because we are closer to them and have more varied and nuanced accounts of their impact, but if presence is about *being* present, to the times and in the moment, those who are most strongly endowed with this quality are likely to be especially sensitised to the changing dynamics of their era.

With the growth of mass media culture and the internationalisation of celebrity, it became much harder for the stars of the entertainment world to stabilise their public image and retain control of it. Their relationship with their audiences was subject to a wider diversity of influences, and the world was changing more rapidly around them. Tapping the deepest emotions and most potent thoughts of an audience is itself a mysterious process. There is no straightforward explanation for why some people can do this to such inspiring effect while others who may be highly skilled performers cannot. Where in politics the mesmeric speaker can go directly to the heart of an audience with words alone, theatrical performers have the support of a dramatic framework that opens out the imaginative terrain to create expanded terms of psychical engagement; this is especially so with opera.

It was Maria Callas who came to epitomise the prima donna as mesmerist. Although the epithet *La divina* was awarded to her, her power over an audience was never that of a supernaturalist, and whilst she may have been a prodigy, any superhuman capacities she exhibited told only more effectively of the wayward humanity that steered her course. One of her earliest teachers, Maria Trivella, describes her impact at the age of thirteen:

> The tone of that voice was warm, lyrical, intense; it swirled and flared like a flame and filled the air with melodious reverberations like a carillon. It was by any standards an amazing phenomenon, or rather it was a great talent that needed control.[80]

The control was in unreliable and intermittent supply, but her waywardness was essential to her dramatic impact as a performer, giving a tantalising edge to her presence. On stage she was keyed up, notoriously prone to crises, but also to moments of incandescent clarity, both vocal and emotional.

Certainly she lived through turbulent times, including the period of Nazi occupation in Athens during the Second World War, when she was in her late teens, but the turbulence she exhibited is not in any evident way related to the larger events of her world. She was no political barometer. Indeed, her obtuseness on matters of political principle was evident from an early stage. After the occupying troops withdrew from Athens, Callas was accused of being a Nazi sympathiser because she had been romantically involved with an Italian soldier, and had given informal recitals for the enemy forces. Nevertheless, the fact that her career took off in the years immediately following the war invites some consideration of how her performances resonated with a certain kind of collective mood, one that, perhaps, was born of exhaustion with the harsh pragmatism of the war years, and sought again the dramatic landscapes of personal emotion offered by the grand operas.

Following her 1954 Chicago appearance in *Lucia di Lammermoor*, it was reported:

> Near pandemonium broke out. There was an avalanche of applause, a roar of cheers growing steadily louder and a standing ovation, and the aisles were full of men pushing as close to the stage as possible.[81]

In the same year Callas gave a performance as Medea that prompted similar outbursts. Conductor Leonard Bernstein commented: 'The place was out of its mind. Callas? She was pure electricity'.[82] Obviously more is going on here than mesmerism *per se*. There is the thrilling vocal performance, the narrative, the emotional power of the music, the visual impact of the figure on stage torn by the passions of love, rage and madness. Stage presence always feeds off the dramatic stature of the character portrayed, and Callas's identification with the heroines of grand opera – Lucia, Medea, Tosca (a role created by Bernhardt), Norma – gave her enormous scope to portray heightened states and generate sympathetic intensity in her audience. Arianna Stassinopoulos recalls being taken to see *Norma* in an open-air performance at Epidaurus, the ancient theatre which had witnessed the birth of Greek drama; she affirms that 'Maria went beyond acting and opera and touched the hearts of thousands who knew nothing of either. From her very first notes, the audience was magnetised by the power she displayed'. Stassinopoulos believes that the power arises from a capacity to draw out 'the deeper, primordial self, home both of the darkness we harbour and of all life-giving forces'.[83]

So are we back, again, to the ancient mysteries? The influence exerted by stage performers who have achieved legendary status for their mesmeric and magnetic powers can be seen to shuttle between the polarities of archaism and urgent contemporaneity. Mesmerism itself can be seen as a form of mystery-mongering escapism, or as a means of cutting through layers of psychical insulation to reach a pulsing vitality that has been smothered. The relationship between mesmerism and stage presence is accordingly paradoxical. Recalling the figure of Rachel chanting the Marseilleise, or Irving making his entrance in *The Bells*, or Nijinsky as the young faun rising from sleep, we can recognise that the impact on an audience was both an intoxication and an awakening. The mesmeriser may be vampirically drawing energy from those packed into the auditorium, or, in accordance with Franklin's principle, themselves be a source of super-concentrated power seeking release into empty vessels. That both images have some validity makes the phenomenon of mesmeric presence more interesting. There is a circuit between the energetic polarities of performer and spectator, and it is established at the moment when the performer arrives on stage and with the very first notes (Callas) or the very first gesture (Irving) brings the present moment into sharp relief, opening the channels of receptivity for the unexpected and the unprecedented.

4

DASH AND FLASH

Lucky possum that you are
You are now a mini star,
A big fish in a tiny pond
Thanks to my magic wand.

Dame Edna Everage

The performer on stage who by his or her very presence generates some kind of mesmeric power over an audience may need little or nothing in the way of spectacle to achieve an impact. There is a personal electricity at work, as anyone who has watched Maria Callas in her televised Hamburg concerts will know. Without the aid of scenery or costume, and moving only from the waist up, she seems to be channelling the dramatic shapes of the music with a concentration so full it is impossible not to share it. Presence can also be associated with silence and stillness, with a figure who, like Prospero, redraws the hyperactive energy fields around him by remaining apart, on another wavelength. What, then, of the stars who belong to the razzle-dazzle tradition of theatre? The sparkle and razzamatazz can serve as a substitute for personal magnetism, or as a distraction from it. Watching a Las Vegas show we may be aware of how the simple mystique of presence can be drowned by all the star-effects produced by modern technology, but there are cases where an individual who surrounds him- or herself with dash and flash actually harbours some corresponding electricity that generates the real charge at the centre of the show.

If both these versions are around in show business, can we tell the difference? Personally, I am always fascinated by this challenge. I love to watch the star of a mass-audience concert or musical as the performance unfolds and to see if I can identify where the energy is coming from, how it is being shaped and managed. There is a special charge in the air when something unexpected is being offered: the Beatles making a new kind of a sound, whose casual inventiveness carried through to the way they dressed and moved, the expressions on their faces; David Bowie, taking stage images that were somehow familiar and twisting them, twisting them again, ratcheting up the strangeness until you really could believe he was a being from another planet; Johnny Rotten attacking a song in a way that promised to tip the live concert experience off the edge of any known cultural world.

Expanding circuits

Recent research demonstrates that lightning does indeed sometimes strike the same person twice. A certain kind of logic would suggest that some people have an affinity with electricity, and some electrical researchers have clearly believed this of themselves, especially those who came to prominence in the charged-up cultural atmosphere of the late nineteenth century. The Serbian born Nikola Tesla – inventor of the induction motor, wireless communication, remote control and neon lighting – is one of the most theatrical figures in the history of science. He consciously exploited the theatricality of electrical experiment to create an aura of the supernatural around himself: if his rival Thomas Edison was known as 'the Wizard of Menlo Park' for his creation of a laboratory that was like a magical illuminated palace, Tesla in his retreat at Colorado Springs evoked the darker side of wizardry. Christopher Nolan's film *The Prestige* (2006) portrays the scene of his work as a vast hangar-like space underneath a ramshackle house surrounded by snow-covered fields in which are planted outsize lightbulbs which all illuminate at once with a dazzling white light.

Tesla makes his entrance from the midst of a crackling mess of lightning emitted by a sphere suspended from the ceiling of his laboratory. It is a scene replicating those captured in photographs taken in the early 1900s and suggestive of the idea that this elegantly presented gentlemen is himself emitting the currents as he appears. In the film, he is engaged in experiments aimed at achieving the transportation of material objects across distances through a process of electrical dematerialisation that is then reversed. A top hat, a black cat and finally a man are charged up and transmitted to a point outside his enchanted precinct. In Tesla's world, all life is translated into voltage. And in an inspired piece of casting, this Tesla is played by David Bowie. What better way to capture the doubleness of a presence that appears now as a conservatively dressed middle aged gentleman, now as an obsessional meddler with extreme energies? We see nothing of Bowie the dash and flash virtuoso in this performance, but his alter-ego Ziggy Stardust ghosts Tesla, like his progeny from a not so distant future.

The historical Tesla developed his skills as a showman through the lectures and demonstrations he gave early in his career to audiences in Paris, London, New York and other major American cities. In a lecture delivered for the Royal Institution in London in 1892, he is said to have held his audience spellbound for a full two hours with an exhibition of dazzling pyrotechnics that he mediated in the most literal sense. He made sparks fly from a wire by touching it, caused wireless tubes to light up as he held them in his hand, and began to manipulate visible currents of crackling electricity like an orchestral conductor. Lamps burst forth in an array of 'magnificent colors of phosphorescent light'; 'sheets of luminescence' streamed through the air, and as a finale he fired up a coil to send a high voltage aura around his body, illuminating two fluorescent tubes that he brandished like light sabres.[1] Further performances, culminating in a week of demonstrations at the World's Fair in Chicago in 1893, drew massive public interest.

Electricity was the dominant attraction of the Chicago World's Fair, with the rival teams of Edison and Westinghouse vying for prominence in the displays. Tesla, working for Westinghouse, was responsible for devising the system for distributing large currents of electricity over a wide distance, so enabling the whole phenomenon of what became known as the 'White City'. Public anticipation of his appearances at the Electricity Hall was whipped up by announcements that he would send 100,000 volts through his body. As the pre-publicity mounted, the figure escalated to 250,000 volts, but in the event Tesla gratified his audiences with something much more nuanced and entrancing: an electromagnetic field encompassing a set of spinning balls and discs that moved around each other like planets in expanding orbits. Transmission of power across distances was the most significant of his inventions, and was to enable a range of technologies subsequently used in entertainment spectacles. Through his influence, the nature of theatrical spectacle altered, from the moving tableaux created by De Loutherbourg, to a more kinetic, high-speed approach in which the human figure was the central element of an illuminated field.

Although Tesla was something of an exhibitionist, he was no simple egotist and the charged-up public persona was part of a philosophy that disavowed autonomous individual power. He professed a universalism that carried echoes of Mesmer's, but was free of the personalised claims to power and capable of explaining himself with an entirely different order of cogency:

Our bodies are of similar construction and exposed to the same external forces. This results in likeness of response and concordance of the general activities on which all our social and other rules and laws are based. We are automata entirely controlled by the forces of the medium, being tossed about like corks on the surface of the waters, but mistaking the resultant of the impulses from the outside for the free will. The movements and actions we perform are always life preservative and though seemingly quite independent from one another, we are connected by invisible links.[2]

Individuals might be more or less potent as transmitters of energy waves from the universal forcefield. Tesla's first impression of the business tycoon George Westinghouse was of a 'tremendous energy' that had not yet found its expression:

But even to a superficial observer, the latent force was manifest. A powerful frame, well proportioned, with every joint in working order, an eye as clear as crystal, a quick and springy step.[3]

Like the painter William Blake, Tesla had perceptual hypersensitivities, with an eidetic imagination (an inability to distinguish between what was seen with the mind's eye and what was actually seen). He worked with an obsessive intensity that caused him to have intermittent bouts of neurasthenic exhaustion in which all his senses were at fever pitch. By his own claims, he was susceptible to phenomenal levels of hyperaesthesia:

In 1899, when I was past forty and carrying on my experiments in Colorado, I could hear very distinctly thunderclaps at a distance of 550 miles. The limit of audition for my young assistants was scarcely more than 150 miles... Yet at that time I was, so to speak, stone deaf in comparison with the acuteness of my hearing while under nervous strain. In Budapest I could hear the ticking of a watch with three rooms between me and the timepiece. A fly lighting on a table in the room would cause a dull thud in my ear... the ground under my feet trembled continuously. I had to support my bed on rubber cushions to get any rest at all... In the dark I had the sense of a bat and could detect the presence of an object at a distance of twelve feet by a creepy sensation on my forehead.[4]

This is nerve power gone haywire, but in a perverse way it may tell us something about the relationship between presence and electricity. The external and spectacular manifestations of dazzle and flash have internal correlations that manifest in sensory and emotional terms, but these can be communicated just as the visible flashes can be transmitted from body to body. Indeed, in Tesla's metaphysics, the human mind is a powerful generative influence, whose activity levels are visible in the luminosity of the eyes.[5] Vision was itself a kinetic and dynamic activity with literally astronomical potential:

> ... the fact that the eye, by its marvelous power, widens our otherwise very narrow range of perception far beyond the limits of the small world which is our own, to embrace myriads of other worlds, suns and stars in the infinite depths of the universe, would make it justifiable to assert, that it is an organ of a higher order.[6]

Such pronouncements display an extravagance of mind that raises the sceptic in a reader from our own times, but Tesla was a curious mix. The flights of hyperactive consciousness are moderated by an exactness of knowledge and attention to detail that is more reminiscent of Sherlock Holmes than Madame Blavatsky. He made no secret of his contempt for those he considered deficient in observation, and if he rivalled Frankenstein in his obsessive and isolated work practices, the inventions he worked on had their viability proved in the commercial and industrial world. His metaphysics drew on a range of ideas current at the time: Edward Bulwer-Lytton's influential novel *Vril*, with its theme of a universal life force; Ernst Mach's theories of cosmic inter-relationship; speculations about life on Mars by leading French astronomer Camille Flammarion. In the later nineteenth century, electricity was one of the life sciences, and interpretations of electrical power as a life force were attracting widespread interest. The plot of Mary Shelley's *Frankenstein*, published in 1818, was founded on the idea that tissue from dead bodies could be reanimated by infusing it with large amounts of electrical current, and the narrator's zealotry gives full reign to the implications. 'Life and death seemed to me ideal bounds, which I should first break through, and pour a torrent of light into our dark world. A new species would bless me as its creator and source'.[7] One of his real-life counterparts was Andrew Crosse, who dedicated himself to lightning collection and experiments in spontaneous generation at his estate in Somerset. In 1836, Crosse became convinced he had observed the spontaneous generation of tiny insects through the electrification of silica crystals in a carefully controlled environment and was invited to report his findings to the Royal Society.[8] Richard Owen, one of the most conservative figures in the British scientific establishment, came around to a view that combined the principle of spontaneous generation with biblical orthodoxy. 'Nerve-force we know to be convertible into electric energy', he argued, and from this premise pointed toward 'an admission of the originating and vitalizing of the primary jelly-speck or sarcode-granule, by the operation of a change of force forming part of the constitution of the Kosmos'.[9]

By the 1870s, a significant proportion of the medical profession subscribed to the notion that human nervous energy was a limited resource that might need topping up with doses of electricity. Full-page advertisements for 'Pulvermacher's Patent Galvanic Chain-bands, Belts, and Pocket Batteries' appeared in *The Illustrated London News*.[10] Entertainment lectures at the Egyptian Hall on 'Electric Light and Force' alternated with presentations on 'bio-magnetism' and offered euphoric visions of a future with unlimited possibilities for the human species, a consequence not just of mechanical invention, but of biological affinity with the newly evident powers.

This kind of thinking did not yield any ready formula for charismatic individualism. Rather, it was focused on interconnection and distribution, the two areas in which Tesla made his international reputation as an inventor. With the adoption of his alternating current (AC) distribution system, the Leyden jar was history, and the idea of one form or body serving as a generative reservoir of power also began to look outmoded. Force was environmental and connective; it was about circuits, not forms. Sensitised individuals might have greater capacities as conductors and transmitters of energy and might quite literally light up in front of an audience, but this did not happen as a consequence of some inherent power source.

The terms 'mesmeric' and 'dazzling' are now so routinely used by critics that they have become virtually interchangeable, but they may belong to quite distinct models of the stage performer. A mesmeric presence is one with holding power, drawing to itself the attention and imagination of an audience; someone who dazzles an audience does so through action and connectivity. This is the difference between Paul Robeson and Sammy Davis Junior, between Edith Piaf and Judy Garland. Of course the boundary is blurred. There were times when Garland stopped the show, let her voice take over, and seemed herself to be falling into a state of enchantment with the song. Nijinsky was a mesmeriser, but his capacity to turn on the dazzle and flash has influenced generations of classical male dancers who have tested their 'cross-over' potential in the glitzier forms of popular dance. In such cases, though, the performer him- or herself would be conscious of operating on different axes. To mesmerise is to go deep, using the situation of co-presence to take the collective attention to levels of intensity not normally experienced. A dazzling effect is more temporary, and on stage is associated with fast movement across the field of vision. It is associated with lighter forms of entertainment and typically involves a surrounding spectacle enabled by electricity.

Tesla's obsession with passing current through himself was symptomatic of a wider cultural fascination with the electrification of the body and the personification of electricity. The desire to switch on like an incandescent bulb, to move at the speed of light, to glitter and sparkle with surface brilliance, was inspired by the new manifestations of electricity. At the World's Fair of 1900 in Paris, 'The Fairy Electricity' was the presiding deity, emblematised in statues and medallions, yet escaping her image to spread as a formless multiplicity of sights and sounds:

> It is Electricity that enables the espaliers of fire to climb the monumental arch... The Seine is violet, pigeon's-throat pink, ox-blood. Electricity is drawn up, compacted, trans- formed, stored in bottles, fed out in cables, wound around drums, then they unleash her into the water, through the fountain jets, they set her free across the roof tops, they pour her out amongst the trees.[11]

The human impersonator of the Fairy Electricity was Loie Fuller, who at her theatre on the avenue near the main entrance performed the *Fire Dance*. This work, of her own devising, exploited the advanced electrical effects newly available to the stage as a result of inventions from Tesla and Edison. The London critic J. Crawford Flitch recorded a description:

> The dancer's dress was a voluminous smoke-coloured skirt, to which strips of the same material were loosely

attached. She danced in the center of a darkened stage before an opening in the floor through which a powerful electric light shot up flame-coloured rays. At first only a pale indecisive bluish flame appeared in the midst of the surrounding darkness; little by little it took shape, quickened into life, trembled, grew, mounted upwards, until it embraced all the stage in its wings of fire, developed into a mighty whirlwind in the midst of which emerged a woman's head, smiling, enigmatical while the shifting phosphorescence played over the body that the lambent flames had held in their embrace.[12]

Loie Fuller was born in Chicago and her career began in popular entertainment venues there and then in New York and London. She played a small part for Bill Cody in *Buffalo Bill's Pledge*, then went on to perform with limited success in various farces and musical dramas. Hers was not a story, like Irving's or Bernhardt's, of personal magnetism requiring only the right part in order to take hold. Her gifts were those of an image-maker rather than a performer, and playing on Broadway gave her an opportunity to see what the new lighting technologies could do. She was particularly astute about the potential for creating effects through inventive approaches to direction and colour. The opportunity to experiment on her own terms came when she was employed to perform a 'serpentine dance' as a solo interlude in a variety programme in a Brooklyn theatre. Fuller created a costume with dozens of yards of fine white silk in the skirt and, performing on a darkened stage, moved through coloured light beams to create what one reviewer described as 'airy evolutions... tinted blue and purple and crimson'.[13] As a young woman, Fuller had discovered a way to create a stage presence that had immediate impact. She proceeded to develop the techniques, extending the costume by ordering silks from India so fine they could be threaded through a wedding ring, and bias cutting the fabric so that hundreds of yards of it could be seamed into the panels attached to her. In order to manipulate these effectively, and create movement on a larger scale, she used lightweight 'wands' of bamboo or aluminium held in each hand and experimented with raised platforms lit from below, or danced on a glass panel over sub-floor lighting, to give an extended vertical axis.

The performances she created were a brilliant aesthetic fusion of electrical technology with magical fantasy. As the personification of 'the Fairy Electricity' she became an international icon, but she remains a curiously anomalous figure in the history of stage stars because of the stark separation between the person and the image. Fuller never had any off-stage glamour, and never shone as a performer without the prosthetics of illumination she had devised. Did she have presence in her own right? The evidence – a lacklustre early career, and a total dependency on technological effects for her impact – suggests that she did not, but the question remains open. In her dances she demonstrated a brilliant complicity between electricity and the performer, pointing the way towards an era of stage entertainment in which electricity, human and technological, was the star. Certainly electricity can enhance the impact of a performer, but can it serve to mask a lack of genuine stage presence?

Razzle dazzle

'Razzle dazzle 'em' is the advice the profiteering lawyer Billy Flynn in *Chicago* gives to his client about handling her court appearance. Roxie, a ditzy blonde up on a murder charge, doesn't have much going for her from a legal point of view, but if she plays it for all she is worth, she'll be able to fool the jury because 'how can they see with sequins in their eyes?' To dazzle people has connotations of sharp practice, hoodwinking, deception. Like mesmerism it can be associated with control and manipulation, but the effects are shallower and more fleeting; and for those who are taken in, there is at least the pleasure of a momentary exhilaration.

The theatre is dependent upon a culture of deception, whether through the illusions of stage spectacle or the role-playing of the performers, but there is a tendency to think of presence as a kind of gold standard or 'the real thing'. All that glitters is not gold, and sparkle is suspicious. Sequins and razzle could in themselves be tell-tale signs that something vital is missing. This is one of the reasons that presence is a quality harder to judge in light entertainers than dramatic actors, or operatic performers, but we may also underestimate the degree to which the star of a vaudeville show is underpinning the stage effects with something entirely human and uniquely their own.

Florenz Ziegfeld, the impresario whose *Ziegfeld Follies* made its first impact on Broadway in 1907, specialised in enhancing the presence of his stars through extravagance in staging and costume. Wearable lighting was amongst his earliest specialities: the show of

1908 featured chorus girls dressed as taxi-cabs, with head-pieces that lit up to say 'for hire' when the stage was darkened; the following year there were headdresses modelled as battleships, with light showing through the portholes. In 1916, an electrified mat was devised so that the tap-dancing chorus line sent sparks flying. For the principals in the show, more romantic effects were created. Kay Laurel as Aphrodite in the 1915 show rose from a pool of water surrounded by golden elephants. Twin Venuses, played by Allyn King and Eleanor Lang, appeared in a 1917 number enclosed in translucent bubbles that floated through a curtain of light (actually created from horse pills dipped in silver paint). Lillian Lorraine starred in the 1918 show, got up as the evening star in a silver lamé gown and surrounded by lesser stars who wore costumes sprinkled with fragments of mirror to reflect her light.[14] Ziegfeld featured many stars, some of whom (including Barbara Stanwyck, Fred Astaire, Louise Brooks, Paulette Goddard, W.C. Fields, Mae West) are best known now for their subsequent careers in film; no doubt most of these had individual stage presence, but the show itself was always bigger than they were.

The most celebrated music hall star of the era, Josephine Baker, did not appear in the Follies until after Ziegfeld's death, and it was one of her least successful performances. *The New York Times* critic accused her of offering 'her presence instead of her talent'.[15] This is a striking remark, given that presence was almost indistinguishable from talent in the fast moving, virtuosity-driven entertainments that dominated Broadway. The most glamorous looks, sharpest comic timing, best singing and most spectacular dancing got the loudest applause, and headline status in the billing. In this milieu, 'star quality' was replacing presence as the premium attribute, and it is curious to see an explicit statement that presence *per se* was not acceptable currency for an established star to trade in.

Yet, if anyone exhibited dash and flash in a form that was catalysed by a potent stage presence, it was Josephine Baker. She tests the defining elements of presence in a domain where they are hardest to distinguish. Born in St Louis, Missouri, in 1906, Baker was an African American with family connections to show business. Her parents both performed at the Booker T. Washington, a theatre specialising in black vaudeville, at a time when assorted song and dance crazes were beginning to cross the cultural divide between black and white. The St Louis World's Fair of 1904 had brought blues singing and New Orleans jazz to wider audiences, spawning a host of jug bands, ragtime bands, marching bands and 'spasm' bands, the latter being a term for New Orleans groups playing on home made instruments. The best known of them were the Razzy Dazzy Spasm Band, who were performing from 1895. The 'razzy dazzy' epithet was a wry contradiction of the rough and ready components they had to work with.

Josephine (her Christian name alone became her stage name) grew up in a rapidly changing cultural world, where surface gloss had a defiant ironic value to a race kept aggressively on the poverty line. She was an unwanted child, sent into service at the age of eight to earn her keep, and at ten she witnessed the horrors of the St Louis race riots. As was the case with Rachel, her early experience of hardship produced in her a determination to turn her perform-ance skills to account as a means of escape, but she did so in an entirely different context. Perhaps in different cultural circum-stances, Josephine might have made a great dramatic actress. She had seen tragedy and brutality, and, compared to Rachel, was in a position to understand more directly the pathos of the outsider's experience. Instead, she channelled her extraordinary vital drive into clowning and shimmy dancing, and her idea of the golden opportunity was a role with the Dixie Steppers' travelling show.

Her career began with the Dixie Steppers in New York well before she had reached the age of sixteen, the minimum for legal employment as a chorus girl, and she did well enough, by embel-lishing her routines with improvised exit gags and grotesque mugging from the end of the line. The 'end girl' in the British-based Tiller establishment was a kind of prefect, keeping order and rhythm, but in New York there was licence to do some comic counter-pointing, and Baker exploited this to draw attention to herself, as if her natural place was centre stage and it was only a matter of time before she could claim it.

So it turned out. She was talent-spotted by the US representative of André Devin, director of the Théâtre des Champs Elysées in Paris, who was seeking to cast a black vaudeville spectacular, and in 1925 found herself in intensive rehearsal with a new company. Charles Hopkins, its bandleader, later recalled her with rather bland praise: 'she did everything well, singing, dancing and fitting into the comedy skits without any effort or strain'. But he also added, 'it was easily apparent that she had exceptional stage pres-ence'.[16] How did this presence manifest itself? Josephine's first sketch in the show was a piece of grotesque mock-primitivism, for which she entered on all fours, finishing with a chaotic minstrel dance – 'the boodle am shake' – that was a cross between the shimmy and the charleston. It was her second appearance that set the style she made her own. Wearing little more than an artful arrangement of pink feathers, she performed with a male dancer in a sinuous athletic *pas de deux* that displayed an extraordinary sense of form in rapid motion. In her own retrospective account, the performance was driven by an improvisatory exuberance: 'Each time I leaped I seemed to touch the sky and when I regained earth it seemed to be mine alone'.[17] Josephine was apparently acutely anxious about the costuming (or lack of it) but, from this point on, there was no question that her stage impact depended on a whole body presence. The artist Paul Colin, who made a number of sketches of her in his studio, claimed:

> I never saw anybody move the way she did. She was part kangaroo and part prizefighter. A woman made of rubber, a female Tarzan.[18]

This description foregrounds the grotesque, but also hints at the protean grace that made Josephine's dancing a departure from the minstrel tradition and something unique in Parisian erotic vaudeville. As she gained confidence and learned to set the terms for her own reception, she began to exhibit some of the capricious off-stage behaviours of the *demi-mondaines* who had ruled the popular stage during the latter part of the nineteenth century, but she also replicated some of their stage techniques. The most celebrated of the *demi-mondaines*, Cora Pearl, was someone with little talent but considerable presence. She knew how to be looked at, and came up with a range of strategies for capturing and holding the attention of restive audiences, shedding what Sacheverell Sitwell called 'an aura of evil radiance'.[19] She made the radiance literal by appearing as Cupid wearing only some transparent drapes crusted with jewels. Like Pearl, Josephine learned to recognise that a beautiful naked body is a presence in its own right, but on stage it needs to be more than a tableau. For the first time in the west she made public a repertoire of movement belonging to female nakedness, albeit expressive of a female sexuality few European women would have recognised in themselves. In a 1925 review, André Levinson wrote:

> The plastic sense of a race of sculptors came to life and the frenzy of African eros swept over the audience. It was no longer a grotesque dancing girl that stood before them but the black Venus that haunted Baudelaire.[20]

The *demi-mondaines* specialised in a repertoire of glances and turns that made mischievous contact with those in the auditorium. Self parody was part of the provocation. It was as if some intimate dialogue were going on between the body and the eyes, an improvised play of point and counterpoint that was riveting to watch and at its most effective when there was no other form of action to distract from it. This kind of parodic by-play was always an element of Josephine's performances; her eyes and her facial expressions had a vital intensity that completed the sense of form and attitude. In photographs taken at various stages of her career this is clearly evident, as is the sharpness of her overall sense of the image she projects. But action, fast and extravagant, was of the essence. Whatever the spectacle surrounding her, there was never any doubt that she was the focal point of the show and the degree to which an audience might be surprised, delighted, shocked or amazed was moment by moment in her control. Her screen performances also display this quality, but without the added impact of the interactive exuberance generated with a live audience.

She was 'a born exhibitionist' according to Paul Colin. Exhibitionism is not generally regarded as a valuable attribute in show business, especially since it may be unaccompanied or insufficiently accompanied by talent, but in certain iconic figures of the popular stage – and Josephine is one of them – exhibitionism and virtuosity are inseparable. Her technical dynamism as a dancer was fused with a genius for presentation and display. Other dancers wore sequins and jewels, but Josephine made it look as though the light that shone out from them was generated from her own body. Here she was closer to Tesla than to Cora Pearl. In the 1927 production of *Un Vent de Folie* at the Folies Bergères, she wore a costume entirely composed of light: lamé tights covered in gleaming bobbles, echoed at her fingertips on the ends of elongated gloves, and a halter of diamanté about her naked torso. The effect, judging from photographs, was a near blinding level of dazzle, yet the personality shines through. The Cameroon writer Simon Njami describes her life story as 'a lesson in luminous humanism'.[21]

Josephine Baker understood the aesthetics of shine like no other performer of this dazzle-crazed era. Everything about her sparkled and glowed. For the stage, she coated her hair with egg white to transform it into a gleaming cap (occasionally covered by a rhinestone cloche), and painted her fingernails silver. When she wore dresses at all she favoured lamé or sequined sheaths, but her hallmark 'costume' was no costume at all, except an artfully sewn arrangement of pearls and diamanté. In *Paris qui Remue* (1930), she appeared as a firefly with eight glittering wings, in a finale titled 'Amour et électricité'. Putting her name in lights was an almost redundant gesture, and the neon silhouette of her installed at her Parisian estate in the 1950s was a pale imitation.

Her grip on the public imagination was associated with the mystique of light in darkness: she was called 'l'étoile noir' and 'le soleil noir'. Physicality and immediacy were the core of her appeal, and Josephine expressed her own weariness with the persistence in reading this through the lens of primitivism:

> They think I'm fresh from the jungle. In fact in some parts of the world, I think they'd like to offer me glass beads. 'Primitive instincts', 'sexual passion', 'animal sexuality', 'delirium', ... they've written all sorts about me. When it comes to blacks, the imagination of white folks is something else.[22]

Nevertheless, there is no doubt she played up to the 'negrophilia' that gripped Parisian audiences, especially with her hallmark Banana Dance, performed in a 'skirt' of dangling bananas. Nijinsky had exploited the relationship between presence and exoticism in the same theatre a generation previously, emphasising his Slavic heritage and setting off an orientalist craze with his image of the snake-eyed Golden Slave in *Le Pavillion d'Armide*. Charlotte Brontë had orientalised Rachel as 'Vashti' and Sarah Bernhardt created a personal brand of exoticism through her off-stage persona. Can we distinguish between 'true' presence and a cultivated aura of lavish otherness designed to capture attention through image? The test surely lies in the performance itself, which involves captivating attention and holding it over time, taking an audience through shifting moods and experiences. Image alone cannot do this.

In the later 1920s, Josephine's Paris seasons were interspersed with visits to other European cities: Berlin, Vienna, Prague, Budapest, Zagreb, Bucharest, Copenhagen, Stockholm. Writing about her reception in Sweden, Ylva Habel stresses the degree to which she had been 'hypervisualised' in Paris due to the white fascination with blackness, so creating an effect of 'overpresence'.[23] In the comparatively small capital of Stockholm, says Habel, Josephine Baker's arrival fed into a 'craving for blackness as a revitalizing force... mediated through the continental and glamorous connotations of Paris'.[24] The Josephine 'fever' that anticipated her arrival was fed with the release of her film *La Sirène des tropiques*, but the impact of this was nothing to that of the live show. One reviewer commented:

> She's got *it*. What is the use of trying to dissect the tricks of this half-caste on stage? It does not matter from which corner of the world she comes or what skin colour she has. You could speak of Negro culture, but that does not capture what makes Josephine. She is her own little culture.[25]

The reception was not all euphoric, however. There were debates in the daily press, setting charges of degeneracy from some readers against impassioned defences from others. One letter asserted that 'those who have a capacity to live in the present and to love its art forms... should be glad to have known Josephine Baker, the international stage revue's most lovable child of nature'.[26]

Habel's detailed account of the Stockholm reception helps to move the discussion away from the focus on European primitivism that has organised so much of the commentary on Josephine Baker. As Andrea Stewart suggests, Josephine's stage persona combined the stereotype of the stage primitive with that of the showgirl, who is 'always other' because she has 'always been linked to racial difference, exoticism, the power of darkness and the corruptions of the blood'.[27] A somewhat pejorative view of exoticism is emphasised here, though. I would prefer to emphasise the upbeat side of the picture, since Josephine was evidently well in control of the images she projected. She also proved she had staying power. In the early 1950s, she made a come-back in her homeland, with shows in Miami, Chicago and New York. Walter Winchell, one of those New York critics who could make or break a reputation with his morning-after review, declared that he'd seen 'a one-gal show, with exquisite gowns, charm, magic and big-time zing'. Jack Schiffman, manager of the Apollo Theater in Harlem, called her 'glamour personified', and described how she 'covered the stage with the agility of a cat and the ease of a seal in water', swirling on in one spectacular entry after another.[28] Hers was a genius for lightness.

It is easy in cultural criticism to forget the lightness of the light entertainer, a quality not readily captured in analysis. There is a tendency to equate it with superficiality and with commercially driven imperatives to appeal to the greatest number with the least substantial ingredients. But lightness involves agility – of mind as well as in physical terms – an alertness and adaptability to collective mood, and a ready energy for converting the mood according to its happier components. In those who have the genius of lightness, there is a quicksilver energy that seems inexhaustible and operates at lightning speed, lifting boredom to amusement, amusement to exuberance, exuberance to outbursts of hilarity and elation. It is no wonder that their off-stage behaviour is often notorious for exhibiting compensatory tendencies: the depressive moods of comedians, the selfish caprice of popular stars (Josephine included), who are lit up with charm only when the houselights are down. Theirs is a form of presence that depends upon control, but a very different form of control from that of the mesmerist, since it involves giving out more than drawing in. For the duration of the performance, they must be all generosity, and if they seek to be paid back immediately in acclamation, it is only to build the overall mood to further heights of jubilation.

This interactive play has an excitement all of its own that musicals created for the cinema often seek to incorporate. Josephine made several films, in which the dancing scenes are essentially a record of her stage performances.[29] The primacy of her commitment to the stage was never in doubt. For those of her contemporaries whose careers crossed decisively from stage to screen, the sense of a live audience remained a key element of their impact, and many of the landmark musicals of the cinema are structured around the climactic drama of the theatrical show. Dazzle and flash, when it belongs to the performance rather than the spectacle surrounding it, needs an audience presence to set it off. This is an essential factor in the symbiotic relationship between stage and screen musicals, a relationship in which stage and screen presence feed into each other whilst remaining fundamentally distinct. Screen presence in this genre depends on the eloquence of the face in close-up, and on the actor's capacity to establish and hold an image; the stage star must be more temporally responsive, building and holding the moment. Theatrical warmth and panache can energise a film performance, while the glamour of screen presence feeds back into the theatre musical, producing a magnified sense of stardom, and of the charismatic personality.

Marlene Dietrich in *The Blue Angel* (1930) exhibited both kinds of presence in her portrayal of the cabaret singer Lola Lola, performing to the camera with unforgettable iconic poses and expressions, and to her on-camera audience with provocative unpredictability. Director Josef von Sternberg cast her in the film after seeing her in a Berlin cabaret act so she was able to transfer the persona from one medium to the other. Through film, she maintained her stage career at one remove, playing a night club singer in *Blonde Venus* (1932), *Seven Sinners* (1940), *The Lady is Willing* (1942) and *A Foreign Affair* (1947).

The stage showgirl as a character in film provides a wonderful vehicle for a star performance, together with a readymade dramatic structure, built around her romance with the audience. She must win them through her irresistible displays of song and dance, and they must provide the climactic moments of excitement through their reception. As in more conventional romances, there may be a false pretender to the admirer's attentions, and there will certainly be crises to overcome before she can experience the moments of ecstatic union.

In *42nd Street* (1933), set in Manhattan during the Depression, the stage show is an enterprise that will make or break fortunes, for the management as well as those clamouring for a place in the chorus line. It is the classic story of a chorus girl Cinderella – Peggy Sawyer, played by Ruby Keeler – displacing a spoilt diva and stealing the show. The scenes of the show in performance, its building impact intercut with backstage hustle and tension, create the dramatic climax of the film. Keeler's own career is ironically echoed in the plot. A contemporary of Josephine Baker, she also began as an underage chorus girl in stage shows.

One of the curiosities of the Broadway musical is its self-consciousness: so many musicals are not only about musicals, but feature the performance of a show from the insiders' viewpoint, with all the dramas of audition and casting, back-stage jostling and rehearsal exhaustion. The line of examples includes *Showboat* (1927), *42nd Street* (1933), *Follies* (1971), *Applause* (1970), *A Chorus Line* (1975) and *Phantom of the Opera* (1986). In the original Harold Prince production of *Cabaret*, the audience faced reflections of themselves in a giant mirror surrounded by frosted lamps, upstage centre. A more technologically sophisticated form of this device was used for the finale of *A Chorus Line*, when a backdrop of mirrors descends, transforming the single line of top-hatted kickers into infinitely receding ranks. Reflection magnifies and multiplies. How often have we seen a star born or re-born through being cast in the role of a star? It is as if the impact of a successful performer in this genre can always be recycled and redoubled, as when Ethel Merman played Annie Oakley (*Annie Get Your Gun*, 1950), Barbra Streisand played Fanny Brice (*Funny*

Girl, 1968) or Liza Minnelli was cast in the revival of *Cabaret* to play the legendary Sally Bowles, reminding critics of her mother Judy Garland's triumph in *A Star is Born*.

There is something contrived about this and there is no doubt that the musical is a form that manufactures stardom. This is not to deny that there are stars of genuine brilliance in the musical tradition, but it does prompt some speculation about where stardom, with all its manufactured components and its aura of celebrity, is a phenomenon distinct from that of stage presence as a supposedly innate and organic quality. We may be suspicious of stardom. How can we be sure the chosen star is the right one? As anyone in show business knows, brilliant talents are constantly being turned down or relegated to the chorus, and for everyone who gets a principal role there is someone else who might have done it better. Here the storyline of *42nd Street* is prototypical. Given the most glamorous costumes imaginable, brilliant choreography, some show-stopping songs and a narrative featuring the romance of breakthrough success, how could the person cast in the central role fail to have impact? Martin Gottfried, one of the most experienced New York theatre critics, notes that 'Broadway directors know very well that an audience will thrill on cue'.[30] In Gottfried's engaging book on the Broadway musical, the featured personalities are not the stars, but those who make the whole thing happen: the directors, composers, lyricists, choreographers and designers. One of the paradoxes about the musical is the presence of the chorus line, supposedly the anonymous back-up team, yet, as the phenomenal success of *A Chorus Line* has demonstrated, it is easy to invert the dynamics so that they become the starring act.

The musical is often at its most effective when it inverts its techniques for cueing the thrill. *Gypsy* (1959) includes a scene in which Mama Rose, played with legendary panache by Ethel Merman, enacts her futile dream of success before an empty theatre to an audience she imagines. As Gottfried comments:

> With this number's devastating power we rise from our seats, and still we are part of Mama Rose's hallucination as she accepts our ghostly standing ovation. We realize this as we are taken to a higher plateau. It is as thrilling a moment as there is in all theatre.[31]

One of the reasons for this is its bringing to consciousness of the present, the here and now of the performance. On the Cinderella principle, anonymity can produce an inverse charisma when it is surrounded by people splitting themselves to be the centre of attention. When the cast-off husband of Roxy Hart in Chicago sings 'Mr Cellophane', this is a show-stopping moment of an unorthodox kind. For a brief interlude, all the razzle dazzle stops and the lone, shuffling figure of a middle aged man assures the audience 'you can look right through me, walk right by me, and never know I'm there'. A human presence is realised, with a warmth and directness made impossible by the conventions of glamour. In reviews of the 1975 opening night, it was this number rather than any of the dazzling set-pieces given to Gwen Verdon and Chita Rivera that got the mentions. Clive Barnes in *The New York Times* remarked that it was 'the only moment of true feeling', delivered by Barney Martin with 'all the corny but real heartbreak of the vaudeville trouper'.[32]

Glamour

Roles such as that of Frank N. Furter in *The Rocky Horror Show*, Jesus or Mary Magdalen in *Jesus Christ Superstar*, Eva Peron in *Evita* or the Phantom in *Phantom of the Opera* produce a demand for charisma which can actually be in conflict with the qualities of concentration and holding-power that are involved in stage presence.

It is a high-risk strategy that can prompt some of the worst brickbats. Douglas Watt opened his review of the Broadway *Evita* with the statement: 'There's a great big gap in the middle of *Evita*, and the name of the gap is *Evita*'.[33] James Spina reported for *Women's Wear Daily* on the 1975 Broadway opening of *The Rocky Horror Show* and went for the jugular. 'Head pretender Tim Curry is only mildly irritating in his sweaty drive to blend the mannerisms of Mick Jagger, Alice Cooper and Fay Wray gone ghoul'. Kim Milford as Rocky fared even worse, targeted by James Spina for having 'the stage presence of a muscle tone eraser and a time consuming wont for exhibitionist calisthenics'.[34] In these cases, glitzy spectacle had become part of the problem.

It seems that if you razzle dazzle 'em some people get all too good at catching wise. With production values riding high and state of the art technological inventiveness, the effect on the performances seems to have been both inflationary and reductive. 'If the material is predictable', wrote Howard Kissel of *Evita*, 'Harold Prince's staging is not... The most exciting moments in the show are two stunningly staged political rallies, where Prince

makes adroit use of every inch of stage space as well as the prodigious, specially designed technology'. (The technology included 'an
enormous mobile movie screen' to amplify the scale of the gathering.) Douglas Watt commented that Prince had created 'a dazzling
stage entertainment' around the offending gap.[35] *Rocky Horror*,
which began life at the tiny 'Upstairs' auditorium of London's
Royal Court Theatre and moved to a semi-derelict converted
cinema on the King's Road as its cult appeal took off, was
evidently not well served by high-end lighting designers. In New
York there was a token attempt to replicate the cabaret ambience,
but the primary impression was Broadway glitz. Martin Gottfried
described 'flashy and fabulous sets that include a bulb-lit runway'
with 'lots of streaming dry ice; neon bolts of lightning; and rear
screen projections'.[36]

The genesis of *Rocky Horror*, though, is a story of avant-garde
theatricality in which the electricity is raw and uncontrolled. Its
original 1973 cast were drawn from the lower ranks of the entertainment world and from the fringes of the nascent punk scene
around the King's Road, and portions of the £200 costume budget
were spent at Vivienne Westwood's shop SEX, which at the time
was specialising in an assortment of S&M rubber wear and
perversely crafted shoes. (Patricia Quinn as Magenta wore
Westwood's black patent pixie boots with stiletto heels and gold
linings.) The visual style of the production combined influences
from *Cabaret*, *A Clockwork Orange*, early David Bowie shows
and a production of Jean Genet's *The Maids*. The staging was, in
the words of Richard Hartley (musical arranger), 'fast, furious and
basic'.[37] Everything was cheap and, from a technical point of view,
a little dangerous. Set elements consisted of some tarpaulins and a
Coca-Cola ice box and most of the action took place on an improvised catwalk, with a concrete pillar to be negotiated at one end.
There was at least one serious collision during a performance.
Electricity strikes and bomb scares caused disruptions, and rain
falling on the tin roof made dialogue almost inaudible. Such, of
course, can be the ingredients of a cult hit, especially in a cultural
milieu that is a hotbed of anarchy and impulse. Amongst the audience members jostling for seats and sharing the toilets with the cast
was an exceptional line-up of celebrity drop-ins, including
Tennessee Williams, Mick Jagger, David Bowie, Rudolf Nureyev,
Lou Reed and Princess Margaret.

This was a classic piece of what Peter Brook has called 'rough
theatre', the kind that 'brings about the most vivid relationships

between people'. Speculating on what best serves this relationship, Brook suggests that asymmetry, even disorder, may be essential to it: 'a beautiful hall may never bring about an explosion of life, while a haphazard hall may be a tremendous meeting place'. That *Rocky Horror* generated vivid relationships and an explosion of life is overwhelmingly attested; it spawned a culture of audience participation that still continues, and bears more resemblance to the dynamics of carnival than those of cabaret. The 'roughness' of rough theatre is sensory. Brook envisages a bucket banged to make the sound effects in a battle scene, flour used to whiten faces, and an arsenal of local jokes, topical references, false noses and padded stomachs.[38]

Substituting torn fishnet tights and corsets for the false noses and padded stomachs, the formula is all there in Transvestite Transylvania. We are a long way from the presentational virtuosity of razzle dazzle, but there is a certain kind of glamour at work. The word 'glamour' in present usage tends to evoke the image-making apparatus of an affluent culture: a glamorous person is someone luxuriously dressed and accessorised; a glamorous life style is one of fashionable indulgence and social cachet. This is the glamour associated with stardom, but the archaic meanings of the word derive from the Scots *gramarye*: magic or enchantment, and the occult knowledge that enables it. In a recent book on the *Rocky Horror* cult, Scott Michaels and David Evans identify this as the kind of glamour that was stalking the King's Road in the punk era, and was evoked in the show.[39] *Gramarye* belongs not to high society but to folk culture; it connotes secret forms of relationship, circles of occult communication. The knowing glances and eloquent body language of Frank N. Furter invite the audience to be initiates, so that there is a relationality at the heart of Tim Curry's performance, a presence born of co-presence. Richard O'Brien in the counterpointing role of Riff Raff, the sepulchral butler, establishes a presence on his own terms through the code of deadpan, which he breaches in moments of fanatical outburst. Nell Campbell or 'Little Nell' was a cult figure before she joined the cast, having established a show business of her own dancing on pub tables and busking to theatre queues. Her role was built up to provide a vehicle for the song and dance routine gone haywire in which she specialised.

Rocky Horror presents an example of how presence does not have to be exclusive to one person on the stage, as in the mesmeric model, even when there is clearly one starring role at the centre of it, drawing the lion's share of focus and aplomb. There is actually some good by-play in the parodic jostling for the next star turn amongst a cast containing at least half a dozen players with compelling individual qualities. The ensemble creates a warmer, more fluid milieu than the hierarchical show structured to maximise the impact of its main star, and the rough theatre ensemble breaks down the formality of the performer/audience relationship so that presence is established on easier, more natural terms. The success of *A Chorus Line* underlines the paradox that audiences are more readily engaged with the sweaty tensions of rehearsal scenes than the achieved perfection of spectacle.

As the Broadway reception of *Rocky Horror* demonstrated, though, it is hazardous to cross the demarcation zones of theatrical typology. Rough theatre does not work in a milieu where polish and technical sophistication are the established currency, and adding some technological polish to the roughness can make an intolerable concoction: expectations become confused, the show cannot establish a workable tenor for audience response, and the performer cannot create a rapport. In terms of generic expectations, *Rocky Horror* fell somewhere between the avant-garde and the commercial, and took some time to replicate its theatrical cult following when it was made into a film. The punk milieu in which it first emerged was charged with a feral spirit of parody which was essential to the performance style of the original show and, I would suggest, to the kinds of presence created in the key performances.

What is parody, in performance terms? As in any other medium, it involves imitation with satirically motivated elements of distortion. Something very familiar must be recognisable, and this recognition creates a conspiratorial understanding between the artist and those attending to the work. In literature or the visual arts, it is up to the individual reader or viewer to respond according to their own mood, frames of reference and sense of humour. In performance there is a collective response which is overt, usually taking the form of laughter, though laughter itself is a complex phenomenon taking many forms. Laughter at parody is sparked by moments of recognition, which can be cued by the performer. As responses are generated, the performance builds to raise the tenor so that there is a dialogue between stage and auditorium. The dynamics of attention here are very different from those in operation when a dramatic actor compels silent attention, but the circuit of play, response and counterplay has its own kinds of electricity in which the presence of the performer is catalytic.

Rocky Horror promoted a consciousness of mode and mannerism as inherently ridiculous, as cultural indulgences that belong in
the realms of fetishism. As live entertainment, parody reinvents the
energies associated with over-familiar theatrical strategies, reorient-
ing peak moments of exuberance and performative triumph. For the
performer it means being in control in a moment-by-moment steer-
age of mood that gains its impact from unpredictable swerves.
Rocky Horror has many fronts of parody: the Frankenstein horror
film, middle class suburbia (through Brad and Janet), decadent
cabaret, the razzle dazzle musical. But in its first production there
was an overarching parodic energy that drew on more fundamental
elements. The mock sexuality and exhibitionism were a twist on the
burlesque traditions of popular theatre, given new edge through the
anarchic burlesque of theatricality itself, and its generic forms of
glamour. Parody of glamour was dominant in Tim Curry's performance, with its repertoire of diva gestures and expressions. He was a
burlesque magus, whose mock allure drew audiences into a conspiracy of perverse style rather than occult knowledge.

Punk had introduced a form of reverse glamour through its
chosen celebrities – Johnny Rotten, Vivienne Westwood, Malcolm
McLaren, Jordan, Sid Vicious, Siouxsie – figures who mugged for
the camera with frayed hair and blotched faces, dressed in moth-
eaten cardigans, rotted vests, rubber underwear and jewellery made
of lavatory chain. They understood instinctively how to trade in
persona rather than personality, the difference being that persona is
personality at one remove, an assumed wardrobe of attitudes and
appearances that can be developed in response to circumstances.

The celebrity at this time who made most effective use of theatrical resources in creating persona was David Bowie, whose mansion
in Beckenham may well have been a model for the *Rocky Horror*
set. There was an ornate staircase, a minstrels' gallery, and an
approach to interior décor that combined art deco with hard rock.
It included a giant Regency bed that Bowie decked out 'like a huge
coffin with a canopy'.[40]

Bowie's 1972 concert at Manchester Free Trade Hall was nomi-
nated as one of 'the 25 gigs of all time' in an article in *The
Observer Music Monthly* in January 2007. 'I was in the eighth row
of the stalls', wrote Paul Morley, and Bowie, 'as single minded as
any performer I've ever seen, was some kind of demon acting like
some kind of superstar ignoring the empty spaces in the hall,
committing himself to turning us on so he could turn himself on'.[41]
The impression in this account is that Bowie was taking himself

seriously, so much so that he virtually forced his own destiny onto a higher – or at least more successful – plane, but Bowie had an early commitment to parody. The kind of glamour affected by the group Hype, which he formed as a teenager, was the crudest burlesque, as described by Tony Visconti:

> David was Rainbowman, dressed in Lurex, pirate boots with diaphanous scarves pinned to his clothes... I was Hypeman in a mock Superman costume with a white leotard, crocheted silver knickers and a big red cape.[42]

In performance, this went over like a lead balloon. Audiences responded with boos and missiles.

Bowie's trademark androgyny and cross-dressing bravura were signals of other forms of crossing. In his self-managed development as an independent performer, he wanted hatred from the crowds in the auditorium, then adoration. He steeped himself in the abrasive milieu of Berlin cabaret, read Dostoevsky, trained with the avant-garde mime artist Lindsay Kemp, then returned to the commercial world with the determination to make himself a superstar. When he did so, it was an enterprise loaded with Nietzschean awareness. Bowie's reading diet crossed between superhero stories in Marvel comics and Nietzsche's writings on the *Übermensch*. He laced his Nietzschean inspiration with the occult ideas of the superhuman taken from Aleister Crowley, the charismatic latter-day magus who founded the Hermetic Order of the Golden Dawn and whose text-book guide to the acquisition of higher powers began with the principle 'Do what thou wilt shall be the whole of the law'.[43]

If anyone knows how to fuse modern glamour with *gramarye* it is Bowie. He is one of those figures who consciously works to learn from the magnetism of other charismatics, in widely different spheres: Crowley, Tesla, Bob Dylan, the comic book Superman, Andy Warhol. From the earliest phase of his career, he studied the lore of presence with an obsessive involvement but could switch to parodic mode when he chose. There is as much Andy Warhol as Aleister Crowley in the invention of Ziggy Stardust, one of the outstanding examples of persona-based staged presence in the twentieth century. From Crowley he learned some of the potency of esoterics, and the art of suggesting that the world was unimaginably large and strange. From Warhol he took the postmodern consciousness of image as a currency to be bought, accumulated, sold and revalued. One of the reviewers of a 1972 concert in

Oxford wrote that 'Bowie's never been a star but he's studied some of the best, like Garbo and Presley, and now he's on top he knows what to do'.[44]

Beyond the Warhol principle, though, Bowie understood that it takes more than iconography to create charisma on the stage. What he derived from the study of stars from such widely different zones of the show business galaxy was a highly developed understanding of stage techniques. Whilst there was much generic raving in Ziggy Stardust's reception, there was also much astute commentary on the craft and judgement he brought to the performances. Michael Watts noted his 'gift for artful mannerism' and flair for 'creating a convincing mise-en-scène' combined with 'a strong sense of biographical drama'. Others praised him for his diction, his pace and timing, the precision of his movements and the way he shifted mood to deepen the dramatic involvement or recharge the energy levels.

The Ziggy Stardust stage show began as rough theatre: the key component of the set was scaffolding, with a catwalk around the top accessed by removable ladders, and the sawdust floor was sprinkled with glitter. Such were the elements used in several alternative theatre productions at the time, including Lindsay Kemp's extraordinary *Flowers* (created in 1968), and to an audience in the know they promised inventive physicality. This Bowie delivered in spades, using sequences of Kemp-inspired mime to offset the loud sexuality of the rock numbers. As the success built, so did the budget. When the show opened at London's Rainbow Theatre in August 1972, the scaffolding was still there but with added platforms and a lighting design that created illusionary levels. A team of Kemp's mime dancers performed routines based on Chinese choreography, in which the ladders were scaled and turned with seamless fluidity. Chris Welch, one of the more experienced and hard nosed of the music journalists, found it 'tremendously effective' and described how Bowie, 'clad in a suit of silver with matching boots... strode out with perfect timing to ankle deep jets of smoke'.[45] *Plays and Players*, the prestige magazine devoted to theatre, did a feature review, beginning:

> Judy Garland hasn't left us! Rematerialised, reincarnated, her spirit today enjoys comic existence with the inner consciousness of one transvestite poseur, namely David Bowie, who recently returned to Earth with something like the impact of nuclear fission.[46]

The Garland association was less about image and persona than about performance qualities – 'the guts, the glitter, the charm, the force, the remoteness' – and, of course, the glamour. Though the sense of parody was something Bowie had that Garland didn't. 'Bowie and his band are nothing if not superb parodists', *Melody Maker* proclaimed, but it was not parody in the form of any overt satirical take-off.[47] It was something much more nuanced and comprehensive: a presentational approach that was always playing with the virtual and the imaginable rather than the actual, a twisting of the familiar codes of glamour to create an aura of strangeness. The starman, after all, was an alien being.

When Bowie arrived for his debut at the Carnegie Hall no-one knew what to expect, though anticipation ran so high that (as was widely reported) even Andy Warhol could not get a ticket. At this point in his career, Bowie's cross-over gifts served him well. Like *Rocky Horror*, the Ziggy Stardust show had begun rough, but its reinvention as a more technically sophisticated production for the Rainbow Theatre was good preparation for a high-end New York venue. He made the cut, even with some of the most stringent judges. *The New York Times* reported that, 'as a performer, Bowie delivered':

> He understands that theatricality has more to do with presence than with gimmickry, and that beautifully coordinated physical movements and well-planned music can reach an audience a lot quicker than high-decibel electronics.[48]

In reviews, Garland was cited repeatedly as the unlikely alter-ego ghosting the performances on the American tour. Robert Hilburn, reporting on the Sanata Monica show, said that Bowie 'established the same delicate, separate sense of communication with the audience that reminds you of Judy Garland'.

It is Hilburn who, of all the many critics trying to convey the impact of those concerts, is most effective in describing the stage presence that was their catalyst. He registered the 'electric moment' and 'an incredible sense of "nowness"' achieved through specific forms of technical mastery:

> Two things were immediately apparent. First, Bowie, with a background in mime, has enormous stage control and is able to accomplish more with the mere movement of his eyes than most performers in rock can do with a whole series of exaggerated movements. His body is so

disciplined that Bowie can create the tension of a wild animal, a tiger or a panther, as he prowls the stage, controlling the pace and direction of the show as he moves.[49]

Evocations of compelling power, electricity and the prowling panther will by now be very familiar to readers of this book. But in the annals of show business reportage, the compelling witnesses are those who respond to the 'unsayable' phenomenon of stage presence by finding new ways of putting it into words: a freshness of observation takes over from the metaphoric repertoire built up through previous generations of writing. What is captured here is that presence arises from present-ness: something is being communicated on stage through the alertness and discipline of movement, which begins with the movement of the eyes. There is 'enormous' control, but also the unpredictability of larger energies.

These qualities are clearly evident in the way Bowie has managed his overall career. On his return from the US, he peremptorily announced the death of the Ziggy Stardust persona, choosing the occasion of a concert at the Hammersmith Odeon in July 1973 to do so, and without forewarning the band who were on stage with him. Subsequently he proceeded to move through a range of other personae, reinventing his style decade after decade. One of the constants was his instinct for persona, a sense of identity that was virtual and changeable; he used make-up as mask and costume as a means of establishing an aesthetic.

Shelton Waldrep features Bowie as a case study in his book on the aesthetics of self invention, where he suggests that Kemp's influence 'helped Bowie fashion a career of ironizing detachment'.[50] It was also an influence that fore-grounded sexuality and gender crossing. Kemp's own performances draw on Japanese traditions of cross-gender playing to generate an aura of distraught pathos around his sexuality: a man playing a woman, expressing feminine sexuality in ways that are both impassioned and fragile, gives himself up to the pain of impossibility. In *Flowers*, Kemp drew on the poetics of Genet to realise this, working with Genet's perverse fusion of pathos with obscenity and exhibitionism. In Bowie's case there is less investment in pathos, but his persona-shifting is similarly underpinned by an existential feeling for the virtuality of identity. Identity is mask – an impossible paradox – so the play between identities, taking off in the spirit of parody, is of the essence.

The traditions of glamour, especially show business glamour, provide a repertoire of easily replicable means for giving a persona the kind of glossy presentation that will make an impression in the eyes of others. The risk here is that it will take over and develop a career of its own, escaping the control of its creator, a prospect swiftly averted when Bowie cut short the career of Ziggy Stardust.

Barry Humphries took no such precaution with Mrs Edna Everage, whose pretentions to glamour he may have failed to see coming during her earliest incarnation as an air-headed suburban housewife. This 'supremo of narcissists', as John Lahr dubs her, revealed her inner demons by degrees, evolving slowly through the 1960s and 1970s as she moved away from her origins in Moonee Ponds to occupy wider spheres in a consummate demonstration of the feedback loop between live stage presence and media celebrity.[51]

In early appearances she wore a correct pastel coat with a sprig on the lapel, accessorised with pearl jewellery, black gloves and a neat silk hat with a touch of black netting over the brow. The spectacles were standard issue, the kind I remember a next-door neighbour wearing in suburban Australia in the early 1960s. She would have turned no heads on a cruise through a Melbourne department store. Thirty years later she was offering advice to the Queen on how to manage just such an excursion: 'Wear a simple headscarf with pictures of dogs with their tongues hanging out and horseshoes all over it... With a funny old coat'. The formula, Edna announces, 'worked like a charm... She passed unnoticed in that beautiful shop. And that was a suggestion of mine... It's amazing what a headscarf can do'.[52] These remarks were made in an interview with Angela Rippon in the early 1990s, by which time Edna's wardrobe had undergone its diamanté revolution and included a Tina Turner-defying fringed red mini dress, a tailored canary yellow ensemble for royal occasions, gowns of pink sequins and multi-coloured embossed satins, a collection of furs and boas, an opera house hat, a harbour bridge tiara and a collection of spectacles that would stand out in a mardi-gras parade. Edna's glamour has a grasping edge to it: it is competitive and inflationary and these are the keynotes in her performances. She is surely the loudest stage presence of our era.

Conceived in the back of a touring bus, when the young Barry Humphries was attempting to amuse his fellow cast members from a repertory production of *Twelfth Night*, Edna has an unorthodox genetic make-up that includes equal parts of vaudeville, dada anarchy and revenge drama. The impetus for revenge grew from a childhood spent under the spell of boredom and banality, one of those forms of enchantment that, like the sleeping spells or frog metamorphoses of fairy tales, suspends life. Humphries and Dame Edna have both given their accounts of the deadly Sundays of post-war suburban life, spent in the lounge rooms of elderly relatives or going for a 'spin' in the family car to see the cream brick veneer bungalows with feature chimneys in the new estate. 'Even today', Edna writes in her autobiography, 'I get a funny, empty, worried feeling on the Sabbath; a spooky feeling of impending doom which harks back to my childhood when my parents were forcibly reminded that they were married to each other'. In this particular chapter of *My Gorgeous Life* the voice of Barry Humphries takes over, offering some devastating vignettes of those living under the pall of deadliness:

> On one of my trips through a poverty-stricken part of Melbourne, I once glimpsed a woman about my mother's age with a beetroot-coloured face, squatting near a tram stop, enjoying a Craven A, and doing little jobs. It was one of those Polaroids a kiddie's mind 'snaps' that never seems to fade...
> 'Look at that!' Daddy would say to us over his shoulder. 'You kids don't know how lucky you are'.[53]

To be lucky was to have a level of social dignity secured by a beautiful home and an array of possessions that signalled a place on the ladder of prosperity: the Axminster carpet, the Electrolux Coronation Model, gladioli in the garden and – for a child – a Malvern Star bicycle.

These were the charms that protected against the spectre of the beetroot faced woman and her like, but of course the charms only worked to lock in the binding spell of deadliness so that it crept through the mind, numbing thought processes and poisoning the culture at large with the imperative of upward mobility. Edna takes over this imperative and reverses the dynamic of control with a drive so powerfully fuelled it can move her status from housewife to superstar, thence to megastar and 'glittering gigastar' and, ultimately, trigger her apotheosis. Underlying this a particular kind of necromancy is at work, born of Humphries' own determination to avenge the blighting of his childhood by the binding spell.

He has admitted to childhood fantasies of being a magician capable of making the stultifying figures around him disappear; and in her later incarnations, Edna, having thrown off the dowdy exterior of the housewife to emerge in full gigastar glory, brandishes a gladiola that lights up like a wand. The glamour, not so much parodied as inflated to the point of combustion, is a weapon, and the drama plays itself out across an auditorium for which back-stage aides have provided a 'victim map'. Edna is the magus turned demented enchantress, the dignitary making a fanatical bid for sovereignty, the messianic presence that stages its second coming 'with a vengeance'. As her brightness increases, those who fill the auditorium recede further into nonentity so that one of the highlights of her show is the moment when someone is picked out from the sea of invisibility to be touched with the gladiolus and materialised for all to see:

> Lucky possum that you are
> You are now a mini star,
> A big fish in a tiny pond
> Thanks to my magic wand.[54]

These are lines from *Dame Edna's Second Coming*, her 1989 Drury Lane show. A decade later in *Dame Edna: the Royal Tour*, the distance between the gigastar and her possums had stretched to a point where a new order of symbolism was required. As Ben Bradley reported for *The New York Times*:

> 'I have to rise above you,' sings Dame Edna in her final musical number, in which she achieves a spectacularly staged apotheosis. 'It's my secret of survival.' But for all her selfishness, the Dame has also somehow taken us up into the empyrean with her... 'C'mon, possums, wave your gladiolas,' she crows. And as the audience obliges, it seems to have been admitted, however briefly, to that exclusive Olympian club of which Dame Edna is the president and sole member.[55]

Such are the delusions of enchantment.

Wherever it is Dame Edna is going, she is out there on her own, and what is very real is the vengeance. This is enacted in various ways, but the heart of it is the section of the show that features audience members picked out from the victim map that shows the seating position of selected types in the front eight rows of the stalls. The fat person, the senior, the middle aged woman, the woman in a red dress and the 'cripple' are called to the stage one by one for a personal chat designed to reveal details of their taste (or lack of it) and life style, so to expose the ways in which they conform to some generic model of nonentity. Having myself seen performances over thirty years apart (in Oxford in 1972 and in Sydney in 2004) I noticed that there was very little change in the format of these interviews. There are some confidential remarks on personal appearance ('How sensible of you to dress for comfort rather than glamour'), which lead into an account of domestic menus, or bathroom décor. There are reassurances about what is in store for them. The woman chosen to perform nude cartwheels has nothing to worry about:

> Because you will not know you are doing these cartwheels, Emma. Do you know why? You'll be in deep shock, Emma. You will. Because whenever we women are very very frightened, our bodies do a funny thing. We secrete an enzyme... Did you know, Emma, that we women have a little wee gland the size of a fingernail tucked in an intimate nook?[56]

And so it goes on. And on and on, until the intimate gland has been conjured up with cinematic magnitude in the minds of the assembled thousands, who are contorted into positions of undignified hysteria in the dark safety of their seats.

The Dame Edna phenomenon exposes one of the taboos underlying the western tradition of stage magnetism, one that is implicit in the Franklin principal of electrical transmission and in the Mesmerist's induction of trance: the concept of the audience as null and void. Their very emptiness is the cause of their attraction towards a source of light and power, and if they offer anything in return it is mere raw matter to feed the vampiric spirit that compels their attention. Some such intimation is behind Charlotte Brontë's portrayal of Vashti/Rachel as the evil enchantress, but Dame Edna is a burlesque version of this and in her game with the possums, however vindictive, it is not human souls that are at stake but personal dignities. Her victims are monstered rather than vampirised.

The redeeming aspect of this scenario is that audiences collectively are almost impossible to victimise. They have too much power. Whilst individual audience members may be deficient in talent, glamour and magnetism (at least in comparison with the figures on stage), an audience *en masse* is a responsive organism of great potency. Theatre history is full of terrifying stories of what can happen when audiences decide to exercise this power in a hostile mood. They can devastate the performer with a range of strategies, from silence and walk-outs up through the scale of yawning, heck-ling, slow clapping, hissing and booing, throwing missiles to full scale homicidal eruption. And so for the performer with hostile intentions, it is a game of bluff. As Humphries tells John Lahr, 'if what you're doing is urged, hurried, apologetic, the audience will smell fear a mile off... You have to act as if you have no fear'.[57] When there is a killer instinct driving a comic performance – and there is something of the killer instinct in most comic geniuses – the audience must be tricked into a sense of complicity with the attack and here laughter acts as a drug with extraordinary biochemical effects.

Lahr, son of the great comedian Bert Lahr, understands Humphries like no other commentator because he knows about this biochemistry. At the opening night of one of his father's perform-ances, Lahr recalls, he saw a man stuffing a handkerchief into his mouth in a bid to control his uncontrollable laughter. This anecdote is introduced as a comparison with the effects Edna produces:

> To watch inspired laughter register with an audience is to be present at a great and violent mystery. Faces convulse, tears stream, bodies collapse not in agony but in rapture. By the poetic power of one performer's personality, people are literally forced 'beside themselves' ... What is released in the explosion of laughter is a deep contradictory thing that is both joy and pain, mischief and madness, pleasure and panic. Jokes can hit the psyche like punches, and the audience receives them as body blows.[58]

This is one of those descriptions that light up across the literature of theatrical commentary when the writer is trying to articulate the supposedly indefinable and indescribable qualities of a brilliant performer. In his account of the bizarre chemical reactions set off in the performer/audience relationship, Lahr also reminds us that presence is an act, and essentially an act of aggression.

In fairness to Dame Edna, though, it should be said that if performers can sometimes win over the most hostile audiences, the reverse may also be possible. Now in her 70s, she appears to have mellowed a little and in promotional publicity for her 2007 appearance in Sydney, Barry Humphries acknowledged:

> I still get nervous. I'm glad I do. It's good. In the end, you just have to get out there. The audience's goodwill is

almost limitless – they want to have a nice time – and once
they laugh at the first joke, you're away.[59]

Smoke and mirrors

Light entertainment has its polarities. At the opposite extreme to
Dame Edna's burlesque practices of enchantment is the theatre of
romantic spectacle, catering to ingenuous wonder and sentimental-
ity. *Phantom of the Opera*, Andrew Lloyd Webber's blockbuster
musical drama, is the quintessential example of this kind of theatre
in the late twentieth century. It is based on a ghost story written in
1911 by Gaston Leroux, and set in the vast historic building of the
Paris Opera. The mystery of stage presence is at the heart of the
story, and the attempt to embody the phantom on stage in an
actual performance is a high-risk enterprise, courting debacle.

Leroux's Phantom is partially modelled on Du Maurier's
Svengali, and from a theatrical point of view may be seen as an
attempt to mend the divide between stage presence and performance talent that underlies the story of Trilby, so placing the
mesmerist centre stage and at the heart of the drama. From an
actor's point of view, then, the stakes are high. How could the
reality live up to the myth? How can a literary presence that is
nothing but a game of smoke and mirrors, a psychological trick of
atmospherics, be realised on stage? Smoke and mirrors, of course,
will have an important part to play in such a venture, but behind it
all there must be an actor, and a performance. This might have
been a role for Irving, but compared to *The Bells*, *Phantom of the
Opera* is a vehicle that puts its star performer in a confronting situation. There are none of those opportunities Irving took to establish a presence through low-key stage business, with time to build
the intensity and the spectacle along with it. With *Phantom*, it is a
case of coming 'in at the top' with his first appearance.

'Half the world' auditioned for the role of the Phantom, and the
casting of Michael Crawford was far out of left field. He had
played numerous roles in musical comedy but was best known as
the star of *Some Mothers Do 'Ave 'Em*, the BBC sitcom in which
he was a Buster Keaton-inspired stooge with a propensity for
making systems of any kind go haywire, and an infantile charm
edging into camp. In the minds of the public, Crawford was Frank
Spencer, and one look at his face was enough to set the laughter
impulse working; to cast him in an overblown melodramatic role
that bordered on the portentous was asking for trouble. John

Barber in *The Daily Telegraph* called *The Phantom of the Opera* 'tosh of a high order' and expressed admiration for 'the colossal nerve it took to mount a show so preposterous without guying it'.[60] And it is worth noting that Rocky Horror is an acknowledged early influence on Andrew Lloyd Webber's vision for a new stage production of Leroux's much dramatised story. If the art of melodrama is the art of resisting burlesque, why load the dice in this tricky enterprise by involving a lead performer so vividly associated with chaotic debacle? Even the staging of *Phantom*, with its plunges through trapdoors leading to subterranean caverns, its sudden ascents far up into the flies and its vast pieces of mechanised scenery, was like something designed to tempt Frank Spencer to do his worst.

Yet this may have been precisely the secret of making it work. Crawford was known for doing all his own stunt work, often at serious risk to life and limb. *Barnum*, the show he had been starring in when he was picked for the Phantom, involved high wire work and some spectacular aerial spins. His experience was that of a scenic virtuoso, able to steer a lightning course between the perfect stunt and physical disaster. In *Phantom*, it is as if he transposed this skill to the realms of dramatic control, modulating his technique so as to pitch the level of his performance with an exactness that enabled him to bring off large, high-risk effects. If he did not have Irving's advantage of being able to build the larger scale of the performance from moments of detail at the outset, he found opportunities to do so at other stages of the drama:

> During early rehearsals, at a point at the very end of the show when Christine leaves the Phantom for the last time, Sarah Brightman's veil fell off. I went over to pick it up, and buried my face in it... It kept in the show because it was a moment to which people completely related. In fact so much of that role came out of little truths. I'm sure the audience always sees through a phony gesture.[61]

While the moving scenery demonstrated 'electrifying showmanship', critics reported on the actor's resourcefulness in drawing focus through touches of subtle naturalism: his 'flickering, desperate hands', emerging from behind the Angel of Music up in the opera house rooftop; the 'subtle vocal intonation and body movement' with which he captured attention on his first appearance behind the mirror in Christine's dressing room.[62]

This was Frank N. Furter reinvented as a straight man, with 'nothing flashy or grotesque' about him, in spite of the slouch hat and all the artwork from the make-up department.[63] It was also a masterpiece of tone control, and a large-scale demonstration of presence as command over the time and space of performance. The scene of the drama is the vast decaying building of the *fin de siècle* Paris Opéra, with added dimensions of dream-space in subterranean caverns, twisting backstage recesses and heights that seem to lose touch with the forces of gravity. All this is the Phantom's domain, to be imprinted with his aura. And, as Crawford says, 'although the Phantom is only on-stage for about thirty five minutes, his invisible presence must suffuse the entire theatre while the show is going on'.[64]

The Lloyd Webber *Phantom* had its première at her Majesty's Theatre in London in October 1986 in a production created by Hal Prince and designed by Maria Björnson. The smoke was dry ice, floating above a sea of candles in the underground grotto; the mirrors were the boundaries of the phantom's domain. When the show transferred to New York, Frank Rich's review for *The New York Times* was an oddly mixed bouquet of roses and brickbats, starting with the backhanded compliment that 'it may be possible to have a terrible time at *The Phantom of the Opera*, but you'll have to work at it', and describing the *tour de force* staging of the subterranean lake as 'Liberace's vision of hell'. Crawford came off clean, with only the roses:

> Mr. Crawford's appearances are eagerly anticipated, not because he's really scary but because his acting gives *Phantom* most of the emotional heat it has... those who have 20-year-old impressions of Mr. Crawford as the lightweight screen juvenile of *The Knack* and *Hello Dolly!* – will be stunned by the force of his Phantom.[65]

The most feared of the New York critics, Rich was not one to put aside his sophistication and weary foreknowledge of every theatrical trick in the book. His testament to Crawford's stage power is in marked contrast to the kinds of accolades Irving won from Victorian critics. While Rich referred to Crawford as a 'mesmerising actor', there was no sense that he had allowed himself to be drawn into the emotional landscape of the performance in the way that Bram Stoker was by Irving. Even Dan Sullivan, who wrote in the *Los Angeles Times* that Crawford 'couldn't give more to his part if it were written by Dante', showed no signs of having been emotionally involved in the drama. Rather, he adopted a stance of sardonic detachment: 'Some of you may recall the strange affair of *The Phantom of the Opera*, a mystery never fully explained'.

Crawford impressed with his technique, his control, his sheer theatrical aplomb. He had worked on his voice as in previous roles he had worked on his body, drawing out of it everything of which it was physically capable. He devoted meticulous attention to the look of the figure and to managing the choreography of shifting scenes. That he had somehow stepped beyond the virtuosity to give some genuine dramatic heart to the production was a matter to be wondered at, but did not bewitch the commentators as Irving or the other great mesmerists had done.

Phantom is a theatrical work in the tradition of dash and flash entertainment, not a sustained drama or even melodrama with the psychological impact of *The Bells*, and the presence at its centre is accordingly mediated. The skills of performance claim predominance in the consciousness of the spectator, so that dramatic involvement is secondary. This is not to say that there is no involvement, but rather that the involvement includes a space for judgement of the kind exercised by a crowd at a sporting match or athletic event, where there is huge collective arousal around high points of skill and virtuosity.

5

BEING PRESENT

What we are is more than what we know.

Herbert Blau

The performer with presence brings a heightened level of vital power to the time and space of performance. The energy at work may be understood as natural vigour, wild animal spirits, elemental force, magnetic drawing power, electrical current or mesmeric command. All these associations are consistent with scientific accounts of the world, but in creating such accounts, scientists had to contend with prior modes of understanding that had a religious and folkloric potency irresistible to the dramatic imagination.

Modernity harbours the archaic within it, maintaining an ambivalent attitude towards this strange familiar of the deep past. Towards 1900, the ambivalence starts to create sharp and overt divisions: between the symbolist, expressionist and surrealist movements committed to exploring the cultural and psychological substrata of human experience, and voices amongst the naturalists, dadaists, futurists and social realists committed to an engagement with rapidly changing external realities. Yet the divisions never quite hold, and many of the most aggressive proponents of realism and naturalism find themselves slipping into wider metaphorical terrain. Presence itself perhaps carries this tendency to slippage, from the registers of social impact to those that carry resonances of the uncanny and the spiritual.

'What we are is more than what we know', the American director Herbert Blau remarks. It may be the actor's vocation to help us expand what we know, but other restrictions come in, born of individual and cultural timidity. 'All science aside, our experience is severely limited, by frailty, screening, lapsed memory, fright'.[1] Nevertheless, the confined sphere of 'what we are' is continually haunted by what resides at its edges.

For all the influence of social naturalism and scientific rationality on modern consciousness, the phenomenon of presence continues to insist on its mystery. There is, after all, something uncanny about the present: 'the now moment', as John Cage called it, is the vanishing point of time and space. The instant of the here and now is almost impossible to bring into focus, yet when some trigger causes it to occur to an assembly of people, the chances are that they will always remember it, as if it were a shift in consciousness resulting in break-through to some normally excluded dimension of experience. Holy theatre seeks to access this, and demonstrates how through extreme rigours of performance technique, the body and the mind are torn from their comfortable lodgement in habit and circumstance. Something of the kind also happens in death and, logically enough, might leave a residual trace of energetic engagement, a haunting presence that is the aftermath of an actual being there.[2] Joseph Chaikin offers a twentieth-century 'take' on haunting: 'Until we can hear the dominant voices of those ghosts whom we contain, we cannot control, to any degree, whom we are to become'.[3]

When in 1890 André Antoine called for a new breed of actors 'who are spontaneous and authentic, in touch with reality through and through', he had in mind the squalid and cruel realities of daily life created by the voracious economic imperatives of the later indus-trial revolution. The realities Vaslav Nijinsky was to live through after the turn of the century, and that lead Artaud to speak of 'the rude and epileptic rhythm of our times', were still unimaginable. It took Nijinsky's nervousness rather than Antoine's logic to get in touch with these rhythms. Responding to a world in the throes of trauma, the various splintering movements of the avant-garde began to discover time as disjointed and jolting segments, and to declaim the aesthetics of catastrophe, rupture, shock. The present, and the experience of being in it, had begun to mean something entirely different from what previous generations had known.

The nervous system

In 1905, the young Sergei Diaghilev took it upon himself to speak 'in the name of a new and unknown culture' which would ulti-mately sweep away all those who created it, and his prediction proved to be accurate.[4] Within ten years the tidal wave had broken, scattering everything in its path. The First World War forced a confrontation with the present as trauma, and Nijinsky in his final performance set out to express it. After a difficult period confined to his mother-in-law's house as an enemy alien in the war, he promised to appear again as a dancer in January 1919. The performance was to be at Suvretta House, a country mansion outside St Moritz, before an invited audience augmented by a few curious travellers. We have his own account of this occasion, since he began writing his diary on the same day.

A few hours before the performance, he eats a lunch of soft-boiled eggs and beans. 'I do not like dry beans', he writes, 'because there is no life in them'. And, of course, he is nervous. *Dry* and *nervous* are words that pull at each other in the opening pages of the diary. To be dry is to have none of the juice of life in you. To be nervous is to crackle with germinating force, but there is violence in this life force. It is highly reactive. By the time he arrives at Suvretta House, Nijinsky is dangerously wound up.

In the eyes of his wife Romola, who also wrote an account of it, the situation unfolds moment by moment across knife-edge tensions. She asks what the pianist is to play first, and provokes a furious outburst. The performance begins. Nijinsky sits on a chair facing the audience. He stays there so long Romola can't bear it and suggests a piece he might perform. There is a worse outburst, and she leaves the room.[5] What happens next is described by another witness:

> First he stretched his arms forward, hands raised vertically, palms outward as if to ward off danger. Then he spread his arms out sideways in a welcoming gesture. Next he brought them up high over his head. Finally he let them drop noisily, as if the joints were broken.[6]

Some people leave. Now Nijinsky decides the audience want to be amused and he does a comic dance. But he stops abruptly and shifts the mood to the other end of the spectrum.

He throws out two rolls of cloth, so they unfurl to make a giant cross on the floor, and stands at the head of it, arms outspread, to deliver a harangue about the war, charging his audience with responsibility for all the killing. 'Now', he says, 'I will dance the war'. As he dances, half with his old brilliance, half with a kind of spasmodic incoherence, the audience becomes terrified and he, eventually, becomes exhausted. Later, he writes in his diary:

> I played nervously today. I played nervously on purpose, because the audience will understand me better if I am nervous. They do not understand artists who are not nervous. One must be nervous.[7]

'One must be nervous'. The stop-start rhythms of Nijinsky's performance were those of his increasingly impulse-driven behaviour in daily life, but they were also the rythms of the time, in a world where the survivors had learned that literally anything can happen next, and the present moment is always one of potential rupture. Nijinsky's last dance is an expression of the imperative to be *in* the present, not just as an individual, but as a single being sharing the larger nervous system of a world in crisis.

During the course of the twentieth century, writers and directors were concerned with the creation of dramaturgical frameworks for a new kind of stage presence, conceived in relation to the conditions of the times. The theatrical voices of the European avant-garde, with their wholesale spirit of rejection, were angrier and more reckless, but also more recklessly humorous than those of previous eras. In the immediate aftermath of the war, Nijinsky's external world was also that of Marinetti and the Futurists, one which, as they declare in their manifestos, 'throbs around us, bombards us with squalls of fragments of interconnected events'.[8] Ten years later, the cultural reaction to all the chaos was taking more diverse and fully articulated directions.

Antonin Artaud in the 1930s rails against a culture that he sees as fostering disjunction in the conditions of life itself:

> If our life lacks brimstone, i.e., a constant magic, it is
> because we choose to observe our acts and lose ourselves
> in considerations of their imagined form instead of being
> impelled by their force.[9]

To be impelled by this force is to be nervous on the larger scale. Artaud calls for a 'theatre of cruelty' that will return to the psychical violence of the ancient mysteries. It is a choice, he declares, between a return to the greater energies of these mysteries and an abandonment to disorder, famine, blood, war and plague. The mission of the theatre must be nothing less than to broker this alternative in favour of the former, so the stakes are the highest, and the actor through whom the energies are concentrated and realised must be like an athlete commanding strength and breath; the actor's business is magnetism, poetry and spellbinding.[10] Artaud makes no concession to scientific modernism and gives no quarter in his demand for the return of the magic generated by the archaic mystery rituals in which presence was once invoked.[11]

This vision for the theatre is diametrically opposed to that of Brecht. Artaud wants a presence on stage that will draw all the potencies of deep myth into connection with the violence of contemporary upheaval. Brecht wants to keep these elements far apart. Where Artaud interprets the trauma of the contemporary world in metaphysical terms, as an episode in the violent creation story that plays itself out in perpetuity, Brecht's viewpoint is one of political rationality. His anger is directed against government and industry, and his determination invested in a form of control that is pragmatic:

> How can the tortured and heroic, abused and ingenious, changeable and world-changing man of this great and ghastly century obtain his own theatre which will help him to master the world and himself.[12]

This mastery is dependent on the explicit rejection of all the elements Artaud places at a premium: mesmerism, emotional stirring, magic and myth. Brecht dismisses these as the 'spiritual dope traffic' of the theatre and asserts the need to strip acting of all its empathic qualities.

In the 'theatre for the scientific age' to which he is committed, the actor is a demonstrator, the polar opposite of Artaud's 'athlete of the heart'. Brecht argues the case for this approach to acting with an uncompromising stringency, as if he is convinced that cognitive function can only be restored to its necessary centrality in the human world if it is quarantined from empathy, fantasy and sensibility. 'Nerves' in this account are not the outriders of sensory intelligence, but rather manifestations of a disorderly emotional life divorced from reality. The effect of emotional acting on the nerves, he insists, is 'a continual menace to the production's educative value'.

Brecht's writings contain an explicit refusal of virtually every quality associated with stage presence in the western theatre tradition. Brechtian theatre – at least in theory – distributes the presence effect across the whole production. The co-presence of actor and audience is fostered through a style of dialogue and action that demands active mental work from the spectator; energetic concentration is harboured in the structure of the drama and the techniques of its demonstration; the sense of being present at a catalytic point in time is the over-riding focus of the theatre event. Yet Brecht's major plays demonstrate a fascination with the charismatic figure, historical or fictional, who occupies a crucial position in epochal transition. Galileo, Arturo Ui (a character based on a satirical amalgamation of Hitler and Al Capone), the legendary highwayman Macheath and Mother Courage are all investigative portraits of the charismatic personality. Brecht reconceives charisma in an atheistical and democratic framework so that it includes the ordinary man or woman with a sense of mission and personal determination that drives them through circumstances, gathering others around them. But he is also interested in the analysis of political and intellectual leaders.

Inevitably, the charisma in his characters draws out the charisma in those who play them, so that, for all his declared antipathy to magnetic acting, Brecht created a repertoire that has made or confirmed the reputations of some of the most powerful dramatic actors of the twentieth century. Helen Weigel, who created the role of Mother Courage on stage, was his own chosen example of the actor-demonstrator. Her stage presence was devoid of charm and deliberately jarring, but she exercised a stern control that had its own compelling effect. She caught Brecht's attention in her portrayal of a maidservant in a Greek tragedy, reporting on the death of her mistress in a way that was 'utterly without lamentation, yet so definite and irresistible that the bare fact of Jocasta's death was more effective at that moment than any sorrow could have been'.[13] Weigel excelled at bringing 'the moment' into sharp relief, whether as the breaking of a major event or the unfolding of a sequence of reaction, expressed through minutely detailed pieces of stage business. As she explained herself:

> Mother Courage's moneybag: that's a conspicuous prop one can exploit in the part. Since the bag makes a clicking sound when you shut it, you discover a great many ways of doing so… I developed a kind of aria of clicking sounds.[14]

Only an actor with a consummately secure grip on the concentration of the audience (comparable with Irving's) could direct it to this kind of detail with instant dramatic effect. Weigel combined precision techniques of detailing with a monumental approach to the role. According to Brecht 'she made every moment into a historic moment, every speech into a famous speech by a historic character'.[15] The democratisation of the heroic role is part of Brecht's agenda, which includes a rejection of ennoblement and aesthetic appeal. His Galileo combines genius with vulgarity and attempts to strip the Renaissance man of any vestiges of either the dignitary or the magus. But in spite of the trenchant dramaturgical principles on which the character is created, there is a kind of glamour about him on stage that tends to rub off on the actor who plays him. *The Resistible Rise of Arturo Ui*, as its title indicates, is an attempt to explode the myth of charismatic inevitability surrounding Hitler and Capone, but in performance the actor playing the lead more often than not proves that the charisma is itself inevitable.

Later twentieth-century interpretations of Brecht have tended to recognise the contradictions in Brecht's views on acting, and to exploit the inherent magnetism of the leading characters. When the British National Theatre Company was casting a new production of Galileo in 1980, it was acknowledged that 'someone was needed who had bottomless vigour, maturity, enough "star quality" to sustain a bravura performance over a long evening, and the nerve not to be put off by the character's flaws'.[16] Michael Gambon was chosen. He was known at the time as a 'middle weight' comic actor and the role transformed his status, inspiring Ralph Richardson to dub him 'the Great Gambon'.[17] A *New York Times* profile of the actor referred to his Galileo as a 'titanic characterisation' with 'the classical grandeur of Laurence Olivier'.[18]

Simon Callow prepared for the role of Arturo Ui by watching recordings of Hitler's rally speeches, which left him in no doubt of the hypnotic effect and the 'psychic energy at work'.[19] His approach, though, was to present this energy without a magnetic centre. The performance 'was to be a series of disconnected impulses, as if his nervous system and his brain had likewise been made up of scraps from the laboratory dustbin'.[20] Callow also describes how, towards the end of the rehearsal process, the disjointedness took on its physical manifestation as he and the designer went through the make-up box:

> ... and quite by chance my eye lighted on a cheap joke-shop false nose with a Hitler moustache attached. I nearly knocked the poor girl over as I leaped across the room. 'That's *it*,' I said, 'that's it.' I put it over the non-fitting wig so that the elastic string stretched at an angle from left to right of my face, thus splitting it up, like a Kokoscha or Rouault... It was abstract, Neanderthal and robot-like all at once'.[21]

This was neither the charismatic Hitler of the rallies nor the dry Brechtian evocation of a man without qualities, but a nightmare figure, equal parts dada and Grand Guignol, both hollow and compelling.

The question must arise, though, of whether by the 1970s directorial sophistication and the virtuosity of fine acting create a theatrical experience that is divorced from the rough urgency of the concerns that prompted Brecht to write *Arturo Ui* in 1941, after he fled Nazi Germany. When the play was revived by the National Actors Theatre in New York in 2002, many of the critics made disparaging remarks about how time had devalued its currency. It was called 'a short course in Brecht', and 'a punishingly didactic text' with a 'plodding plot'. This gave the whole production, and in particular the starring performance, a compensatory dynamic. Since Al Pacino was in the title role, the star-power was exceptional and here the critics were unanimous. 'If any American actor inspires obsession, not for his looks, but for his overall presence', Brendon Lemon wrote in *The Financial Times*, 'it is Al Pacino'. The words 'magnetic' and 'mesmerising' recurred across the spread of reviews; *The Washington Post* declared that Pacino had proved himself the equal as a dramatic actor of Ian McKellan and Michael Gambon and was fit to be 'the charismatic lynch pin' of a new national theatre; as the *New York Daily News* concluded, the audience had 'not really come to study the sources of evil' but had 'paid $100 to see high powered stars'.[22]

Ben Brantley summed up the situation in *The New York Times*, commenting that the production 'unfolds as a neck-and-neck race between the tedium of the material and the entertaining chutzpah of its presentation'. Even the chutzpah of the central character was borrowed from a show business heritage brought by the lead actor.

> Mr. Pacino sometimes seems to be channeling most of his more celebrated roles. It's as if his entire professional life were passing before your eyes in a series of juicy, iconographic acting bites.[23]

There were echoes of Michael Corleone, Scarface, Herod (a role Pacino played in a production of Wilde's *Salome*) and Pacino's Richard III in the film *Looking for Richard*. Brecht's idea of creating a Hitler image stripped of the charisma effect now manifested as a problem to be overcome. 'Unlike Mack the Knife', Elysa Garden wrote in *USA Today*, 'the title character is not the kind of stylish thug-hero who inspires popular story'. In her view, Pacino triumphed by nevertheless raising the performance to 'a level of piercing intensity' and transforming the nonentity into 'a mesmerising demagogue'. She saw this as true to the Brechtian vision because the effect was to create 'sensory assaults' and to 'jolt rather than seduce'.

But what kind of jolting and assault are we talking about here? New York audiences in 2002 may have lived through some trauma, but this was not the protracted, unrelenting assault on the nerves experienced by Brecht and others who had lived under the Nazi regime. Nor was it the kind of jolt in consciousness so familiar to those who remained in East Germany after the war. The anonymous critic of the *New York Daily News* recalled seeing a production of *Arturo Ui* in East Berlin in 1965: 'My German was minimal. What most fascinated me was the eerie mood of the audience'. A fierce engagement with the present is, by definition, not repeatable at another time, when political and cultural tensions are quite different. To mainstream theatre audiences in 2002, Brecht had become a 'style', and Simon McBurney, the director of the New York production, was praised for his fidelity to it through the creation of what Brantley described as an 'electrified artificiality'. But style is born of formal principles and techniques. Wedded as he may have been to certain formalities, Brecht was not driven by stylistic concerns but by the urgency of an inflamed reaction to circumstances. The distancing effect he demanded from actors included a sense of rupture and disruption that shot through the whole nervous system, albeit with a more gradual effect than anything the Futurists envisaged.

No doubt Pacino understood this. Brantley registered his 'scary energy and focus' and reported:

> Here is a purely animal presence, a brute whose hands hang at his sides like dead weights and whose eye sockets register as hungry black holes. This man is all id.[24]

In its very immediacy, though, this is a presence not working at distance but compensating for it. Suppose Brecht had mounted his own production of *Arturo Ui* at the time of writing (it was not actually staged until 1958) and suppose there had been a male equal to Helen Weigel to play the title role, it is doubtful that audiences would have been treated to anything like the ferocious virtuosity of Pacino, but the presence of the present itself would have been evoked to do the work on their nerves.

On his own admission, Brecht was dissatisfied with his actors, perversely so because they scored great successes in his plays. In a 'dialogue' published in 1928, he interrogated himself on the reasons for this:

> Because they act badly?
> No. Because they act wrong.
> How ought they to act then?
> For an audience of the scientific age.[25]

Catering to such an audience, he said, meant communicating 'consciously, suggestively, descriptively' instead of 'by means of hypnosis'. The tradition of mesmeric acting was anathema to him because it interfered with the spectator's independence of mind and judgement. He sought to maintain a double consciousness in the audience: of the imagined world of the drama and the actual situation of the performance in the here and now.

Brecht had a model for effective stage presence, going back to his youth at the turn of the century, when he witnessed a cabaret appearance by Frank Wedekind. Wedekind was to become better known (or, rather, more notorious) as a dramatist, but when Brecht wrote an obituary in 1919, it was the cabaret artist who left the indelible impression:

> His vitality was his finest characteristic. He had only to enter a lecture hall full of hundreds of noisy students, or a room or a stage, with his special walk, his sharply cut bronze skull slightly tilted and thrust forward, and there was silence... There he stood, ugly, brutal, dangerous, with close-cropped red hair, his hands in his trouser pockets, and one felt that the devil himself couldn't shift him...No singer ever gave me such a shock, such a thrill. It was the man's intense aliveness, the energy which allowed him to defy sniggering ridicule and proclaim his brazen hymn to humanity, that also gave him his personal magic.[26]

Wedekind was one of The Eleven Executioners, a Munich cabaret group formed in 1901 and dedicated to the death sentencing of the anti-democratic regime of Wilhelm II, with its crushing censorship laws. The Eleven Executioners were part of a dissident culture surge of which Wedekind and later Brecht were figureheads. The surge swept up from the fringes of a milieu characterised by intimidated compliance and aesthetic sterility, generating a forced confrontation with the present. As Brecht's description of Wedekind signals, the ruptured aesthetic was as much of a key factor in this as any of the political messages the artists sought to deliver. Wedekind stood out from the group as a one man shock-effect, his whole persona working against the grain of prevailing taste, galvanising an unprecedented collective encounter with the actualities of a brutalised society.

Brecht's demand for a grip on modernity, and specifically scientific modernity, was motivated by a recognition that the experience of being present was not a taken-for granted condition, but rather a sudden and un-nerving occurrence. And it is curious that, averse as he may have been to supernaturalism for its offence against science and realism, he is still tempted to speak of magic in his highly charged verbal portrait of Wedekind. Naturalism escalates into supernaturalism through a twist of rhetoric such as even Brecht is ready to employ. His evocation of Wedekind as a match for the devil himself is just a humorous flourish, but there is an unmistakable suggestion of a crackle in the air as Wedekind makes his entry; there is something preternatural, if not supernatural, about the energy he brings with him, and about its power to convert one state of the world into another. The uncanny keeps on creeping back.

The vanishing point

The uncanny keeps on creeping back because its points of access can never be sealed off. Even Barry Humphries cannot resist the call to speak from beyond the grave. Throughout her career, Dame Edna has been ghosted by a co-star whose spectral appearances shift the hysterical mood of her show into another register. Sandy Stone's death is hard to pinpoint on the calendar. It was a seamless passing from a life so evacuated it had become almost transparent, yet so tenacious in its anchorage to a litany of last things that they passed across with him, to be recounted from the realms of eternity. In 1968 he announced he had just had 'a little op' in 'a strange place with strange womenfolk coming and going'.[27] In 1971 he spoke from his bed, voicing a series of letters to his absent wife Beryl. The last of them begins, 'Just a note to let you know I'm still in the land of the living', and concludes: 'I haven't forgotten to stop the *Women's Weekly* or defrost the Silent Knight...The Harpic is cleansing while I sleep'.[28] After a pause and a blackout, another letter was read in voice-over, from Beryl's friend Gweneth, offering condolences on her husband's death. Sandy's next performance is given three years later, from Limbo. He has dreamed he dropped off the twig. By 1978, though, he is ready to state, 'I am deceased' before going on to provide the details of life as it continues to be lived by Beryl in spite of his failure to defrost the fridge before fading away. Nearly twenty years later, in 2007, Sandy is still making his presence felt in the middle of Edna's shows.

The Sandy Stone monologues are widely regarded as Humphries's finest writing. If Sandy is unable to quite die away, this is because of his continuing testament to an inability to quite be alive. There is always the fridge to worry about, and the Harpic, and the cancellation of the *Women's Weekly*. There is always the recollection that he has forgotten these things, so their insistent life cycles will go on and on, free from human intervention. Vitality is elsewhere, all vacuumed up into the ever brightening presence of Edna. And yet it is Sandy who stops the show, makes time stand still, so that the here and now looms large for all those packed into the auditorium; and the fragile voice, the seated figure in the dim spill of light, have a drawing power on another frequency. 'Moment to moment reality', Joseph Chaikin says, 'becomes a circle of concentration'.[29] We may be watching Sandy Stone as a witness to how this reality escapes in the drip by drip passing of daily life, but the process of watching and witnessing is itself a confrontation with the present moment. There is a strong flavour of Beckett in Sandy Stone, and Humphries acknowledges he was reading Beckett's novels at the time when the first sketch was written. 'Do you believe in the life to come?' Clov asks Ham in *Endgame*, to which the reply is 'Mine was always that'.[30]

Life is always in communication with death, whether through imperceptible leakage or when the expanded life cycle of the ancient mysteries is opened suddenly, in an instant of unexpected awareness. The creation of such openings may be the core business of the actor, whose situation is precariously held in the world of physics and biology. As Herbert Blau envisages it:

> The history of theatre is a calculus of changing focus on a subject which is increasingly mist. The thing which moves us is on the edge of disappearance. Whether in or out of perspective, we are always at the vanishing point.[31]

One of the strangest paradoxes of stage presence is that, the more powerfully it draws us into the here and now, the more palpably it seems to connect us to a time zone that stretches beyond the boundaries of natural life, to invoke the supernatural. Why do ghosts, which the French call *'revenants'* – those who return – come back to the places from which they are supposed to have departed, and how do they achieve the presence effect? This is a question with which scientists would have no patience but, with a little poetic licence, it helps to raise some other questions that are of the essence in an enquiry into stage presence. Are the ghosts looking for something that is or was missing to them? Is their presence a recompense for some kind of failure to be present in life? And since the places where ghosts haunt are themselves invested with an aura of the uncanny, are these points of spectral appearance also vanishing points?

Presence involves a 'here' as well as a 'now' and the stage, as the place privileged for the conjuration of presence, may also have something uncanny about it, as Simon Callow learned when he stepped out on the stage of the Old Vic as a teenager and found it 'throbbing with energies and a curious power – an altar without a tabernacle'. And when he spoke some lines from *Hamlet,* he recalls:

> It was a shock to hear my own voice so loud and resonant; but just as shocking was the physical, or even the psychical, power released, a small earthquake.[32]

Is this how it feels to be a ghost? Presence, after all, is a quality actors and ghosts have in common. And actors seem to communicate it with special force when playing scenes in which they are faced with a ghost. One thinks of Betterton as Hamlet seeing his dead father walk, Garrick staring out Banquo in *Macbeth,* Irving's Mathias seeing his murder victim in his mind's eye. Ghosts like theatres. All the older theatres of London's West End boast they have one, and some, like the Phantom of the Paris Opera, find their way back to centre stage in living performances. The stage is, in Peter Brook's account, 'the empty space', but nature abhors a vacuum, so perhaps this emptiness also calls for something beyond the natural to fill it. We might call the emptiness uncanny, with the doubleness of meaning that Freud points to in that term: *heimlich* (of home and origin) and *unheimlich* (strange, alien).

One of the fascinations about Callow's recollection of his early encounter with the strange presence of the empty space is that it is a reminder of how even the most powerfully confident stage performers can maintain this connection to the energising fear of just being out there. Callow in his prime is a robust, humorous performer, hardly best known for uncanny qualities, though they emerge from time to time in his repertoire. In *The Mystery of Charles Dickens*, a one-man show created in collaboration with the writer Peter Ackroyd, he travelled across Dickens's extraordinary range of moods, from the florid caricature of Mrs Gamp to the supernatural atmospherics of Edwin Drood. Dickens himself gave readings of his work with, as Callow says, 'a degree of histrionic energy that drew the stunned admiration of the theatrical profession'. Callow's performance evoked the mesmeric quality of the original readings, including a quite literal sequence of hypnotic command to the audience: 'Keep your eyes on me. Look at me. Now my eyes are on you. I need to be connected to you, and you to me. Then I can come alive'.[33] There is a sense of some boundary being crossed here, between the actor and his audience but also between the actor and his role, so that there is even a suggestion of possession. 'Inhabiting his world', Callow writes, 'becoming his characters, becoming him, I am seized by the suprahuman vitality which so overwhelmed his contemporaries'. The channelling is of a kind closer to spiritualist demonstrations than to conventional acting. 'I set out to catch, to lure this strange genius into the auditorium for a couple of hours. Sometimes it is a little spooky'.[34]

In the case of Dickens, as of Brecht, there is a burning contemporaneity at the core of the dramatic vision. The episodes of social brutality on which his novels turn were triggered by things he witnessed in the streets. Whilst writing *The Chimes*, he recorded: 'I am in regular, ferocious excitement... get up at seven; have a cold bath before breakfast; and blaze away, wrathful and red hot'.[35] This is the absolute antithesis of the hard headedness and cold theatrical energy favoured by Brecht and it creates a very different situation for the actor, who can use the psychic electricity of mesmerism to close the distance between himself and the one he is impersonating, so collapsing also the distance in time. For the audience, the experience is that of reliving the episode recounted as if it were happening and judging from the number of hysterical outbursts and collapses recorded amongst Dickens's audience, his ability to conjure persons and events into the present was equivalent to Irving's.

Callow's Dickens is both hypnotist and conjurer. Actual conjuring tricks were included in his performance, where the transition from one character or state of consciousness to another had to be as immediate and complete as a conjuring trick. In the first instance, this trick had to be played on the actor by himself. Callow describes a number of almost ritualised preparations he carries out before a show, and central amongst them is the moment of transformation:

> Transformation is not disguise, but the revelation of alter-native possibilities in the muscular disposition of the face and the body. Whichever approach you favour, the assumed or the osmotic, as you stand in front of the mirror, SOMEONE ELSE LOOKS BACK. This is voodoo. The embodiment of another person is black magic, the raising of spirits. Being this person, you will be able to do things you cannot do. You will be able to lift weights you cannot. You will be able to dance steps you cannot.[36]
>
> [*Callow's emphasis*]

The mirror is a vanishing point and one through which spectres (including the Paris Phantom) traditionally make their appearance. Callow's use of capitals to signal the shock of the moment after the transition has occurred also denotes another order of alienation from that envisaged by Brecht.

But are the two orders really incompatible? Brecht's attack on mesmerism and supernaturalism is born of a particular kind of vitalism, a conviction of the need for an awakening to life. Joseph Chaikin expresses this well. 'I believe Brecht must be performed in relation to what *is* vital, rather than what *was*', he writes. '... A person is whom he pretends to be. While I put off taking any action for or against what I see, my life recedes before me. It passes. It passes. It passed'. When the person one pretends to be vanishes into the mirror to be replaced by someone else, the passing and recession are suddenly arrested. Time itself is halted as the new presence – and presentness – is manifested. There is an awakening which, if it is properly managed from a theatrical point of view, can reactivate cognitive awareness of the kind Brecht is so determined to jolt into life. 'A theatre event', says Chaikin, 'should burn into time, as a movement cuts into space'.[37]

The theatre event should be a matter of life and death. In a theatre responding to the conditions of modernity, this does not mean that bodies will pile up on stage, as in Jacobean revenge drama, or off it, as in Greek tragedy. Following the Second World War, Beckett led the way with a new dramatic minimalism, focused on the minute by minute, second by second ticking away of a life span tensed between birth and death. In his plays, the living and the dead are virtually indistinguishable, and death is an indeterminate threshold across which all the dead voices continue to make themselves heard:

> *Estragon*: They talk about their lives.
> *Vladimir*: To have lived is not enough for them.
> *Estragon*: They have to talk about it.
> *Vladimir*: To be dead is not enough for them.
> *Estragon*: It is not sufficient.[38]

'They give birth astride of a grave', as Pozzo says in *Waiting for Godot*, 'the light gleams an instant, then it's night once more'. But the play shows the interminable stretching out of the instant:

> *Pozzo*: I don't seem to be able ... (long hesitation)... to depart.
> *Estragon*: Such is life.[39]

The quietus may be devoutly to be wished, but the flatline eludes Beckett's characters. 'Finished', announces Clov at the beginning of *Endgame*, then immediately backtracks: 'nearly finished, it must be nearly finished'.[40] Lucky's speech in *Godot* tracks the ever-stretching distance to the finish line as man, in spite of the tennis, football, running, cycling, swimming, flying and golf over eighteen holes, continues to shrink and dwindle, 'the dead loss per caput since the death of Bishop Berkeley being to the tune of one inch four ounce per caput'.[41] This is Zeno's paradox with a twist: it is not space that is infinitely divisible but the life force and the resources that sustain it. For the quartet in *Endgame*, the biscuit rations are halved and then quartered, and every day there is a bit less light, less mobility, less sensory connection to a world that is systematically losing its content. The point of extinction is never reached because the gradations of decline are distended into ever fainter signs of life, while the shades of the dead continue to come and go in the world.

A fullness of presence may be suggested in some figures – Hamm, Pozzo, Winnie in *Happy Days* – because they carry the highly coloured remnants of what they were, but what we actually see is the process of slow evacuation, the intolerable capture, instant by instant and breath by breath, of living as a journey

LIVERPOOL JOHN MOORES UNIVERSITY
LEARNING SERVICES
173

into dying. Against the backdrop of western theatrical tradition, this is perverse; or is it an approach that exposes the perversity of all that magnetism, mesmerism and electrical voltage towards which the art of the actor has been dedicated? Blau, who has directed many productions of Beckett's plays, including the landmark performance of *Godot* at the San Quentin prison in 1957, writes:

> With mortality as a base, Presence is fragile, subject to change (and chance), yet persisting through that. Breath blood nerves brains, the metabolism of perception.[42]

If presence is seen not as the property of the exceptional individual, but as a quality all human beings manifest, the staging of it requires a sensibility very different from that cultivated through classical training. Perhaps it is not a quality of fullness at all.

Evidently the fullness of the traditionally trained actor was an embarrassment to Beckett. As a director, he became notorious for his techniques of subduing and restraining actors, as if there was something distasteful to him about everything they did. In a 1973 letter to his biographer Dierdre Bair, he admitted: 'The best possible play is one in which there are no actors, only the text'. Yet he had strong affection for particular actors, notably Jack MacGowran and Billie Whitelaw, with whom his working relationship bordered on obsession. In general star actors did not get on well with him or his roles. As John Fletcher observes, the plays have tended to be best served by lesser known actors. He cites the example of Alfred Lynch, who played Estragon in a 1964 production of *Godot*, as being 'all the more eloquent... because he was less famous, more self-effacing, and allowed the character to come alive through him'. MacGowran as Lucky, according to a review in the *New Statesman*, 'acted himself so far into Beckett's mind' he seemed to become part of its imagery. The *Guardian* critic Hugh Herbert observed Beckett speaking with the actors in rehearsals and described it as 'like a parliament of moths. All you can hear is that soft, fluttering sound of the muted voices'.[43]

It was not that Beckett was averse to theatricality: shades of vaudeville are evident throughout *Godot* and *Endgame*, and in the latter Hamm can be seen as a wry tribute to the ham actor. But Beckett evokes a theatricality worn away to shreds and patches, easily ruined by any attempt to introduce stronger fibres and always in the process of wearing thinner.

Hamm: Don't sing.
Clov: (*turning towards Hamm*) One hasn't the right to
    sing any more?
Hamm: No.[44]

Yet there is a tenacity in the refusal itself – and the sustaining of stage activity following it – that is perversely entertaining, and tensely dramatic. In Beckett's world, the sense of privation becomes a primordial drive.

The later works present a succession of characters who voice at length their 'gnawing to be gone'.[45] They hover on a bandwidth just above one degree zero of the life force, always a breath and a few more words away from the flatline, even when they are shades of the already dead. 'The lower the order of mental activity, the better the *Company*', states the narrator of *Company*, 'up to a point'. There are always flutterings in the nerve ends, flickerings of image and memory, stirrings in the muck heap. A voice comes in the dark, a faint voice at loudest, which slowly ebbs till almost out of hearing, and at each slow ebb hope slowly dawns that it is dying.[46] The death of hope and the hope of death are mutually exclusive. All the things there are no more of – hair, teeth, ideals, eyesight, sugar plums, rugs, bicycle wheels, pain killer, coffins – just pile up waiting for the last rat, the last flea, the last half biscuit, the last gleam of light to be added to them.[47]

As the vital sphere of the characters shrinks, so does the radius of operation for the actor. James Knowlson describes how this begins with *Godot*:

> When Vladimir and Estragon go off stage, they are merely beating their wings like birds, trapped by the strands of the net, bouncing back as if on elastic into the stage space to which they are inextricably tied.[48]

After leashing Didi and Gogo to the dirt mound, Beckett imprisoned two of the characters in *Endgame* in dustbins, buried Winnie in *Happy Days* up to her waist and then her neck, and confined the trio of players in *Play* to 'identical grey urns about one yard high... the neck held fast by the urn's mouth'.[49] Yet this physical confinement was like a literalisation of how he sought to constrain the performative freedom of the actors, whether as the official director of a production or through authorial involvement when he attended rehearsals. He refused to engage in issues of interpretation, and

focused exclusively on controlling the execution of the performance, as Ruby Cohn testifies:

> At his first meeting with the actors, he never speaks about
> the play but plunges right into it. Work on scenes begins at
> once, and Beckett shakes his head at questions that stray
> from concrete performance. On the other hand, no
> concrete detail is too small for his attention. [50]

When the German cast working under his direction on *Endgame*
asked about the meaning of the pauses, Horst Bollmann (cast as
Clov) recalls:

> He told us 'Act as if you were in a boat with a hole in it
> and water is coming in and the boat is slowly sinking. You
> must think of things to do; then there is a pause; then you
> get the feeling you have to do something else…'[51]

Brenda Bruce, cast in the 1962 London production of *Happy
Days*, found the physical challenge of being enclosed in the mound
was surpassed by the strictures of performing according to
Beckett's instructions, with his insistence on the observation of
every punctuation mark. 'I found that the lines of dots were
absolutely part of the play and that if I didn't attend to them on the
split second I had to go right back to the beginning again'. Then
there was the introduction of the metronome, which, she says,
made her 'absolutely hysterical'. She describes the lead-up to the
opening night as a crisis of fierce intensity summarily resolved by
her entrance on stage:

> My heart was hammering so hard that it hurt. [Jocelyn
> Herbert] and George Devine helped me downstairs and then
> they put me in that mound and the stage manager came and
> shut it behind me and put the bolt in. It was dreadful. There
> was the claustrophobia of sitting there trapped, I couldn't
> ease it by walking across the stage. It is complete exposure
> because with the lighting there is no shadow anywhere. You
> begin to get mesmerised by the lights.[52]

This is like a programmed inversion of the power of the player:
mesmerised and reduced to hysteria, then wheeled out in a trap to
be confronted with the audience. It was an exercise in elimination
that also brought audiences to the limits of toleration.

In 1974 Peggy Ashcroft appeared in a revival of *Happy Days* under the direction of Peter Hall, who had to mediate some tensions when Beckett attended the rehearsals. 'The slightest feeling disturbs Sam', Hall records in his diary, 'and he speaks of his need for monotony, paleness, weakness'. Ashcroft herself was circumspect in her account: 'I'm not sure he altogether approved of my interpretation. He might have thought it too "humanised"'.[53] What might have disturbed Beckett, however, impressed the critics. Irving Wardle in *The Times* praised the performance for its alternation of darkened moods with 'radiant thanksgiving', and 'gentle wistfulness', and a delivery 'full of Ashcroft music'.[54]

Beckett himself was driving towards the achievement of productions devoid of this kind of dramatic nuance and human dimension, and Hall recognised that 'physical precision' was at the heart of his method. 'I want him to tell us everything by doing it', he stated. 'There is no notation which can describe the precision of the physical business'.[55] As a director, Beckett evidently had notations of his own reflecting a spatial and temporal exactness that would have made Laban blanch, but he kept these mainly in his head, memorising the text as an intricate performance score. E.M. Cioran says that, in conversation, Beckett visualised the most insignificant details of the staging 'minute by minute – I was about to say second by second'.[56] The quasi-apologetic form of Cioran's statement is curious, since there was no such thing as an insignificant detail in Beckett's plays, and his demand for exactness in timing went well into the division of seconds. The result was a confrontation with unfolding time that made the physical presentness of the actor into a burning issue.

Happy Days and *Not I* became the forcing grounds for the realisation of Beckett's quest for a kind of being on stage that could only be experienced as an ordeal by the performer. Jessica Tandy was the first to be cast as the Mouth in *Not I*, following an appearance in *Happy Days*, which prepared her for some of the rigours involved. According to Deirdre Bair, Tandy challenged Beckett about the extraordinary technical demands in the role of Winnie, showing him 'how difficult it would be to project a variety of mood and inflection with her neck elongated into the unnatural position the mound demanded', but her concerns evidently made no impression on him. When it came to working out the staging conditions for *Not I*, Beckett instructed the director Alan Schneider to ensure that the actress would be completely immobilised except for her mouth, which was the only part of her to be seen. Dressed in a black cloth shroud, she was enclosed in a box together with a technician who held the spotlight trained on her mouth. An iron brace attached to the back of the box held her head in place, after the use of a forehead strap had proved too much of an impediment to the muscular freedom she needed for vocal projection. Tandy was instructed to consider herself as nothing other than the mouth, 'an organ of emission, without intellect', and to perform the piece strictly according to the rehearsed rhythms and intonations, so that the experience from her point of view was almost robotic.[57]

When the French director Pierre Chabert saw a video recording of Billie Whitelaw in *Happy Days*, his comment was: 'She appears somewhat like a mechanical puppet whose strings, one knows, are being pulled by Beckett himself'.[58] This is easily said, and something of a hackneyed image, but the arresting fact is that it was actually done. Eva-Katharina Schultz, who played Winnie under his direction in the 1971 German production, recalls a moment of truth during rehearsals:

> I was very much in despair very soon with the whole thing and he said, 'OK, I'll read it for you.' He had his note-books... But he was the best Winnie he ever had. When he was reading it, it was very flat, he didn't have any modulations. Yet it was so lively in a way in which I would have liked to have been capable of.[59]

If Beckett was the best Winnie he ever had, Whitelaw was the actress who came closest to channelling his performance in the most arduous of all his roles, the mouth in *Not I*. From the beginning of the rehearsal process at the Royal Court Theatre, Beckett began to take a close interest, giving instructions so minute and insistent that the interpretative constraints were as severe as those imposed by the apparatus in which she was physically confined on stage. There could hardly be a more comprehensive denial of the presence of an actor, yet what was being created was a stage presence of an unprecedented kind, forged at the outer limits of human endurance. In an incident that has now become part of stage lore and gossip, Whitelaw suffered a nervous collapse during a run-through. Given Beckett's already well-established reputation for taking actors to breaking point, and given the relentless instruction to which she had submitted, the obvious conclusion is that he had broken her. His reaction – 'Oh Billie, what have I done to you, what have I done to you?' – has itself become notorious. But in

Whitelaw's account, it was a turning point rather than a breaking point, and one that produced a technical recognition:

> If you are blindfolded and have a hood over your face, you hyperventilate, you suffer from sensory deprivation. It will happen to you. And I hung on and hung on until I couldn't any longer. I just went to pieces because I was convinced I was like an astronaut tumbling out into space... and that's when I fell down; I couldn't go on.[60]

The crisis was resolved by some adjustments to the apparatus surrounding her, and, like so many of Beckett's characters, she discovered that when one realises one can't go on, the only response is to go on. On stage, the mouth of *Not I* becomes the vanishing point, but also the point of genesis, with its emission of words 'out... out into this world', trailing images and frail traces of lost narrative. This is a minimalism that borders on the alchemical, perhaps even feeling its way towards making a full circle with the ancient mystery dramas, though here the extended life cycle that connects the living with the dead contracts to an instant, a point in space between states of being and unbeing.

'It's possible you haven't lived until you've watched Billie Whitelaw die', Frank Rich wrote in a *New York Times* review of a 1984 revival of *Rockaby*, in which, as he summarised, 'she plays a woman in a rocking chair rocking herself to the grave'. She rocks to a halt. Her words cease. The light fades over her whitened features.

> During the long silence, the actress doesn't so much as twitch an eyelash – and yet, by the time the darkness is total, we're left with an image different from the one we'd seen a half a minute earlier. Somehow Miss Whitelaw has banished life from her expression: what remains is a death mask, so devoid of blood it could be a faded, crumbling photograph. And somehow, even as the face disintegrates, we realize that it has curled into a faint baby's smile.[61]

The times

The present is an instant, but it is also 'the times', the swing of events at large that can suddenly shift direction or change register, pitching a critical mass of the public into a new cultural dynamic. Since the Renaissance there has been a succession of cultural shifts, from those that mark an era – the Enlightenment, Romanticism, Modernism, Postmodernism – to those that have more local or specific impact as change movements fuelled by the impulse to break with the past.

Now that we are in a position to look back on it, the twentieth century can be seen as an age characterised by accelerating bands of such movement, beginning with the tail end of the decadence ethos, taken over by the thematic drive of the symbolists and expressionists; the sudden outbreak of dada prompted by the massive trauma of the First World War, then the breaking wave of surrealism; a backlash of analytical realism led by Piscator and Brecht across the mid century; the jazz culture growing in momentum, fusing with the energies of popular commercial entertainment and leading them towards the activism of the civil rights movement; the civil rights movement spreading into the wider demand for 'liberation' that swept through a whole generation during the 1960s before breaking up into the new decadence of hippie culture; the onslaught of punk, over in a flash but with an aftermath that still resonates; postmodernism capturing the agenda with an initial exhilaration that soon lost itself in the confusions of excessive debate; hip-hop reasserting the power of the street.

'The very notion of modernity', Peter Conrad states at the beginning of his marathon study *Modern Times, Modern Places*, 'refers to that irrevocable breach with the past'. But towards the end of the book he observes that 'to repeat the past, like Beckett's Krapp poring miserably over his tapes, is our only option'.[62] Time and again through the last century, a new movement would stage its own dramatic birth as a claim, over-riding that of all predecessors, to the territory of the present and the future. Such claims require someone to embody them: a figurehead – or several – with a persona that is catalytic, and expressive of the energies from which the culture surge arises. The stage they occupy is the wider public space sometimes referred to as the 'world stage', once reserved for figures of Napoleonic command, but rapidly diversifying through the reach provided by mass media communications. Some, though, have an actual stage as their home territory.

Bob Dylan's capacity for making and taking a stage was demonstrated early on. A fellow student remembers him doing it at teenage parties: 'He was very powerful... You'd go to a party and Bob would get a chair and move right into the centre of the room'. Another describes him as being 'nervous as a cat... energy just flowing'.[63] Greil Marcus witnessed his appearance in a local Joan Baez concert in 1963:

> This person had stepped onto someone else's stage, and while in some ways he seemed as ordinary as any of the people under the tent or the dirt around it, something in his demeanor dared you to pin him down... From the way he sang and the way he moved, you couldn't tell where he was from, where he'd been, or where he was going.

On that occasion, as Dylan sang 'With God on Our Side' he was 'retelling the story of American history' in a way that brought the present into crackling immediacy.[64] The legend, though, is retrospectively constructed. Dylan entered the contemporary music scene with some faltering moves, and responses to his appearances were very mixed. The recording of a 1960 performance in Minneapolis, according to Paul Williams, 'does not itself suggest the coming of a major artist'.[65]

It was a coming that, when it happened, swept a self conscious teenage poseur who had seemed, in the view of Irish singer Liam Clancy, 'totally blank' and 'ready to suck up everything that came within his range' into prophetic authority as the voice of his generation.[66] There were both circumstantial and intrinsic factors at issue here. Howard Sounes in his biography of Dylan marks the transformation point as the summer of 1962, when the civil rights movement escalated in response to the imprisonment of Martin Luther King, and the Cuban missile crisis prompted widespread anxiety about the imminence of nuclear war. Dylan wrote 'A Hard Rain's A-Gonna Fall' and performed it live at the Gaslight Club in New York. As Sounes comments, 'the apotheosis of Bob Dylan had begun'.[67] Or, in Dylan's own words, 'America was changing. I had a feeling of destiny and I was riding the changes... My consciousness was beginning to change, too, change and stretch'.[68]

During this time, he was quite literally finding his voice, a development from what Williams calls the 'weird Okie voice' he had experimented with while still at school. It was not the voice of a young man. Watching the visual recordings of the early performances in Martin Scorsese's *No Direction Home*, where they are juxtaposed with the speaking image of Dylan at sixty, I am struck by the discrepancy between the young Dylan's voice and his face. In its pitch and tenor, the singing voice seems to carry a weight of experience and the songs themselves are loaded with an almost preternatural sense of knowing. They are dramatic monologues: narratives, lyric complaints, tirades, sermons and prophecies. Learning to manage this voice may have had as much to do with his 'apotheosis' as any circumstantial events in the world. 'I wrote the songs to perform the songs', says the older Dylan in Scorsese's film.[69] In Dylan's own renditions, dramatic interpretation dominates the tempo and the melody of the songs; he uses repetition – both verbal and melodic – to create variation, so that their unfolding is improvised line by line with a fresh interpretative attack. This is what sets him apart from the leading pop singers of his generation, and displays his affiliation with blues and folk traditions. It is also what has kept him connected, throughout his career, to live audiences as his primary orientation, since this is where the impromptu energy is generated:

> I never promised anybody anything. I used to get up on the stage when I first began playing concerts, and not even know what I was going to do. I used to just walk in from the streets. Anything could happen.[70]

If he began to produce the voice of the times, it was because he knew how to use the tip of the moment in live performance. Greil Marcus experienced the singing of 'With God on Our Side' as 'one of those uncanny performances, in which the whole of what is happening comes through instantly and irrevocably'.[71] But this might be to do with specific forms of performance mastery. Like most of Dylan's songs from this period, this one has a simple rhythmic shape (the melody is traditional) with short rhyming stanzas and a chorus that repeats like a slogan. In live delivery, Dylan uses this to find unexpected tone colours and attitudes, stretching the tempo this way and that to set the repeating lines and rhythms on a continually changing edge. When he sings it in duet with Joan Baez at the 1963 Newport Festival, you can see him forced to pull it back into the melodic shape she excels at and embellishes, and this turns it into an anthem. At that point, the anthem is what the crowd wants. They want Dylan to give them 'We Shall Overcome' in multiplying variants, but the prophesy is in the dramatic monologues.

Dylan exhibited Nijinsky's propensity for both capturing the spirit of the times and going against the grain of popular taste. Whatever was dictating his next move, it was not the wave of adulation that had greeted him at Newport, or the idealistic convictions that gave rise to the wave, and he paid a price for resisting that overwhelming collective momentum. There were the boos and heckles that greeted his move to electric instruments, the incessant challenges from journalists and commentators about his renegade behaviour, and the massive intrusions on his private life from myth-hunters who refused to admit that the scent had gone cold. In his autobiography *Chronicles* he indulges in some rhetorical frustration over all this, but at the same time suggests that something was indeed dictating his moves, something that crossed the *Zeitgeist* with particular kinds of musical chemistry.

Evidently his sense of the times, far from being an echo of what was surging up in the collective mood of his generation, was drawn from deep tradition. The arrow pointing at the future was drawn from a very long bow. He makes allusion to reading *Beyond Good and Evil*, where 'Nietzsche talks about feeling old at the beginning of his life… I felt like that too'.[72] Some of the most remarkable passages in *Chronicles* are those describing his time in New Orleans working on the album *Oh Mercy* in 1989. This is a city where the spirit empire reigns:

> The past doesn't pass away so quickly here. You could be dead for a long time. The ghosts race towards the light, you can almost hear the heavy breathing – spirits, all determined to get somewhere. New Orleans, unlike a lot of those places you go back to and that don't have the magic any more, has still got it.[73]

For Dylan the past is a continuing drama. His relationship to it is not the arid repetition Peter Conrad sees as the curse of late modernity; rather it serves as an ever-firing catalyst for new directions, providing epiphanies just when his creative pulse seems to have flatlined.

At one such time, when, as he says, 'my own songs had become strangers to me, I didn't have the skill to touch their raw nerves', he walked past the door of a tiny bar and 'something was calling me to come in'. A jazz singer was performing, an older man who sang with a natural power:

> Suddenly and without warning, it was like this guy had an open window to my soul. It was like he was saying, 'You should do it this way.' All of a sudden, I understood something faster than I ever did before. I could feel how he worked at getting his power, what he was doing to get at it.

Dylan refers to a 'technique' he rediscovers from this experience, but the way he describes it, the resulting effect is more like the cracking of an arcanum:

> I had a premonition something would happen. At first it was hard going, like drilling through a brick wall. All I did was taste the dust. But then, miraculously, something internal came unhinged... now I knew I could perform any of these songs without them having to be restricted to the world of words.

From here, Dylan takes off into an account of his art as if it were that of a necromancer: 'I conjured up some different type of mechanism to jump-start the other techniques... cast my own spell to drive out the devil... everything came back and it came back in multidimension... Immediately I was flying high'.[74]

Somehow the voice of this narrative remains that of the dramatic monologue, trying on visions and expressions to see where they might go, keeping just enough dry parody in the mix to rescue it from portentousness. He writes of hypnotism and self hypnotism, of 'incantation' and 'manifest presence', all in the tone of a man spinning a yarn in a bar.[75] Dylan converts the prophetic voice into something so familiar it is hard to accept you can't continue it in your own head. In performance, though, it is hard to sustain and precarious to attempt. Is it a matter of remaining true to some kind of inspiration? Or of practising a technique that releases a natural power? Or is it to do with the *Zeitgeist* itself, and the strength of the current released from tapping into it? It is of course all these things, but the balance alters with each performance and can be lost at any time. The performer has no control over the manifest presence of the times, which is at once the most potent and least predictable element in the mix.

After writing at length about the volatile process of trying to find the songs again through his collaboration with the New Orleans based producer Daniel Lanois, Dylan makes an admission that the times have passed on, and the songs they once delivered are elsewhere:

> I couldn't get to those kinds of songs for him or for anyone else. To do it, you've got to have power and dominion over the spirits. I had done it once, and once was enough. Someone would come along eventually who would have it

again – someone who could see into things, the truth of things – not metaphorically either – but really see, like seeing into metal and making it melt...[76]

Earlier in the book, he admits that he once read Albertus Magnus, but is dismissive about him. 'Magnus seemed like a guy who couldn't sleep'. All the same, he seems to have crept into Dylan's consciousness and found a niche there from which to feed out the alchemical talk. There is more than a little of the magus in Dylan.

As for his successor as the laureate of 'the times', he or she never really arrived. Not that there weren't others who came forward to take the world stage and give it a good shaking: he himself names Ice T, and there was also Tupac, or in another cultural dimension John Lydon aka Johnny Rotten, who surely had one of the worst voices ever heard on a stage. The times that spoke through him were rude and epileptic.

England in the mid 1970s was 'repressed and horrible' in the summation of John Savage, whose chronicle *England's Dreaming* remains the best analysis of the punk movement.[77] For those who grew up in the new post-war high rise blocks of west London, material poverty was less of an affliction than the grinding banality of the way of life offered to them. Theirs was a world whose tedium even Beckett missed, precisely because it *did* contain all those things Clov announced there were no more of. High rise dwellers did not 'go without' in the way that their slum-dwelling parents and grandparents probably had. In general, they did not lack for biscuits, bicycle wheels, pain killer, coffins – or even teeth and eyesight, thanks to the new National Health System – but the problem was that these had become the defining elements of their existence.

Against this backdrop, there was a sudden outbreak of theatricality. It was fomented in the art schools, though it did not take the aesthetic guise of bohemian precedents. To begin with it was costume-based but the dandies of the punk movement had found an anti-aesthetic, defined through rejection of all the poetic affectations of the hippy movement and the 1960s fashion world. Instead of lace and crochet, there were rubber t-shirts; wide velvet pants gave way to drain pipe jeans, worn with brothel creepers that would have sent a shiver up the spine of any cowboy-booted rockstar; dangling jewellery was replaced by skewers, typically in the form of large safety pins, worn through earlobes and any other folds of soft flesh. In the tradition of avant-garde break-outs, punks attacked bourgeois respectability but their hatred of that was subordinate to their contempt for the hippies, with all their idealism and their artistic pretensions.

The scene was set before Johnny Rotten made his entry, with a lethal instinct for the kind of voice required to galvanise the action. 'The kids want misery and death', he said, 'they want threatening noises, because that shakes you out of your apathy'.[78] What was required was an assault on the nervous system, but no-one had yet come up with a way to deliver it on a satisfying scale, as an onslaught on the country at large. There was a vacancy at the microphone.

In spite of the upfront call for threatening noises, for the expression of anger and hatred, and in spite of the various exercises in mayhem being conducted around the venues that were the punks' headquarters, no-one knew quite what had hit them when Rotten took the stage. The killer stare (supposed to be the consequence of a childhood bout of meningitis) and the facial expression of a psychotic rodent were offset by a hunchback stance borrowed from Olivier's film performance as Richard III. And when the mouth opened, what came out was full-throttle, toneless yelling. The effect, according to a journalist from *Record Mirror*, was 'about as subtle as a sawn-off shot-gun'.[79]

As a performer, John Lydon had only one register and that was extreme. Any trained singer or actor knows the need for techniques of conserving and modulating energy, for building and maintaining intensity. Lydon apparently had no techniques at all. The assault he mounted from the stage must have had a brutal impact on his own nervous system, not to mention his vocal chords, which appeared to be strung through right to the fists that grasped the microphone.

Lydon's story is the genius myth in reverse. Every telling of it (and there are many contesting versions) stresses the fact that he and the Sex Pistols were aiming at nothing but chaos. It was the declared intention of Malcom McLaren, their manager, that they 'were going to be obnoxious'. Their first concert appearance at St Martin's College was cut short when the stage manager unplugged them. 'They were bloody awful', he testified later.[80] Lydon was brought in as the lead singer after a late night karaoke style audition to the accompaniment of the juke box in Vivienne Westwood's shop at 430 King's Road, because he had the right look and attitude about him. As Johnny Rotten's anthems and the group's agenda of 'Anarchy in the UK' began to hit the headlines, the tabloid response ratcheted up. To cry chaos was outrage enough, but to do it in a toneless voice at top volume, wearing a moth-eaten jumper, was explosive. Concerns were raised at local government level, and a member of the Greater London Council let rip, declaring that the whole phenomenon was nauseating and the group would be 'vastly improved by sudden death'.[81]

Where most of the analyses in this book are concerned with the intricate – and integral – relationship between stage presence and performance skills of an exceptional order, the case of Johnny Rotten might prompt the question of whether it is possible to make a major impact as a presence on stage with no talent. Amongst actors and those concerned with the actor's art, debate moves back and forth through the ages over the question of control. Is the actor an agent or a mere conduit? A mesmerist or a hypnotic subject? When some power is being channelled – whether it is understood as the power of the gods, the elements or of human passions – is the actor in control of this or under its sway? It would be easy to contribute to this debate with a suggestion that stage presence is essentially a quality of control, an attribute of the player who commands, controls and directs forces. Someone who is at the mercy of these forces might make a lot of sound and fury, but would have little impact as a presence. So, at least, runs one line of an enduring argument amongst theorists of acting and performance, yet there is no doubt of the catalytic effect Rotten had on audiences.

'One of the greatest dangers threatening the actor is, of course, lack of discipline, chaos', Grotowski warned. 'One cannot express oneself through anarchy'.[82] Rotten may have proved him wrong. In Caroline Coon's view, what he was doing was 'dramatizing rage'.[83] He was the materialisation of something feared throughout the history of western acting: total abandon on stage, the rule of the passions, and the worst passions at that. Rotten letting rip in 'Anarchy in the UK' was a calling into presence of human nature stripped of all civilising influence. When Edward Gordon Craig made his call for the replacement of the human player by the über-marionette, he characterised the actor as a vehicle for pandemonium, a being possessed:

> ...he moves as one in a frantic dream, or as one distraught, swaying here and there; his head, his arms, his feet, if not utterly beyond control, are so weak to stand against the torrent of his passions, that they are ready to play him false at any moment... As with the movement, so it is with the expression of his face... Instantly, like lightning, and before the mind has had time to cry out and protest, the

hot passion has mastered the actor's expression... It is the same with his voice as it is with his movements. Emotion cracks the voice of the actor. It sways his voice to join in the conspiracy against his mind.[84]

A Sex Pistols concert would have been beyond Gordon Craig's imagining, yet the description here fits the Johnny Rotten phenomenon quite well.

Except that it *is* a style, consciously cultivated, and the conspiracy theory of the passions as assassins of the mind doesn't quite wash. The Rotten persona was held on a knife-edge balance: it was both a conscious, decided act and an outbreak of uncontrollable pandemonium from which he was himself at risk to life and limb. He cried havoc and unleashed the dogs of a ferocious culture war, but the cry and the unleashing were fully premeditated. The 'no talent' myth is just that. Photographs of Johnny Rotten at the time provide enduring evidence of an extraordinary sense of image. If the 'look' owes something to the accident of childhood meningitis, this does not explain it away, or account for how this particular figure immediately captures the attention over everyone else around him. It is a look that belongs to a persona, and a persona that is born of a particular kind of energy charge. When Lydon/Rotten took the stage, he did so with an attack that belies his apparent lack of technique. Who else could deliver 'Anarchy in the UK' or 'Pretty Vacant' with the unrelenting force and pile-drive rhythm he commanded?

Presence is often bound up with paradox, a holding together of contraries, as if the one who embodies it is a convergence point for opposing forces. An alchemist would have understood this also as a switching point, the *coniunctio oppositorum*, through which transformation occurred. Even as I write this, I envisage Rotten's stage face twisting itself in contempt. He is no magus, but a hard-headed social realist with all the savagery of the underdog to fuel his determinations. His is a presence that, like Dylan's, captures a cultural turning point. But where Dylan is associated with larger power shifts and with realignments that have metaphysical resonances, Rotten is a gunpowder apparition who occupies a flashpoint, gone almost as soon as it appears, yet leaving a burning after-image.

A term as loaded and as nebulous as 'presence' can be a way of labelling whatever we most value in performance but, like the medium of theatre itself, it should be taste proof. For anyone who has steeped themselves in the transforming atmosphere of holy theatre, it is easy to denigrate the raw talent that walks in off the street in a filthy mood. It is easy to look to the east, and find a deep centre of gravity in some unbroken tradition which can still command the present moment, as American philosopher William Segal conveys in his luminous description of the entry of a Noh actor:

> This slowly moving figure produced a vibration that seemed to speak to each one in the audience. One could not escape the fact of being present to something different from our ordinary existence, a change in the conditions that were a result of the being of the player. Time was surely being examined in front of our eyes.[85]

The movement is not always slow and the vibration not all low, but something like this account might be given of exceptional performers from western traditions across the spectrum from the holy to the rough theatre, the classical to the vaudeville.

NOTES

INTRODUCTION

1 Patrice Pavis, *Dictionnaire du Théâtre* (Paris: Messidor, 1987), 301.
2 Arianna Stassinopoulos, *Maria Callas* (London: Arena, 1985), 10.
3 Simon Callow, *Being an Actor* (London: Vintage, 2004), 6–7.
4 Bob Dylan, *Chronicles*, Vol. I (New York: Simon and Schuster, 2004), 44.
5 Antonin Artaud, 'The Alchemical Theatre', in *The Theatre and its Double*, trans. Mary Caroline Richards (New York: Grove Press, 1981), 48–52.
6 Antonin Artaud, 'Metaphysics and the Mise en Scène', in Richards, 46–7.
7 Edward Gordon Craig, 'The Actor and the Über-marionette', in *On The Art of the Theatre* (London: Heinemann, 1912), 92.
8 Ibid., 70.
9 Paul Valéry, 'La Conquète de l'ubiquité', quoted in Walter Benjamin, 'The Work of Art in the Age of Mechanical Reproduction', in *Illuminations*, ed. Hannah Arendt (New York, Schocken Books, 1968), 217.
10 Benjamin, 218, 220–1.
11 Martin Heidegger, 'The Turning', in *The Question Concerning Technology and Other Essays*, trans. William Lovitt (New York: Harper and Row, 1977), 37.
12 Jacques Derrida, *Of Grammatology*, trans. Gayatri Chakravorty Spivak (Baltimore: Johns Hopkins University Press, 1974), Chapter 2.
13 Philip Auslander, *From Acting to Performance* (London: Routledge, 1997), 63.
14 Joseph Roach, 'It', *Theatre Journal* 56 (2004), 559.
15 Colley Cibber, *An Apology for the Life of Colley Cibber* (London: R. Dodsley, 1750), 88.
16 Philip Auslander, *From Acting to Performance* (London: Routledge, 1997).
17 Joseph Roach, *It* (Michigan: University of Michigan Press, 2007).
18 George Christoph Lichtenberg, in Philip Highfill, Jr, Kalman A. Burnim and Edward A. Langhans, eds, *A Biographical Dictionary of Actors, Actresses, Musicians, Dancers, Managers and Other Stage Personnel in London, 1660–1800*, Vol. 6 (Carbondale and Edwardsville: Southern Illinois University Press, 1978), 69.

NOTES

19 Giordano Bruno, *De la causa*, quoted in Frances Yates, *Giordano Bruno and the Hermetic Tradition* (London: Routledge, 2002), 321.
20 'Presence, n.' *The Shorter Oxford English Dictionary* (third edition), ed. G.W.S. Friedrichsen (Oxford: Clarendon Press, 1973), 1659.
21 Yates, 180.
22 Patrice Pavis, *Dictionnaire du Théâtre* (Paris: Messidor, 1987), 301–2.
23 Constantin Stanislavski, *An Actor Prepares*, trans. Elizabeth Reynolds Hapgood (Harmondsworth: Penguin, 1967), 22, 38, 232.
24 Stanislavski, 234, 252, 266.
25 Michel Saint-Denis, *Training for the Theatre*, ed. Suria Saint-Denis (London: Heinemann, 1982), 35.
26 Simon Callow, Foreword to Michael Chekhov, *To the Actor* (London: Routledge, 2002), xxii.
27 Joseph Chaikin, *The Presence of the Actor* (New York: Theatre Communications Group, 1991), 1.
28 Cibber, quoted in Roach, 82.
29 Joseph Roach, *Cities of the Dead: Circum-Atlantic Performance* (New York: Columbia University Press, 1996), 76. 'Mimic State' is Charles Gildon's expression.
30 Roach, 73 and 76.
31 George Farquhar, quoted in Roach, 80.
32 William Gilbert, *De Magnete*, trans. P. Fleury Mottelay (New York: Dover, 1958), xlviii.
33 Johann Wolfgang von Goethe, 'Rules for Actors', recorded by Pius Alexander Wolff and Karl Franz Grüner, in A.M. Nagler, ed., *A Sourcebook in Theatrical History* (New York: Dover, 1959), 432.
34 Julie Holledge, email interview, 6 June 2007.

1 THE SUPREME ATTRIBUTE

1 Joseph Roach, 'It', *Theatre Journal* 56 (2004), 555.
2 Roach, 562, 567.
3 Colley Cibber, *An Apology for the Life of Colley Cibber* (London: R. Dodsley, 1750), 88.
4 Simon Callow, interview with Carol Zucker in Carol Zucker, *In the Company of Actors* (London: A & C Black, 1999), 32.
5 Peter Brook, *The Empty Space* (Harmondsworth: Penguin, 1979), 33–4.
6 Jane Lapotaire in Zucker (1999), 79–80.
7 Johann Wolfgang von Goethe, 'Rules for Actors', recorded by Pius Alexander Wolff and Karl Franz Grüner, in A.M. Nagler, ed., *A Sourcebook in Theatrical History* (New York: Dover, 1959), 432.
8 Eugenio Barba, *Dictionary of Theatre Anthropology* (London: Routledge, 1991), 74–94.
9 Barba, 79.
10 Barba, 94.
11 Julie Holledge, email correspondence with Jane Goodall, 6 July 2007.
12 Charles Gildon, *The Life of Thomas Betterton, the Last Eminent Tragedian* (London: Robert Gosling, 1710), 52.

13 Janet Suzman, in Zucker (1999), 207.
14 Jean-Paul Ryngaert, quoted in Pavis, 301.
15 Pol Polletier's Six Laws were demonstrated in a workshop at York University in November 1998 and reported in *The York University Gazette*, vol. 29, no. 11, 18 November, 1998.
16 Michael Chekhov, *To the Actor* (London: Routledge, 2002), 7–12.
17 Lincoln Kirstein, *Thirty Years of the New York City Ballet* (London: Adam & Charles Black, 1979), 259.
18 Robert Lindsey, Introduction to Brando, viii.
19 Guy Brown, *The Energy of Life* (London: Flamingo, 2000), 87.
20 Peter Brook, *The Shifting Point, 1946–1987* (New York: Harper and Row, 1987), 231.
21 Michael Kustow, *Peter Brook, a Biography* (London: Bloomsbury, 2005), 664.
22 Brown, 89.
23 Brook, *The Empty Space*, 50, 63.
24 Plotinus, *Ennead* IV, 3, xi, quoted in Frances Yates, *Giordano Bruno and the Hermetic Tradition* (London: Routledge, 2002), 68–9.
25 Dio of Prusa, quoted in Walter Burkert, *Ancient Mystery Cults* (Cambridge, Massachusetts: Harvard University Press, 1987), 83.
26 Burkert, 89.
27 Marvin W. Meyer, ed., *The Ancient Mysteries* (San Francisco: Harper and Row, 1987), 18.
28 Hippolytus, *Refutation of all Heresies*, paraphrased in Meyer, 19.
29 Burkert, 93.
30 Plutarch, quoted in Burkert, 91.
31 Meyer, 7–8.
32 Eliphas Levi, *The History of Magic*, trans. A.E. Waite, London: Rider, 1988), 122.
33 Levi, 34.
34 David Garrick, Letter to Mr. Powell, 12 December 1764, in Toby Cole and Helen Crich Chinoy, *Actors on Acting* (New York: Crown Publishers, 1970), 137.
35 William Hazlitt, [1816] 'A View of the English Stage', *The Complete Works of William Hazlitt*, vol. V, ed. P.P. Howe (London: Dent, 1930), 312.
36 Penrhyn Stanley, quoted in Rachel M. Brownstein, *The Tragic Muse: Rachel of the Comédie Française* (New York: Alfred A. Knopf, 1993), 187–8.
37 Nina Auerbach, *Private Theatricals: the Lives of the Victorians* (Cambridge, Massachusetts: Harvard, 1990), 78.
38 Geoffrey Whitworth, quoted in Richard Buckle, *Nijinksy* (Harmondsworth: Penguin, 1980), 96.
39 Rolf Lieberman, tribute to Maria Callas, quoted in Arianna Stassinopoulos, *Maria Callas* (London: Arena, 1980), 400.
40 Harold Hobson, quoted in Michael Billington, 'Bringing Magic to the Stage', *The Telegraph Sunday Magazine,* 14 February 1982; Ian McKellan, 'I Always Wanted to be on Broadway', *The New York Times*, 27 September 1981.

41 Kenneth Tynan, *A View of the English Stage* (St Alban's: Paladin, 1976), 27–8.
42 Tynan, 15, 17.
43 Antonin Artaud, 'The Alchemical Theatre', in *The Theatre and its Double*, trans. Mary Caroline Richards (New York: Grove Press, 1981), 52.
44 I have discussed this more fully in Jane Goodall, *Artaud and the Gnostic Drama* (Oxford: Oxford University Press, 1994), chapter 1, 20–47.
45 Anna de Noailles, quoted in Derek Parker, *Nijinsky: God of Dance* (London: Equation, 1988), 63.
46 Laurence Olivier, interview with Kenneth Tynan, reprinted in *Actors on Acting*, 410.
47 Marlon Brando, *Songs My Mother Taught Me* (New York: Random House, 1994), 147, 83, 21.
48 Brando, 211.
49 Edward Gordon Craig, 'The Actor and the Über-marionette', in *On The Art of the Theatre* (London: Heinemann, 1912), 86.
50 Craig, 86.
51 Brook, *The Empty Space*, 67–8.
52 Kustow, 211.
53 Ibid., 71–2.
54 Ted Hughes, quoted in John Heilpern, *Conference of the Birds: The Story of Peter Brook in Africa* (Harmondsworth: Penguin, 1979), 26.
55 Ted Hughes, interview with Tom Stoppard, quoted in Kustow, 207.
56 Peter Brook, preface to Jerzy Grotowski, *Towards a Poor Theatre*, ed. Eugenio Barba (London: Methuen, 1975), 11.
57 Ibid., 34.
58 Ibid., 23, 35.
59 Ibid., 52–3.
60 Josef Kelera, review of *The Constant Prince*, 11 October 1965, reprinted in Grotowski, 64–5.
61 Franz Marijnen, notes printed in Grotowski, 161.
62 Grotowski, 18.
63 Franco Ruffini, 'The Dilated Mind', in Eugenio Barba and Nicola Savarese, *The Secret Art of the Performer: a Dictionary of Theatre Anthropology* (London: Routledge, 1991), 64.
64 Grotowski, 16.
65 Stanislavski, 20–21.
66 Callow, 69.
67 Anthony Sher, in Zucker (1999), 172.
68 Norman Mailer, *The Spooky Art* (New York: Random House, 2004), 202–4.
69 Mailer, 205.
70 Holledge, op. cit.
71 Janet Suzman, in Zucker (1999), 207.
72 Ian Richardson, in Zucker (1999), 131–2.
73 Barba, 64.

74 Constantin Stanislavski, 'Direction and Acting', in Toby Cole, ed., *Acting: A Handbook of the Stanislavski Method* (New York: Crown, 1975), 32.
75 Christine Gledhill, 'Signs of Melodrama', in Christine Gledhill, ed., *Stardom: Industry of Desire* (London: Routledge, 1991), 224.
76 Carole Zucker, *Figures of Light: Actors and Directors Illuminate the Art of Film Acting* (New York: Plenum, 1995), 4–5.
77 Dustin Hoffman, interview with Mitch Tuchman in Bert Cardullo, Harry Geduld, Ronald Gottesman and Leigh Woods, eds, *Playing to the Camera: Film Actors Discuss Their Craft* (New Haven: Yale University Press, 1998), 300.
78 Max Weber, *Theory of Social and Economic Organization*, in S. Eisenstadt, ed., *Max Weber on Charisma and Institution Building* (Chicago: Chicago University Press, 1968), 48.
79 Charles Lindholm, *Charisma* (Oxford: Blackwell, 1990), 17.
80 Friedrich Nietzsche, *Twilight of the Idols* (Harmondsworth: Penguin, 1977), 97.
81 Lindholm, 5.
82 Ian Kershaw, *Hitler: 1889–1936, Hubris* (London: Penguin, 2001), 280.
83 Ibid., xxvii.
84 Ibid., 148.
85 Ibid., 145–6.
86 Richard Corliss, 'Ol' Man Charisma: Paul Robeson 1898–1976', *Time*, vol. 151, no. 16, 20 April 1998, 7.
87 Charles L. Blockson, 'Melody of freedom: Paul Robeson', in *American Visions: 13.1*, February/March 1998, 14, 15.
88 Martin Duberman, *Paul Robeson, A Biography* (New York: The New Press, 1989), 69.
89 Paul Robeson, *Here I Stand* (Boston: Beacon Press, 1988), 15.
90 Duberman, 126.
91 Duberman, 125.
92 Duberman, 218.

2 DRAWING POWER

1 Jean-Antoine Roucher, 'Les Mois', poème en douze chants (Paris: Quillau, 1779), vol. 1, 318.
2 William Shakespeare, *As You Like It*, Act II, scene 7.
3 Walter Raleigh, quoted in Frederick Turner, *The School of Night*, Corona 4, p. 4. Online text at www.montana.edu/corona/4/school14.html.
4 Turner, 12–13.
5 Sir Kenelm Digby, writing in 1645. Quoted in the Biographical Memoir prefacing P. Fleury de Mottelay's edition of William Gilbert, *De Magnete* (New York: Dover Publications, 1893), xviii.
6 William Shakespeare, *The Tempest*, Act 4, scene 1, l.147–156, Arden edition, ed. Frank Kermode (London: Methuen, 1980), 104.
7 Thomas Hobbes, *Leviathan*, Part I, Chapter X, extract in Scott McMillin, ed., *Restoration and Eighteenth-Century Comedy* (New York: Norton, 1973), 347.

8 Hobbes, 348–9.
9 Jeremy Collier, *A Short View of the English Stage*, extract in McMillin, 398.
10 James Thomas Kirkman, *Memoirs of the Life of Charles Macklin, Esq.*, vol. I (London: 1799), 86.
11 Kirkman, 258.
12 Philip H. Highfill, Jr, Kalman A. Burnim and Edward A. Langhans, *A Biographical Dictionary of Actors, Actresses, Musicians, Dancers, Managers and Other Stage Personnel in London, 1660–1800* (Carbondale and Edwardsville: Southern Illinois University Press, 1978), 77.
13 Colley Cibber, *An Apology for the Life of Colley Cibber* (London: R. Dodsley, 1750), 87.
14 Anon., 'An Excellent Actor', 1615 essay generally attributed to John Webster. Extract printed in *Actors on Acting*, 88. See also Stanley Wells, *Shakespeare and Co.* (London: Allen Lane, 2006), 46.
15 *The Universal Magazine*, 1748, quoted in Patricia Fara, *Newton: The Making of a Genius* (London: Picador, 2002), 2.
16 Fara, *Newton*, 155.
17 Ian McIntyre, *Garrick* (London: Penguin, 1999), 126.
18 William Hazlitt, 'On Actors and Acting', *The Examiner*, 5 January 1818.
19 Quoted in Fara, *Newton*, 154.
20 Immanuel Kant, *The Critique of Judgement* (Oxford: Oxford University Press, 2007), 6.
21 Colley Cibber, 'Apology for his Life', in *Actors on Acting*, 107.
22 David Garrick, letter to Helfrich Peter Sturz, 3 January 1769, in David M. Little and George M. Kahrl, *Letters of David Garrick*, Vol. III (London: Oxford University Press, 1963), 634–5.
23 Catherine Clive, letter to David Garrick, 23 January 1774, in *Actors on Acting*, 139.
24 William Hazlitt, 'The Indian Jugglers', in Jon Cook, ed., *William Hazlitt, Selected Writings* (Oxford: Oxford University Press, 1998), 133.
25 Hazlitt, *Selected Writings*, 34–5.
26 Anonymous writer in *The Laureat* [1740], extract in A.M. Nagler, *A Sourcebook in Theatrical History* (New York: Dover, 1952), 219; Fanny Burney, quoted in McIntyre, 469; Sarah Siddons, 'Remarks on the Character of Lady Macbeth' [1834], in *Actors on Acting*, 144.
27 Hazlitt, 'The Indian Jugglers', 137.
28 William Hazlitt, 'A View of the English Stage' [1816], in *The Complete Works of William Hazlitt*, vol. V, ed. P.P. Howe (London: Dent, 1930), 174.
29 Anonymous writer in *The Occasional Paper*, vol. III, Number 10, 1719.
30 Adam Mickiewicz, quoted in Adam Zamoyski, *Holy Madness: Romantics, Patriots and Revolutionaries, 1776–1871* (London: Pheonix, 1999), 201.
31 Charlotte Brontë, [1853] *Villette* (Harmondsworth: Penguin, 1981), 341.

32 J.L. Heilbron, *Electricity in the 17th and 18th Centuries: A Study in Early Modern Physics* (New York: Dover, 1999), 24, 50, 45.
33 Gilbert, 77, 97–8.
34 Heilbron, 55.
35 Fara, *Newton*, 8.
36 Heilbron, 52.
37 Gilbert, 97.
38 Fara, *Newton*, 78, 86.
39 Cibber, 97.
40 Alexander Carlyle, quoted in McIntyre, 118.
41 Highfill, 18.
42 Letter from Hannah More to James Stonehouse, forwarded to David Garrick on May 21 1774, in *Letters*, vol. III, 1357.
43 Cibber, 186.
44 Gilbert, 91.
45 Patricia Fara, *Fatal Attraction* (London: Icon Books, 2005), 10.
46 Sarah Siddons, lines from an epilogue delivered at Bath in 1782, reprinted in Lewis Melville, *More Stage Favourites of the Eighteenth Century* (London: Hutchinson & Co., 1929), 88.
47 Oscar Wilde, *Phrases and Philosophies for the Use of the Young*, first published in the Oxford student magazine *Chameleon*, December 1894.
48 Leonard Digges, Preface to the 1640 First Folio of William Shakespeare, quoted in Wells, 14.
49 Isaac Newton, *Correspondence*, vol. 1, quoted in Heilbron, 4.
50 *Actors on Acting*, 84.
51 William Shakespeare, *Hamlet*, Act 3, scene 2, Arden edition, ed. Harold Jenkins (London: Methuen, 1982), 287.
52 David Garrick, letter to William Powell, 12 December 1764, in *Actors on Acting*, 136.
53 David Garrick, 'An Essay on Acting' (1744), in *Actors on Acting*, 135.
54 Ibid., 135.
55 Ibid., 133–5.
56 René Descartes, 'The Passions of the Soul' [1649], in John Cottingham, Robert Stoothoff and Dugald Murdoch, eds, *Descartes: Selected Philosophical Writings* (Cambridge: Cambridge University Press, 1988), 218.
57 Descartes, 229.
58 Jessica Riskin, *Science in the Age of Sensibility* (Chicago: The University of Chicago Press, 2002), 2.
59 Riskin, 7.
60 Riskin, 2–3.
61 John Hill, 'The Actor: A Treatise on the Art of Playing' [1750], in *Actors on Acting*, 126.
62 François-Joseph Talma, 'Reflections on the Actor's Art', 1825, translated in 1915 for the Dramatic Museum of Columbia University, available online at Classicaltheatre.com.
63 Joseph R. Roach, *The Player's Passion: Studies in the Science of Acting* (London and Toronto: Associated University Presses, 1985), 27.

NOTES

64 Heilbron, 53–4.
65 'The History of the English Stage', 1741, attributed (probably wrongly) to Betterton, in Nagler, 222.
66 Aaron Hill, 'An Essay on the Art of Acting', in *Actors on Acting*, 117.
67 Ibid., 124.
68 David Garrick, letter to Helfrich Peter Sturz, 3 January 1769, in David Garrick, *Letters*, vol. I (London: Oxford University Press, 1963), 634–5.
69 Newton, 1713 notes, quoted in Heilbron, 240.
70 Heilbron, 28, 267.
71 Handbill for 'Electrical Fire', lectures and experiments by Ebenezer Kinnerly, 16 March 1752, reprinted in Brandon Brame Fortune and Deborah J. Warner, *Franklin and his Friends* (Washington: Smithsonian National Portrait Gallery, 1999), 76.
72 Benjamin Wilson, 'Observations upon Lightning', *Philosophical Transactions*, vol. 63, 1773–54, 50.
73 Recounted by Fara in *An Entertainment for Angels*, 74.
74 Percival Stockdale, *Memoirs* (1809), quoted in McIntyre, 41.
75 The mezzotint is reproduced in Nagler, 366.
76 Garrick, *Letters*, vol. 2, 800; vol. 3, 1189.
77 Thomas Gainsborough, Letter to David Garrick, quoted in McIntyre, 489.
78 Hill, 130.
79 These experiments are widely reported with varying dates and numbers. I have taken the details here from Heilbron, 319–20.
80 Benjamin Wilson, 'Farther Experiments in Electricity', in *Philosophical Transactions*, vol. 51, 1759–1760, 898.
81 Tracy C. Davis, 'Reading Shakespeare by Flashes of Lightning: Challenging the Foundations of Romantic Acting Theory', *English Literary History*, 62.4 (1995), 3.
82 *Memoirs of Charles Macklin*, quoted in Highfill, 69.
83 Thomas Davies, *Memoirs of the life of David Garrick* (London: published by the author, 1784), 46, 49.
84 Davies, 51.
85 Talma, op. cit.
86 Abraham Fleury, *The French Stage and the French People*, extract in Nagler, 300–1.
87 James Ballentyne, quoted in Michael R. Booth, 'Sarah Siddons', in Michael R. Booth, John Stokes and Susan Bassnett, *Three Tragic Actresses* (Cambridge: Cambridge University Press, 1996), 57.
88 Sarah Siddons, extract in Lewis Melville, *More Stage Favourites of the Eighteenth Century* (London: Hutchinson, 1929), 124.
89 Riskin, 77.
90 Henry Nelson Coleridge, *Specimens of the Table Talk of Samuel Taylor Coleridge* (London: John Murray, 1836), 13.
91 William Hazlitt, 'Whether Actors Ought to Sit in the Boxes', from *Table Talk, Essays on Men and Manners*, vol. II (1822), in Duncan Wu, ed., *The Selected Writings of William Hazlitt*, vol. 6 (London: Pickering and Chatto, 1998), 249.

3 MESMERISM

1 Charlotte Brontë, letter to Sydney Dobell, 28 June 1851, in Margaret Smith, ed., *The Letters of Charlotte Brontë*, vol. 2, 1848–1851 (Oxford: Clarendon Press, 2000), 652.
2 Alexander Herzen, *The Other Shore*, trans. Richard Wollheim (Oxford: Oxford University Press, 1979), 145.
3 Jules Janin, quoted in Philip Mansel, *Paris Between the Empires, 1814–1852* (London: John Murray, 2001), 384.
4 Herzen, *From the Other Shore*, 43.
5 Jules Janin, *Rachel et la Tragédie* (Paris: Adolphe Delahays, 1864), 48.
6 Janin, 469.
7 Robert Darnton, *Mesmerism and the End of the Enlightenment in France* (Cambridge, Massachusetts: Harvard University Press, 1968), 40.
8 Jean-Sylvain Bailly, *Exposé des experiences qui ont été faites pour l'examen du magnétisme animal*, 1784, quoted in Riskin, 189.
9 Adam Zamoyski, *Holy Madness: Romantics, Patriots and Revolutionaries 1776–1871* (London: Phoenix, 1999), 159.
10 George du Maurier, *Trilby* (Oxford: Oxford University Press, 1998), 23.
11 Du Maurier, 27.
12 Anonymous verse, quoted in Darnton, 22. (My translation.)
13 Derek Forrest, *Hypnotism: A History* (London: Penguin, 1999), 45.
14 Joseph Priestley, *The History and Present State of Electricity*, part II, Third Edition (London: Bathurst and Lowndes, 1775), 16.
15 Darnton, 47.
16 Eliphas Levi, *The History of Magic* [1860], trans. A.E. Waite (London: Rider, 1982), 293.
17 Levi, 66.
18 Forrest, 79.
19 A.E. Waite, introduction to Levi, *The History of Magic*, 29.
20 Levi, 44, 292.
21 Stephen Connor, *Dumbstruck: A Cultural History of Ventriloquism* (Oxford: Oxford University Press, 2000), 13.
22 *Actors on Acting*, 174.
23 Véron, quoted in Nina H. Kennard, *Rachel* (London: W.H. Allen, 1885), 31. 3
24 Edwin Forrest, quoted in Kennard, 20.
25 Charlotte Brontë, letter to Ellen Nussey, 24 June 1851, in Margaret Smith, ed., *The Letters of Charlotte Brontë*, vol. 2, 1848–1851 (Oxford: Clarendon Press, 2000), 648.
26 David Leeming, *The Oxford Companion to World Mythology* (New York: Oxford University Press, 2005), 23.
27 Ibid.
28 Philip Scaff, ed., *Saint Chrysostom: Homilies on the Epistles of Paul to the Corinthians* (Edinburgh: T&T Clark, 1889), 7.
29 Connor, 74.
30 Virgil, *The Aeneid*, Book Six, lines 47–50, quoted in Connor, 60.
31 Janin, 54.

32 Ibid., 59.
33 Ibid., 64.
34 Ibid., 45.
35 Ibid., 66, 53.
36 Kennard, 42. The story is also recounted in 'Rachel', *Harper's New Monthly Magazine*, vol. 11, no. 65, 1 October 1855.
37 George Henry Lewes, *On Actors and the Art of Acting* (New York: Grove Press, 1957), 31–3.
38 Rachel M. Brownstein, *The Tragic Muse: Rachel of the Comédie Française* (New York: Alfred A. Knopf, 1993), 40.
39 Charlotte Brontë [1853], *Villette* (Harmondsworth: Penguin, 1981), 307.
40 Brontë, *Villette*, 339.
41 Mary Shelley, *Frankenstein* (Oxford: Oxford University Press, 1993), 30–1.
42 Peter Ackroyd, *Dickens* (London: Vintage, 1999), 258–9, 470.
43 Laurence Irving, *Henry Irving: The Actor and his World* (London: Columbus Books, 1989), 39, 41.
44 Irving, 171.
45 Bram Stoker, *Personal Reminiscences of Henry Irving* (London: William Heinemann, 1906), 29–31.
46 Bram Stoker, *Dracula*, ed. Glennis Byron (Ontario: Broadview Press, 1998), 49.
47 Barbara Belford, *Bram Stoker* (London: Phoenix, 1997), 4.
48 Stoker, *Henry Irving*, 55–6.
49 Stoker, *Dracula*, 70, 346.
50 Edward Gordon Craig, *Henry Irving* (London: Dent, 1930), 59.
51 Craig, *Henry Irving*, 60.
52 Edward Gordon Craig, *On the Art of Theatre* (London: Heinemann, 1912), 264.
53 Rainer Maria Rilke, extract in Ulrich Baer, *The Poet's Guide to Life: the Wisdom of Rilke*, trans. Ulrich Baer (New York: The Modern Library, 2005), 20.
54 James Agate, contribution in H.A. Sainsbury and Cecil Palmer, eds, *We Saw him Act: A Symposium on the Art of Henry Irving* (London: Hurst and Blackett, 1939), 45.
55 Cornelia Otis Skinner, *Madame Sarah* (London: Michael Joseph, 1967), 291.
56 James T. Boulton, ed., *The Letters of D.H. Lawrence*, vol. I (Cambridge: Cambridge University Press, 1979), 59.
57 Lytton Strachey, *Books and Characters: French and English*, third edition (London: Chatto & Windus, 1924), 23–4.
58 Arthur Symons, *Plays, Acting and Music* (London: Jonanthan Cape, 1928). Online text at http://ia331326.us.archive.org/2/items/playsactingandmu13928gut/132928-8.txt
59 Ellen Terry, quoted in Maurice Baring, *Sarah Bernhardt* (London: Peter Davies, 1933), 25.
60 Arthur Gold and Robert Fizdale, *The Divine Sarah: A Life of Sarah Bernhardt* (London: HarperCollins, 1992), 144–5.
61 Symons, op. cit.

62 Gold and Fizdale, 317.
63 Levi, 292.
64 Friedrich Nietzsche, *Ecce Homo*, trans. R.J. Hollingdale (Harmondsworth: Penguin, 1979), 77.
65 Nietzsche, *Ecce Homo*, 102, 73.
66 Ibid., 104.
67 Oscar Wilde, letter to Leonard Smithers, 2 September 1900, in Rupert Hart-Davis, ed., *The Letters of Oscar Wilde* (London: Rupert Hart-Davis, 1962), 834.
68 Richard Buckle, *Diaghilev* (New York: Atheneum, 1979), 87.
69 Bronislava Nijinska, *Early Memoirs*, trans. Irina Nijinksa and Jean Rawlinson (London: Faber and Faber, 1981), 270.
70 Jean Cocteau, quoted in Richard Buckle, *Nijinksy* (Harmondsworth: Penguin, 1971), 219.
71 Peter F. Ostwald, *Vaslav Nijinsky: A Leap into Madness* (New York, NY: Carol Publication Group, 1991), 14–15.
72 Buckle, *Nijinsky*, 325, 230.
73 Ibid., 337.
74 Ibid., 285.
75 Lincoln Kirstein, *Nijinsky Dancing* (London: Thames and Hudson, 1975), 41.
76 Buckle, 357.
77 Jacques Rivière in Kirstein, 168.
78 Nietzsche, 105.
79 Nietzsche, 45.
80 Nicholas Petsalis-Diomidis, *The Unknown Callas* (New York: Amadeus Press, 2001), 96.
81 Claudia Cassidy, quoted in Arianna Stassinopoulos, *Maria Callas: The Woman Behind the Legend* (London: Arena, 1988), 146.
82 Stassinopoulos, 137.
83 Stassinopoulos, 255–6, 138.

4 DASH AND FLASH

1 Marc J. Seifer, *The Life and Times of Nikola Tesla* (New York: Citadel Books), 85, 89.
2 Nikola Tesla, *My Inventions: the Autobiography of Nikola Tesla,* ed. Ben Johnston (Vermont: Hart Brothers, 1982), 106.
3 Seifer, 51.
4 Tesla, *Autobiography*, 59–60.
5 Nikola Tesla, 'On light and other high frequency phenomena', lecture delivered to the Franklin Institute, Philadelphia, February 1893, in *Nikola Tesla, Lectures, Patents, Articles* (Belgrade: Nikola Tesla Museum, 1956).
6 Ibid., 108.
7 Mary Wollstonecraft Shelley, *Frankenstein or The Modern Prometheus*, ed. James Rieger (Chicago: University of Chicago Press, 1982), 49.
8 James A. Secord, 'Extraordinary Experiment: electricity and the creation of life in Victorian England', in David Gooding, Trevor Pinch

and Simon Schaffer, eds, *The Uses of Experiment* (Cambridge: Cambridge University Press, 1989), 344.

9   Richard Owen, *On the Anatomy of Vertebrates* (London: Longmans, Green, 1868), Vol. III, 819.

10 *The Illustrated London News*, 25 March 1871, 302.

11 Paul Morand, '1900', in *Oeuvres* (Paris: Flammarion, 1981), 351–2.

12 J.E. Crawford Flitch, *Modern Dancing and Dancers* (London: Grant Richards, 1912), 86.

13 Review for *Spirit of the Times*, quoted in Richard Nelson Current and Marcia Ewing Current, *Loie Fuller: Goddess of Light* (Boston: Northeastern University Press, 1997), 35.

14 Richard and Paulette Ziegfeld, *The Ziegfeld Touch: the Life and Times of Florenz Ziegfeld Jr.* (New York: Harry N. Abrams, 1993), 217–73.

15 Ean Wood, *The Josephine Baker Story* (London: Sanctuary, 2000), 249.

16 Wood, 89.

17 Josephine Baker and Jo Bouillon, *Josephine* (Paris: Editions Laffont, 1976), 51.

18 Wood, 96.

19 Sacheverell Sitwell, *La Vie Parisienne* (London: Faber and Faber, 1937), 37.

20 Quoted in Petrine Archer-Straw, *Negrophilia: Avant-Garde Paris and Black Culture in the 1920s* (London: Thames and Hudson, 2000), 118.

21 Simon Njami, 'Forward to Benetta Jules-Rosette', *Josephine Baker in Art and Life: the Icon and the Image* (Chicago: University of Illinois Press, 2007), xiv.

22 Baker and Bouillon, 85.

23 Ylva Habel, 'To Stockholm with Love: the Critical Reception of Josephine Baker, 1927–35', in *Film History*, vol. 17, 2005, 125.

24 Habel, 126.

25 Review in *Dagens Nyheter*, quoted in Habel, 128.

26 Correspondence in *Stockholms Dagblad*, ibid., 130.

27 Andrea Stuart, *Showgirls* (London: Jonathan Cape, 1996), 82.

28 Wood, 323 and 337.

29 See Jules-Rosette, *Josephine Baker*, 72–3.

30 Martin Gottfried, *Broadway Musicals* (New York: Harry N. Abrams, 1984), 136.

31 Gottfried, 107.

32 Clive Barnes, 'Chicago Disappoints', review for *The New York Times*, and Douglas Watt, 'Bold and Cynical Chicago', review for *The Daily News*, 4 June 1975, reprinted in Steven Suskin, ed., *More Opening Nights on Broadway* (New York: Schirmer Books, 1997), 168.

33 Suskin, 274.

34 Ibid., 792–3.

35 Ibid., 274–5.

36 Ibid., 791–2.

37 Ibid., 93.

NOTES

38 Peter Brook, *The Empty Space* (Harmondsworth: Penguin, 1979), 73, 75.

39 Scott Michaels and David Evans, *Rocky Horror: From Concept to Cult* (London: Sanctuary, 2002), 16.

40 Martin Aston, 'Scary Monster', in *60 Years of David Bowie*, Mojo Classic, vol. 2, no. 2, 2007, 24.

41 Paul Morley, 'The Best 25 Gigs of all Time', in *The Observer Music Monthly*, 21 January 2007, 35.

42 Mark Paytress, 'Inventing Glam Rock', in *60 Years of David Bowie*, 20.

43 Aston, 25.

44 Peter Holmes, 'Gay Rock', in *Gay News*, July 1972. Online at www.5years.com/gayrock.htm.

45 Chris Welch, 'David Bowie', in *Melody Maker*, 26 August 1972. Online at www.5years.com/DBCW.htm.

46 Alexander Stuart, 'Starman over the Rainbow', *Plays and Players*, November 1972. Online at www.5years.com/playplayers.htm.

47 Anonymous review, 'Caught in the Act', *Melody Maker*, 19 February 1972. Online at www.5years.com/mmfeb19.htm.

48 Don Heckman, 'A Colourful David Bowie', *The New York Times*, 1 October 1972. Online at www.5years.com/heckman72.htm.

49 Robert Hilburn, 'David Bowie Rocks in Santa Monica', *Los Angeles Times*, 23 October 1972. Online at Online at www.5years.com/hilburn72.htm.

50 Shelton Waldrep, *The Aesthetics of Self-Invention: Oscar Wilde to David Bowie* (Minneapolis: University of Minnesota Press, 2004), 108.

51 John Lahr, *Dame Edna Everage and the Rise of Western Civilisation* (London: Flamingo, 1992), 2.

52 Dame Edna, quoted in Lahr, 32–3.

53 Dame Edna Everage, *My Gorgeous Life* (Sydney: Pan Macmillan, 1989), 80–1.

54 Dame Edna Everage, lines from *Back with a Vengeance: the Second Coming*, quoted in Lahr, 176.

55 Ben Brantley, 'A Comic Megastar, Possums, and Don't You Forget it', *The New York Times*, 18 October 1999. Online at http: //theatre2. nytimes.com/.

56 Lahr, 78.

57 Ibid., 179.

58 Ibid., 207.

59 Simon Plant, 'A Gala Spectacle', interview with Barry Humphries in *The Daily Telegraph*, 17 May 2007, 36.

60 John Barber, *The Daily Telegraph*, 11 October 1986.

61 Michael Crawford, *Parcel Arrived Safely: Tied with String. My Autobiography* (London: Century, 1999), 275.

62 Frank Rich, *The New York Times*, 27 January 1988; Michael Billington, *The Guardian*, 11 October 1986; Richard Barkley, *Sunday Express*, 12 October 1986.

63 Michael Coveney, *The Financial Times*, 10 October 1986.

64 Crawford, 274.

65 Frank Rich, *The New York Times*, 27 January 1988.

5 BEING PRESENT

1 Herbert Blau, *Take Up the Bodies* (Urbana: University of Illinois Press, 1982), 2.
2 I have explored this more fully in 'Haunted Places', in Gay McAuley, ed., *Uncertain Ground* (Brussels: Peter Lang, 2006), 111–2.
3 Joseph Chaikin, *The Presence of the Actor* (New York: Theatre Communications Group, 1991), 14.
4 Richard Buckle, *Diaghilev* (New York: Atheneum, 1979), 87.
5 Romola Nijinsky, *Nijinsky* (Harmondsworth: Penguin, 1960), 337.
6 Richard Buckle, *Nijinsky* (Harmondsworth: Penguin, 1980), 494.
7 Joan Acocella, ed., *The Diary of Vaslav Nijinsky*, trans. Kyril FitzLyon (Chicago and Illinois: University of Illinois Press, 2006), 6.
8 F.T. Marinetti, E. Settimelli and B. Corra, from 'The Futurist Synthetic Theatre' (1915), trans. R.W. Flint, in Richard Drain, ed., *Twentieth-Century Theatre: A Sourcebook* (London: Routledge, 1995), 20.
9 Antonin Artaud, preface to *The Theatre and its Double*, trans. Mary Caroline Richards (New York: Grove Press, 1958), 8.
10 Artaud, 'No More Masterpieces', in *The Theatre and its Double*, 80.
11 Artaud, 'The Theatre of Cruelty: First Manifesto', in *The Theatre and its Double*, 91.
12 Bertolt Brecht, 'On Experimental Theatre', trans. John Willett, in Eric Bentley, ed., *The Theory of the Modern Stage* (London: Penguin, 1989), 104.
13 Bertolt Brecht, 'On a Great German Actress', trans. John Berger and Anna Bostock, in Bentley, 105.
14 Helen Weigel, 'Rehearsing the Part', in *Actors on Acting*, 315.
15 Bertolt Brecht, 'On a Great German Actress', 107.
16 Jim Hiley, *Theatre at Work: The Story of the National Theatre's Production of Brecht's 'Galileo'* (London: Routledge, 1981), 10.
17 Hiley, 12, 223.
18 Unattributed review, 'A Virtuoso who Specializes in Everything', *The New York Times*, 23 August 1987.
19 Simon Callow, *Being an Actor* (London: Vintage, 2004), 91.
20 Callow, 91.
21 Ibid., 185.
22 Peter Marks, '*Arturo Ui*: Hail, Hail, the Gang's all Here', *The Washington Post*, 22 October 2002; Brendan Lemon, 'Intelligent Artificiality', *The Financial Times*, London, 25 October 2002; anonymous review, 'Meaty Performances, but the Jokes Wear Thin', *New York Daily News*, 23 October 2002.
23 Ben Brantley, 'Scarface? The Godfather? Nope, It's a Hitlerian Thug', *New York Times*, 22 October 2002. Online at: theater2.nytimes.com/mem/theater/ treview.html.
24 Ibid.
25 Bertolt Brecht, 'A Dialogue about Acting', trans. John Willett, reproduced in Henry Bial, ed., *The Performance Studies Reader* (London: Routledge, 2004), 185.
26 Bertolt Brecht, obituary for Frank Wedekind, quoted in Lisa Appignanesi, *Cabaret: the First Hundred Years* (London: Methuen, 1975), 45.

27 Barry Humphries, 'Sandy's Stone' [1968], in *A Nice Night's Entertainment* (London: Granada, 1982), 109.
28 Barry Humphries, 'Sandy Stone: the Land of the Living' [1971], ibid., 134–5.
29 Chaikin, 36.
30 Samuel Beckett, *Endgame* (London: Faber and Faber, 1973), 35.
31 Blau, 28.
32 Callow, 6–7.
33 Callow, 330, 331.
34 Ibid., 334.
35 Peter Ackroyd, *Dickens* (London: Vintage, 1999), 465.
36 Callow, 184.
37 Chaikin, 40, 62.
38 Samuel Beckett, *Waiting for Godot* (London: Faber and Faber, 1973), 63.
39 Beckett, *Godot*, 89, 47.
40 Samuel Beckett, *Endgame* (London: Faber, 1973), 12.
41 *Waiting for Godot*, 44.
42 Blau, 84.
43 John Fletcher, *About Beckett: the Playwright and the Work* (London: Faber, 2003), 38, 40, 73.
44 Beckett, *Endgame*, 46.
45 Samuel Beckett, 'Worstward Ho', in *Nohow On* (New York: Grove Press, 1996), 113.
46 Samuel Beckett, 'Company', in *Nohow On,* 7 and 11.
47 Also see Jane Goodall, 'Lucky's Energy', in S.E. Gontarski and Anthony Uhlmann, eds, *Beckett After Beckett* (Gainesville: University of Florida Press, 2006), 193.
48 James Knowlson, *Damned to Fame: The Life of Samuel Beckett* (London: Bloomsbury, 1996), 102.
49 Samuel Beckett, *Play* (London: Faber, 1968), 9.
50 Fletcher, 124.
51 Horst Bollmann on 'Beckett as Director', in James and Elizabeth Knowlson, eds, *Beckett Remembering Remembering Beckett* (London: Bloomsbury, 2006), 181.
52 Fletcher, 163.
53 Peter Hall, *Peter Hall's Diaries*, ed. John Goodwin (London: Hamish Hamilton, 1983), 127, 141.
54 Irving Wardle, review of 'Happy Days', *The Times*, 15 March 1975, quoted in Fletcher, 143.
55 Hall, 124.
56 Fletcher, 86–7.
57 Bair, 624–5.
58 Fletcher, 166.
59 Knowlson, 188.
60 Knowlson, 169.
61 Frank Rich, 'A Whitelaw Beckett', *The New York Times*, 17 February 1984.
62 Peter Conrad, *Modern Times, Modern Places* (London: Thames and Hudson, 1998), 7, 714.

63 Howard Sounes, *Down the Highway: the Life of Bob Dylan* (London: Black Swan, 2002), 89.
64 Greil Marcus, *Like a Rolling Stone* (London: Faber & Faber, 2005), 18–19.
65 Paul Williams, *Bob Dylan Performing Artist: 1960–1973* (London: Omnibus Press, 2004), 13.
66 Liam Clancy, quoted in Williams, 9.
67 Sounes, 153–5.
68 Bob Dylan, *Chronicles*, vol. I (New York: Simon and Schuster, 2004), 73.
69 Bob Dylan, interview in Martin Scorsese, dir., *No Direction Home* (Apple and Paramount Pictures, 2005).
70 Bob Dylan, 1965 interview with Allen Stone, quoted in Marcus, 48.
71 Marcus, 19.
72 Dylan, *Chronicles*, 73.
73 Ibid., 180.
74 Ibid., 150–1, 153.
75 Ibid., 161.
76 Ibid., 219.
77 John Savage, *England's Dreaming* (London: Faber and Faber, 1991), 9.
78 Savage, 122.
79 Review in *Record Mirror*, 10 December 1976, quoted in Stephen Cosgrave and Chris Sullivan, *Punk. A Life Apart* (London: Cassell, 2001), 90.
80 John Robb, *Punk Rock: An Oral History* (London: Ebury Press, 2006), 116, 120.
81 Cosgrave and Sullivan, 103.
82 Jerzy Grotowski, *Towards a Poor Theatre* (London: Methuen, 1975), 177.
83 Caroline Coon, interviewed in John Lydon, *Rotten* (New York: Picador, 1994), 77.
84 Edward Gordon Craig, 'The Actor and the Übermarionette', in J. Michael Walton, ed., *Craig on Theatre* (London: Methuen, 1983), 83.
85 William Segal, *A Voice at the Borders of Silence* (Woodstock and New York: Overlook Press, 2003), 225.

BIBLIOGRAPHY

Ackroyd, P. (1999) *Dickens*, London: Vintage.

Acocella, J. (ed.) (2006) *The Diary of Vaslav Nijinsky*, trans. K. FitzLyon, Chicago and Illinois: University of Illinois Press.

Agate, J. (1939) 'Contribution', in H.A. Saintsbury and C. Palmer (eds) *We Saw Him Act: A Symposium on the Art of Henry Irving*, London: Hurst and Blackett.

Anonymous (1972) 'Caught in the act', *Melody Maker*, 19 February. Online. Available www.5years.com/mmfeb19.htm (accessed 19 May 2007)

Anonymous (1719) 'Of Genius', *The Occasional Paper*, III.10.

Anonymous (1740) *The Laureat*, reprinted in A.M. Nagler (ed.) (1952) *A Sourcebook in Theatrical History*, New York: Dover.

Anonymous (2002) 'Meaty performances, but the jokes wear thin', *New York Daily News*, 23 October.

Anonymous (1855) 'Rachel', *Harper's New Monthly Magazine*, 11.65: 681–7.

Anonymous (1987) 'A virtuoso who specializes in everything', *The New York Times*, 23 August.

Appignanesi, L. (1975) *Cabaret: the First Hundred Years*, London: Methuen.

Archer-Straw, P. (2000) *Negrophilia: Avant-Garde Paris and Black Culture in the 1920s*, London: Thames and Hudson.

Artaud, A. (1981) *The Theatre and its Double*, trans. M.C. Richards, New York: Grove Press.

Aston, M. (2007) 'Scary monster', in *60 Years of David Bowie*, Mojo Classic, 2.2: 24.

Auerbach, N. (1990) *Private Theatricals: The Lives of the Victorians*, Cambridge, Mass.: Harvard University Press.

Auslander, P. (1997) *From Acting to Performance*, London: Routledge.

Baer, U. (2005) *The Poet's Guide to Life: the Wisdom of Rilke*, trans. U. Baer, New York: The Modern Library.

Bailly, J.S. (1784) (2000) *Exposé des experiences qui ont été faites pour l'examen du magnétisme animal*, Paris: Imp. Royale; reprinted in J.

Riskin (2000) *Science in the Age of Sensibility*, Chicago: University of Chicago Press.

Baker, J. and Bouillon, J. (1976) *Josephine*, Paris: Editions Laffont.

Barba, E. (1991) *Dictionary of Theatre Anthropology*, London: Routledge.

Baring, M. (1933) *Sarah Bernhardt*, London: Peter Davies.

Barnes, C. (1975) 'Chicago disappoints', *The New York Times*, 4 June; reprinted in S. Suskin (ed.) (1997) *More Opening Nights on Broadway*, New York: Schirmer Books.

Beckett, S. (1968) *Play*, London: Faber.

—— (1973) *Endgame*, London: Faber and Faber.

—— (1973) *Waiting for Godot*, London: Faber and Faber.

—— (1996) 'Worstward Ho', in *Nohow On*, New York: Grove Press.

—— (1996) 'Company', in *Nohow On*, New York: Grove Press.

Belford, B. (1997) *Bram Stoker*, London: Phoenix.

Betterton, T. (attr.) (1741) *The History of the English Stage*, 8 vols, London: printed for E. Curll; reprinted in A.M. Nagler (1952) *A Sourcebook in Theatrical History*, Toronto: Dover.

Billington, M. (1982) 'Bringing magic to the stage', *The Telegraph Sunday Magazine*, 14 February.

Blau, H. (1982) *Take Up the Bodies*, Urbana: University of Illinois Press.

Blockson, C.L. (1998) 'Melody of freedom: Paul Robeson', *American Visions*, 13.1: 14–15.

Bollman, H. (2006) 'Beckett as director', in J. and E. Knowlson (eds) *Beckett Remembering/Remembering Beckett*, London: Bloomsbury.

Booth, M.R. (1996) 'Sarah Siddons', in M.R. Booth, J. Stokes and S. Bassnett, *Three Tragic Actresses*, Cambridge: Cambridge University Press.

Boulton, J.T. (ed.) (1979) *The Letters of D.H. Lawrence*, Vol. I, Cambridge: Cambridge University Press.

Brando, M. (1994) *Songs My Mother Taught Me*, New York: Random House.

Brantley, B. (1999) 'A comic megastar, possums, and don't you forget it', *The New York Times*, 18 October. Online. Available http://theatre2.nytimes.com/ (accessed 2 June 2007).

—— (2002) 'Scarface? The Godfather? Nope, it's a Hitlerian thug', *New York Times*, 22 October. Online. Available http://theater2.nytimes.com/mem/theater/treview.html (accessed 22 April 2007).

Brecht, B. (1989) 'On experimental theatre', trans. J. Willett, in E. Bentley (ed.) *The Theory of the Modern Stage*, London: Penguin.

—— (1989) 'On a great German actress', trans. J. Berger and A. Bostock, in E. Bentley (ed.) *The Theory of the Modern Stage*, London: Penguin.

—— (2004) 'A dialogue about acting', trans. J. Willett, in H. Bial (ed.) *The Performance Studies Reader*, London: Routledge.

Brontë, C. (1981) *Villette*, ed. M. Lilly, Harmondsworth: Penguin.

—— (2000) *The Letters of Charlotte Brontë, Vol. 2, 1848–1851*, ed. M. Smith, Oxford: Clarendon Press.

Brook, P. (1975) 'Preface', in J. Grotowski, *Towards a Poor Theatre*, ed. E. Barba, London: Methuen.
—— (1979) *The Empty Space*, Harmondsworth: Penguin.
—— (1987) *The Shifting Point, 1946–1987*, New York: Harper and Row.
Brownstein, R.M. (1993) *The Tragic Muse: Rachel of the Comédie Française*, New York: Alfred A. Knopf.
Bruno, G. (2002) *De la causa*, in F. Yates, *Giordano Bruno and the Hermetic Tradition*, London: Routledge.
Buckle, R. (1979) *Diaghilev*, New York: Atheneum.
—— (1980) *Nijinksy*, Harmondsworth: Penguin.
Burkert, W. (1987) *Ancient Mystery Cults*, Cambridge, Mass.: Harvard University Press.
Callow, S. (2002) 'Foreword', in M. Chekhov, *To the Actor*, London: Routledge.
—— (2004) *Being an Actor*, London: Vintage.
Chaikin, J. (1991) *The Presence of the Actor*, New York: Theatre Communications Group.
Chekhov, M. (2002) *To the Actor*, London: Routledge.
Cibber, C. (1750) *An Apology for the Life of Colley Cibber*, London: R. Dodsley.
Clive, C. (1970) 'Letter to David Garrick, January 23 1774', in T. Cole and H. Crich Chinoy (eds) *Actors on Acting*, New York: Crown Publishers.
Cole, T. and Crich Chinoy, H. (eds) (1970) *Actors on Acting*, New York: Crown Publishers.
Coleridge, H.N. (1836) *Specimens of the Table Talk of Samuel Taylor Coleridge*, London: John Murray.
Collier, J. (1698) *A Short View of the English Stage*, London: n.p.; reprinted in S. McMillin (ed.) (1973) *Restoration and Eighteenth-Century Comedy*, New York: Norton.
Connor, S. (2000) *Dumbstruck: A Cultural History of Ventriloquism*, Oxford: Oxford University Press.
Conrad, P. (1998) *Modern Times, Modern Places*, London: Thames and Hudson.
Corliss, R. (1998) 'Ol' Man Charisma: Paul Robeson 1898–1976', *Time*, 20 April, 151.16: 7.
Cosgrave, S. and Sullivan, C. (2001) *Punk. A Life Apart*, London: Cassell.
Craig, E.G. (1912) 'The actor and the über-marionette', in *On The Art of the Theatre*, London: Heinemann; reprinted in J.M. Walton (ed.) (1983) *Craig on Theatre*, London: Methuen.
—— (1912) *On The Art of the Theatre*, London: Heinemann.
—— (1930) *Henry Irving*, London: Dent.
Crawford, M. (1999) *Parcel Arrived Safely: Tied with String. My Autobiography*, London: Century.
Crawford Flitch, J.E. (1912) *Modern Dancing and Dancers*, London: Grant Richards.

Current R.N. and Current, M.E. (1997) *Loie Fuller: Goddess of Light*, Boston: Northeastern University Press.

Darnton, R. (1968) *Mesmerism and the End of the Enlightenment in France*, Cambridge, Mass.: Harvard University Press.

Davies, T. (1784) *Memoirs of the Life of David Garrick*, London: Thomas Davies.

Davis, T.C. (1995) 'Reading Shakespeare by flashes of lightning: Challenging the foundations of Romantic acting theory', *English Literary History*, 62.4: 933–54.

Derrida, J. (1974) *Of Grammatology*, trans. G.C. Spivak, Baltimore: Johns Hopkins University Press.

Descartes, R. (1988) 'The passions of the soul', in J. Cottingham, R. Stoothoff and D. Murdoch (eds) *Descartes: Selected Philosophical Writings*, Cambridge: Cambridge University Press.

Digges, L. (2006) 'Preface to the 1640 first folio of William Shakespeare', in S. Wells, *Shakespeare and Co*, London: Allen Lane.

du Maurier, G. (1998) *Trilby*, Oxford: Oxford University Press.

Duberman, M. (1989) *Paul Robeson: A Biography*, New York: The New Press.

Dylan, B. (2004) *Chronicles*, Vol. I, New York: Simon and Schuster.

Evans, D. and Michaels, S. (2002) *Rocky Horror: From Concept to Cult*, London: Sanctuary.

Everage, Dame E. (1989) *My Gorgeous Life*, Sydney: Pan Macmillan.

Fara, P. (2002) *An Entertainment for Angels: Electricity in the Enlightenment*, New York: Columbia University Press.

—— (2002) *Newton: the Making of a Genius*, London: Picador.

—— (2005) *Fatal Attraction*, London: Icon Books.

Fletcher, J. (2003) *About Beckett: the Playwright and the Work*, London: Faber.

Fleury, F. (1952) 'The French Stage and the French People', in A.M. Nagler (ed.) *A Sourcebook in Theatrical History*, New York: Dover.

Forrest, D. (1999) *Hypnotism: A History*, London: Penguin.

Friedrichsen, G.W.S. (1973) *The Shorter Oxford English Dictionary*, 3rd edn, Oxford: Clarendon Press.

Garrick, D. (1963) *Letters of David Garrick*, Vols I–III, ed. D.M. Little and G.M. Kahrl, London: Oxford University Press.

—— (1970) 'An essay on acting', in T. Cole and H. Crich Chinoy (eds) *Actors on Acting*, New York: Crown Publishers.

—— (1970) 'Letter to William Powell, 12 December 1764', in T. Cole and H. Crich Chinoy (eds) *Actors on Acting*, New York: Crown Publishers.

Gilbert, W. (1893) *De Magnete*, ed. P. Fleury de Mottelay, New York: Dover.

Gildon, C. (1710) *The Life of Thomas Betterton, the Last Eminent Tragedian*, London: Robert Gosling.

Gledhill, C. (1991) 'Signs of melodrama', in C. Gledhill (ed.) *Stardom: Industry of Desire*, London: Routledge.

Gold, A. and Fizdale, R. (1992) *The Divine Sarah: A Life of Sarah Bernhardt*, London: HarperCollins.

Goodall, J. (1994) *Artaud and the Gnostic Drama*, Oxford: Oxford University Press.

—— (2006) 'Haunted Places', in G. McAuley (ed.) *Uncertain Ground*, Brussels: Peter Lang.

—— (2006) 'Lucky's energy', in S.E. Gontarski and A. Uhlmann (eds) *Beckett After Beckett*, Gainesville: University of Florida Press.

Gottfried, M. (1984) *Broadway Musicals*, New York: Harry N. Abrams.

Grotowski, J. (1975) *Towards a Poor Theatre*, London: Methuen.

Guiry, S. (1998) 'Pol Pelletier demonstrates "six laws of theatre"', *The York University Gazette* 29.11 (18 November 1998). Online. Available www.yorku.ca/ycom/gazette/past/archive/111898/issue.htm (accessed 5 June 2007).

Habel, Y. (2005) 'To Stockholm with love: the critical reception of Josephine Baker, 1927–35', *Film History*, 17: 125–38.

Hall, P. (1983) *Peter Hall's Diaries*, ed. J. Goodwin, London: Hamish Hamilton.

Hazlitt, W. (1818) 'On actors and acting', *The Examiner*, 5 January.

—— (1930) 'A view of the English stage', in P.P. Howe (ed.) *The Complete Works of William Hazlitt*, Vol. V, London: Dent.

—— (1988) 'Whether actors ought to sit in the boxes', in *Table Talk, Essays on Men and Manners*, Vol. II, in D. Wu (ed.) *The Selected Writings of William Hazlitt*, Vol. 6, London: Pickering and Chatto.

—— (1998) 'The Indian jugglers', in J. Cook (ed.) *William Hazlitt, Selected Writings*, Oxford: Oxford University Press.

Heckman, D. (1972) 'A colourful David Bowie', *The New York Times*, 1 October. Online. Available www.5years.com/heckman72.htm (accessed 10 May 2007).

Heidegger, M. (1977) *The Question Concerning Technology and Other Essays*, trans. W. Lovitt, New York: Harper and Row.

Heilbron, J.L. (1999) *Electricity in the 17th and 18th Centuries: A Study in Early Modern Physics*, New York: Dover.

Heilpern, J. (1979) *Conference of the Birds: The Story of Peter Brook in Africa*, Harmondsworth: Penguin.

Herzen, A. (1979) *From the Other Shore*, trans. R. Wollheim, Oxford: Oxford University Press.

Highfill, Jr, P.H., Burnim, K.A. and Langhans, E.A. (1978) *A Biographical Dictionary of Actors, Actresses, Musicians, Dancers, Managers and Other Stage Personnel in London, 1660–1800*, Carbondale and Edwardsville: Southern Illinois University Press.

Hilburn, R. (1972) 'David Bowie rocks in Santa Monica', *Los Angeles Times*, 23 October. Online. Available www.5years.com/hilburn72.htm (accessed 10 May 2007).

Hiley, J. (1981) *Theatre at Work: The Story of the National Theatre's Production of Brecht's 'Galileo'*, London: Routledge.

Siddons, S. (1970) 'Remarks on the character of Lady Macbeth', in T. Cole and H. Crich Chinoy (eds) *Actors on Acting*, New York: Crown Publishers.

Sitwell, S. (1937) *La Vie Parisienne*, London: Faber and Faber.

Sounes, H. (2002) *Down the Highway: the Life of Bob Dylan*, London: Black Swan.

Stanislavski, C. (1967) *An Actor Prepares*, trans. E. Reynolds Hapgood, Harmondworth: Penguin.

—— (1975) 'Direction and acting', in T. Cole (ed.) *Acting: A Handbook of the Stanislavski Method*, New York: Crown.

Stassinopoulos, A. (1988) *Maria Callas: the Woman Behind the Legend*, London: Arena.

Stockdale, P. (1999) *Memoirs*, in I. McIntyre, *Garrick*, London: Penguin.

Stoker, B. (1906) *Personal Reminiscences of Henry Irving*, London: William Heinemann.

—— (1998) *Dracula*, ed. G. Byron, Ontario: Broadview Press.

Strachey, L. (1924) *Books and Characters: French and English*, 3rd edn, London: Chatto & Windus.

Stuart, A. (1972) 'Starman over the rainbow', *Plays and Players*, November. Online. Available www.5years.com/playplayers.htm (accessed 12 May 2007).

—— (1996) *Showgirls*, London: Jonathan Cape.

Symons, A. (1928) *Plays, Acting and Music*, London: Jonanthan Cape. Online. Available http://ia331326.us.archive.org/2/items/playsactin-gandmu13928gut/-8.txt (accessed 14 February 2007).

Talma, F.J. (1915) 'Reflections on the Actor's Art', *Papers on Acting*, 4.2. Available on line at Classicaltheatre.com (accessed 5 February 2006).

Tesla, N. (1956) 'On light and other high frequency phenomena: lecture delivered to the Franklin Institute, Philadelphia, February 1893', in Nikola Tesla Museum (ed.) *Nikola Tesla, Lectures, Patents, Articles*, Belgrade: Nikola Tesla Museum.

—— (1982) *My Inventions: the Autobiography of Nikola Tesla*, ed. B. Johnston, Vermont: Hart Brothers.

Turner, F. *The School of Night*, Corona 4: 4. Online. Available www.montana.edu/corona/4/school14.html (accessed 3 September 2006).

Tynan, K. (1976) *A View of the English Stage*, St Alban's: Paladin.

Valéry, P. (1968) 'La Conquète de l'ubiquité', in W. Benjamin, 'The Work of Art in the Age of Mechanical Reproduction', in *Illuminations*, ed. H. Arendt, New York: Schocken Books.

von Goethe, J.W. (1959) 'Rules for actors', in A.M. Nagler (ed.) *A Sourcebook in Theatrical History*, New York: Dover.

Waldrep, S. (2004) *The Aesthetics of Self-Invention: Oscar Wilde to David Bowie*, Minneapolis: University of Minnesota Press.

Wardle, I. (2003) Review of 'Happy Days', *The Times*, 15 March 1975, in J. Fletcher, *About Beckett: the Playwright and the Work*, London: Faber.

Hill, A. (1970) 'An essay on the art of acting', in T. Cole and H. Crich Chinoy (eds) *Actors on Acting*, New York: Crown Publishers.

Hill, J. (1970) 'The actor: A treatise on the art of playing', in T. Cole and H. Crich Chinoy (eds) *Actors on Acting*, New York: Crown Publishers.

Hobbes, T. (1973) *Leviathan*, in S. McMillin (ed.) *Restoration and Eighteenth-Century Comedy*, New York: Norton.

Hoffman, D. (1998) 'Interview with M. Tuchman', in B. Cardullo, H. Geduld, R. Gottesman and L. Woods (eds) *Playing to the Camera: Film Actors Discuss Their Craft*, New Haven: Yale University Press.

Holledge, J. (2007) 'Presence', email (6 June 2007).

Holmes, P. (1972) 'Gay rock', *Gay News*, July 1972. Online. Available www.5years.com/gayrock.htm (accessed 15 May 2007).

Humphries, B. (1982) 'Sandy Stone: the land of the living', in *A Nice Night's Entertainment*, London: Granada.

—— (1982) 'Sandy's stone', in *A Nice Night's Entertainment*, London: Granada.

The Illustrated London News, 25 March 1871.

Irving, L. (1989) *Henry Irving: The Actor and His World*, London: Columbus Books.

Janin, J. (1864) *Rachel et la Tragédie*, Paris: Adolphe Delahays.

Kant, I. (2007) *The Critique of Judgement*, Oxford: Oxford University Press.

Kennard, N.H. (1885) *Rachel*, London: W.H. Allen.

Kershaw, I. (2001) *Hitler: 1889–1936, Hubris*, London: Penguin.

Kinnerly, E. (1999) Handbill, 'Electrical fire', 16 March 1752, in B. Brame Fortune and D.J. Warner, *Franklin and His Friends*, Washington: Smithsonian National Portrait Gallery.

Kirkman, J.T. (1799) *Memoirs of the Life of Charles Macklin, Esq.*, Vol. I, London: n.p.

Kirstein, L. (1975) *Nijinsky Dancing*, London: Thames and Hudson.

—— (1979) *Thirty Years of the New York City Ballet*, London: Adam & Charles Black.

Knowlson, J. (1996) *Damned to Fame: The Life of Samuel Beckett*, London: Bloomsbury.

Kustow, M. (2005) *Peter Brook, a Biography*, London: Bloomsbury.

Lahr, J. (1992) *Dame Edna Everage and the Rise of Western Civilisation*, London: Flamingo.

Leeming, D. (2005) *The Oxford Companion to World Mythology*, New York: Oxford University Press.

Lemon, B. (2002) 'Intelligent artificiality', *The Financial Times*, London, 25 October.

Levi, E. (1982) *The History of Magic*, trans. A.E. Waite, London: Rider.

Lewes, G.H. (1957) *On Actors and the Art of Acting*, New York: Grove Press.

Lindholm, C. (1990) *Charisma*, Oxford: Blackwell.

Lindsey, R. (1994) 'Introduction', in M. Brando, *Songs My Mother Taught Me*, New York: Random House.

Lydon, J. (1994) *Rotten*, New York: Picador.

McIntyre, I. (1999) *Garrick*, London: Penguin.

McKellan, I. (1981) 'I always wanted to be on Broadway', *The New York Times*, 27 September.

Mailer, N. (2004) *The Spooky Art*, New York: Random House.

Mansel, P. (2001) *Paris Between the Empires, 1814–1852*, London: John Murray.

Marcus, G. (2005) *Like a Rolling Stone*, London: Faber & Faber.

Marinetti, F.T., Settimelli, E. and Corra, B. (1995) 'The Futurist synthetic theatre', trans. R.W. Flint, in R. Drain (ed.) *Twentieth-Century Theatre: a Sourcebook*, London: Routledge.

Marks, P. (2002) '*Arturo Ui*: Hail, hail, the gang's all here', *The Washington Post*, 22 October.

Melville, L. (1929) *More Stage Favourites of the Eighteenth Century*, London: Hutchinson & Co.

Meyer, M.W. (ed.) (1987) *The Ancient Mysteries*, San Francisco: Harper and Row.

Morand, P. (1981) '1900', in *Oeuvres*, Paris: Flammarion.

More, H. (1963) 'Letter from Hannah More to James Stonehouse, forwarded to David Garrick, 21 May 1774', in D.M. Little and G.M. Kahrl (eds) *Letters of David Garrick*, Vol. III, London: Oxford University Press.

Morley, P. (2007) 'The best 25 gigs of all time', *The Observer Music Monthly*, 21 January.

Nietzsche, F. (1977). *Twilight of the Idols*, Harmondsworth: Penguin.

—— (1979) *Ecce Homo*, trans. R.J. Hollingdale, Harmondsworth: Penguin.

Nijinska, B. (1981) *Early Memoirs*, trans. I. Nijinksa and J. Rawlinson, London: Faber and Faber.

Nijinsky, R. (1960) *Nijinsky*, Harmondsworth: Penguin.

Njami, S. (2007) 'Foreword', in B. Jules-Rosette, *Josephine Baker in Art and Life: the Icon and the Image*, Chicago: University of Illinois Press.

Ostwald, P.F. (1991) *Vaslav Nijinsky: A Leap into Madness*, New York: Carol Publication Group.

Otis Skinner, C. (1967) *Madame Sarah*, London: Michael Joseph.

Owen, R. (1868) *On the Anatomy of Vertebrates*, Vol. III, London: Longmans, Green.

Parker, D. (1988) *Nijinsky: God of Dance*, London: Equation.

Pavis, P. (1987) *Dictionnaire du Théâtre*, Paris: Messidor.

Paytress, M. (2007) 'Inventing glam rock', in *60 Years of David Bowie, Mojo Classic*, 2.2: 20.

Petsalis-Diomidis, N. (2001) *The Unknown Callas*, New York: Amadeaus Press.

Plant, S. (2007) 'A gala spectacle: interview with Barry Humphries', *The Daily Telegraph*, 17 May.

Plotinus (2002) *Ennead IV*, in F. Yates, *Giordano Bruno and the Hermetic Tradition*, London: Routledge.

Priestley, J. (1775) *The History and Present State of Electricity*, Part II, 3rd edn, London: Bathurst and Lowndes.

Rich, F. (1984) 'A Whitelaw Beckett', *The New York Times*, 17 February.

—— (1988) 'Phantom of the Opera', *The New York Times*, 27 January.

Riskin, J. (2002) *Science in the Age of Sensibility*, Chicago: The University of Chicago Press.

Roach, J.R. (1985) *The Player's Passion: Studies in the Science of Acting*, London and Toronto: Associated University Presses.

—— (1996) *Cities of the Dead: Circum-Atlantic Performance*, New York: Columbia University Press.

—— (2004) 'It', *Theatre Journal*, 56: 555–68.

—— (2007) *It*, Ann Arbor, Mich.: University of Michigan Press.

Robb, J. (2006) *Punk Rock: An Oral History*, London: Ebury Press.

Robeson, P. (1988) *Here I Stand*, Boston: Beacon Press.

Roucher, J.A. (1779) *Les Mois, poème en douze chants*, Vol. 1, Paris: Quillau.

Ruffini, F. (1991) 'The dilated mind', in E. Barba and N. Savarese, *Secret Art of the Performer: a Dictionary of Theatre Anthropology*, London: Routledge.

Saint-Denis, M. (1982) *Training for the Theatre*, ed. S. Saint-Denis, London: Heinemann.

Savage, J. (1991) *England's Dreaming*, London: Faber and Faber.

Scaff, P. (ed.) (1889) *Saint Chrysostom: Homilies on the Epistles of Paul to the Corinthians*, Edinburgh: T&T Clark.

Scorsese, M. (dir.) (2005) *No Direction Home*, Apple and Paramount Pictures.

Secord, J.A. (1989) 'Extraordinary experiment: electricity and the creation of life in Victorian England', in D. Gooding, T. Pinch and S. Schaffer (eds) *The Uses of Experiment*, Cambridge: Cambridge University Press.

Segal, W. (2003) *A Voice at the Borders of Silence*, Woodstock and New York: Overlook Press.

Seifer, M.J. (1996) *The Life and Times of Nikola Tesla*, New York: Citadel Books.

Shakespeare, W. (1980) *The Tempest*, Arden edn, ed. F. Kermode, London: Methuen.

—— (1982) *Hamlet*, Arden edn, ed. H. Jenkins, London: Methuen.

—— (2006) *As You Like It*, Arden edn, ed. J. Dusinberre, London: Shakespeare.

Shelley, M.W. (1982) *Frankenstein or The Modern Prometheus*, ed. J. Rieger, Chicago: The University of Chicago Press.

—— (1993) *Frankenstein*, ed. M. Butler, Oxford: Oxford University Press.

Watt, D. (1975) 'Bold and cynical Chicago', *The Daily News*, 4 June; reprinted in S. Suskin (ed.) (1997) *More Opening Nights on Broadway*, New York: Schirmer Books.

Weber, M. (1968). 'Theory of social and economic organization', in S. Eisenstadt (ed.) *Max Weber on Charisma and Institution Building*, Chicago: Chicago University Press.

Weigel, H. (1970) 'Rehearsing the part', in T. Cole and H. Crich Chinoy (eds) *Actors on Acting*, New York: Crown Publishers.

Welch, W. (1972) 'David Bowie', *Melody Maker*, 26 August. Online. Available www.5years.com/DBCW.htm (accessed 10 May 2007).

Wells, S. (2006) *Shakespeare and Co*, London: Allen Lane.

Wilde, O. (1894) 'Phrases and philosophies for the use of the young', in *Chameleon*, 1.1.

—— (1962) *The Letters of Oscar Wilde*, ed. R. Hart-Davis, London: Rupert Hart-Davis.

Williams, P. (2004) *Bob Dylan Performing Artist: 1960–1973*, London: Omnibus Press.

Wilson, B. (1759) 'Farther experiments in electricity', *Philosophical Transactions (1683–1775)*, 51: 896–906.

—— (1773) 'Observations upon lightning', *Philosophical Transactions (1683–1775)*, 63: 49–65.

Wood, E. (2000) *The Josephine Baker Story*, London: Sanctuary.

Zamoyski, A. (1999) *Holy Madness: Romantics, Patriots and Revolutionaries, 1776 – 1871*, London: Phoenix, 1999.

Ziegfeld, R. and Ziegfeld, P. (1993) *The Ziegfeld Touch: the Life and Times of Florenz Ziegfeld Jr.*, New York: Harry N. Abrams.

Zucker, C. (1995) *Figures of Light: Actors and Directors Illuminate the Art of Film Acting*, New York: Plenum.

—— (1999) *In the Company of Actors: Reflections on the Craft of Acting*, London: Adam & Charles Black.

INDEX

INDEX

mystery: 'holy theatre' 36–8, 159, 189; and presence 9, 10, 19, 26–34, 158–9, 161; *see also* supernaturalism
mystery cults 27–30
myth-making process 32–3, 33–4

Napoleon I, emperor of France 61–2, 86
naturalism vs. supernaturalism 11, 13
neo-Platonism 26–7
nervous energy: and electricity 127; Nijinsky 15, 116, 118, 159–61; Tesla 125
nervous system 159–68
Newton, Sir Isaac: aethers and effluvia 63–4, 67, 72, 74, 89; and forces of attraction 67, 73, 74; as genius 57, 58; magnetism 62, 65
Nietzsche, Friedrich Wilhelm 45, 47, 111–12, 118, 145, 182
Nijinsky, Bronislava 114, 116
Nijinsky, Romola 160
Nijinsky, Vaslav 11, 14, 86, 112, 121, 128; exoticism 135; experimental approach 15, 115, 116–18, 160–1; mystery and myth-making 31, 32, 33; nervous energy 15, 116, 118, 159–61; radiance 23, 31, 114; superhuman talent 113–18
Njami, Simon 134
No Direction Home (film) 181–2
Noailles, Countess Ann de 33
Noh theatre 189
Nolan, Christopher 123
Nollet, Jean Antoine 77–8, 89
Northumberland, Earl of 52

Occasional Paper (1719) 61
occult: and glamour 142; and magnetism 62–4, 66, 72–3, 92; and mesmerism 92, 93, 94–107, 171; and science of equilibrium 93; *see also* supernaturalism
Olivier, Laurence 11, 18, 31–2, 33
Orghast (performance piece) 35–6

oriental theatre and stage presence 3–4
orientalism 4, 135
Owen, Richard 127

Pacino, Al 15, 165–6
parody: Bowie 145, 146, 147, 148; *Rocky Horror Show* 15, 143–4
passions: and humours 70–1; motive power 72–3; sensibility 71–2
Pavis, Patrice 9, 19, 22
Pearl, Cora 133
Pelletier, Pol 22
personality: cults of 118–19; flashiness and personality-driven theatre 34; Irving's personal magnetism 14, 101–4, 105–7, 121; 'magnetic personalities' 91
Phantom of the Opera, The (stage musical) 15, 140, 154–7
phlogiston 90
physics: and powers of attraction 14, 61–6, 67, 73; science of equilibrium and mesmerism 93; *see also* electricity; magnetism
Piaf, Edith 86, 128
Plotinus 27
Plutarch 29
pneuma 25–6, 71, 72
poetics of presence 7, 12; and science 100–1
'poor theatre' 36
Pope, Alexander 76, 83
presence: meaning and usage of term 7–8, 20; as objective quality 3–6; poetics of presence 7, 100–1; unnameable quality 17–19
present: presence and present time 15, 158–89
Prestige, The (film) 123
Priestley, Joseph 90
primitivism and Josephine Baker 135, 136
Prince, Hal 138, 140–1
prodigies 18–19, 93, 107–21
Prometheus myth 100, 101

221